Historical Protestantism

WILLIAM A. SCOTT
Le Moyne College
Syracuse, New York

Historical Protestantism: An Historical Introduction to Protestant Theology

Prentice-Hall, Inc., *Englewood Cliffs, New Jersey*

To the memory of
my father and mother

Prentice-Hall International, Inc., *London*
Prentice-Hall of Australia, Pty. Ltd., *Sydney*
Prentice-Hall of Canada, Ltd., *Toronto*
Prentice-Hall of India Private Limited, *New Delhi*
Prentice-Hall of Japan, Inc., *Tokyo*

© 1971 by Prentice-Hall, Inc.
Englewood Cliffs, N.J.

LIBRARY OF CONGRESS CATALOG CARD NO.: 76–123085
PRINTED IN THE UNITED STATES OF AMERICA

13-389171-2 (p)

13-389205-0 (c)

CURRENT PRINTING (LAST NUMBER):
10 9 8 7 6 5 4 3 2 1

Preface

This book is intended to be an initial introduction to Protestantism and thereby a contribution to the developing dialogue between Protestant and Roman Catholic Christians. It attempts to appraise historical Protestantism from the point of view of a Roman Catholic. To do this, a study is presented of Protestantism in historical perspective. Chapters one through four are a discussion of the initial vision of Protestantism at the time of the Reformation of the sixteenth century as it was expressed by Martin Luther and John Calvin, and by the other two forms that Protestantism took at that time, Anabaptism and Anglicanism.

But it is not enough to study beginnings. One must also see what history has made and is making of those beginnings. What history has made of the Reformation is dealt with in chapters five through seven where Puritanism, Methodism, and nineteenth century liberal Protestantism are studied as representative expressions of Protestant Christianity in the seventeenth, eighteenth, and nineteenth centuries. What history is now making of the Reformation is the subject of chapters eight through twelve where five twentieth century Protestant theologians: Karl Barth, Dietrich Bonhoeffer, Rudolf Bultmann, Reinhold Niebuhr, and Paul Tillich are considered as representative expositors of the meaning of contemporary Protestantism.

Let it be said at the outset that the term Protestantism as used in this book carries a double connotation, one negative, the other positive. The Reformation began as and continues to be a protest *against* certain aspects of late medieval Roman Catholicism. This is the negative implication of the term and until quite recently this has been the sense in which Catholics generally thought of Protestants. In this view, the only acceptable Catholic attitude toward Protestantism was hostility or, at least, wariness, since it was opposed to Catholic beliefs and practices. The chapters which follow will attempt to discuss and evaluate the content of this protest against Roman Catholicism.

But there is another sense in which one can protest. One can protest *for*, speak out in favor of, something. This is by far the more important meaning of the word to Protestants. It is the meaning that needs to assume much more importance in the Catholic view of Protestantism. Sixteenth and twentieth century Protestants alike feel that their primary task has always been to bear witness to a Christianity that is discovered in the Word of God alone. An insistence on the original apostolic faith as that faith is embodied in the Scriptures and an opposition to any form of Christianity which is a deformation of that faith, these, in that order of importance, are the two basic thrusts of Protestantism. These two emphases recur again and again in the pages that follow. To grasp them is to touch the heart of Protestantism.

My grateful thanks are due to Le Moyne college for a faculty research grant and a year's leave of absence which provided me with the assistance and the time needed to complete this book. My gratitude goes out also to my students at Le Moyne over the past five years who have, by their interest and their questions, helped me to work out the ideas which follow. I am grateful, too, to two of my colleagues, Father James Carmody, S. J., and Father Avery Dulles, S. J., for their critical reading of the manuscript. Their suggestions considerably clarified and corrected a number of ideas which might otherwise have remained unclear or incorrect. Last of all, I extend my thanks to Frances E. Morrison, for her careful stylistic reading of the text. What style or clarity is here, owes much to her careful editing.

William A. Scott

Contents

CHAPTER ONE

Martin Luther

How an insistence on biblical Christianity came to be the hallmark of Protestantism is best understood from a study of the first great Reformer, Martin Luther (1483-1546). It was because Luther set himself against the corruption of Christianity that he found in the church of his time, and because he determined to restore Christianity to the form he found it to have in the New Testament that Protestantism became and remained dominated by two principles of life: (1) *Ecclesia semper reformanda*—the church stands always under the necessity of reform. This is the negative protest; (2) reform must always find its source in a return to God's Word, the Scripture. That is the positive protest.

LUTHER'S PROBLEM

Martin Luther's problem which led him to a radical re-thinking of the Christian message was the problem of salvation: How can I be certain I will be saved? How can I come to the assurance that God looks on me with favor? His questions were theological ones: Who is God? Who am I? How do I relate to Him? His answer was a personal one: I must believe that God is at work in Christ saving me as His Word tells me.

These were the questions and this the answer that dominated and shaped his life. All else is to be read in that light. He could be coarse and vulgar in speech; he could marry a woman who had been a nun; but this and all else in his life, good and bad, can only be seen in perspective if it is seen as flowing from the central core of his life: his strong and sincere quest for a right relation with God. The vehemence and the vulgarity were weapons in defense of what he saw as religious truth. The leaving of the

1

monastery and the subsequent marriage he saw as the logical explication of his deepest religious convictions. He was above all a man of religion. This is the key to understanding him.

Gifted with an intense, scrupulous nature, Luther very early in his life came face to face with his problem: knowing myself for what I am, a sinner, and God for what He is, all just, how can I ever hope to win His favor? His church offered him answers to his problem and he tried them with all the passion of his sincerely religious nature.

Monasticism for the church of that time was the road above all others to God. For the generous soul wanting to give God proof of his love and thereby gain God's approval in return, it was the surest way to salvation. And so in 1505, at the age of 21, he entered the Augustinian Friars at Erfurt. Once in the religious life he gave himself wholeheartedly to it. He was a good monk.

> I was a good monk and I kept the rule of my order so strictly that I may say that if ever a monk got to heaven by his monkery it was I. All my brothers in the monastery who knew me will bear me out. If I had kept on any longer, I should have killed myself with vigils, prayers, reading, and other works.[1]

Austerities became central to his life; nightlong vigils of prayer, corporal punishment, fasting. But none of them gave him the security he sought. Always the question returned: how can I be sure I am doing enough? Is not my sinfulness too great to win His forgiveness? It is impossible for me to become worthy of His love. Thus self-effort, strenuously worked at for a long time (he had already been a monk for twelve years when he posted his ninety-five theses in Wittenberg in 1517) could not give him his assurance. Where else could he turn? There was also the mass and the sacrament of forgiveness for sins. And to these also he gave himself ardently.

Perhaps what one could not earn for oneself could be won through presenting the merits of Christ to the Father. If I offer mass, he thought, that re-presentation of Christ's sacrifice for us to God, He will deign to look on me favorably because of those merits. So, as an ordained priest, he offered the Mass piously and reverently. But the old problem kept returning to torment him. The sacrifice provided only one more occasion for self-doubt. He felt it first on the occasion of his first Mass in 1507. It would return many times thereafter to torment him. It was again the problem of his own unworthiness before God. His own words on that occasion typify the reaction that the Mass tended more and more to arouse in him. As he began the first words of the offertory prayers, the awfulness of what he was about to do burst upon him.

At these words I was utterly stupefied and terror-stricken. I thought to myself, With what tongue shall I address such Majesty, seeing that all men ought to tremble in the presence of even an earthly prince? Who am I, that I should lift up mine eyes or raise my hands to the divine Majesty? The angels surround him. At his nod the earth trembles. And shall I, a miserable little pygmy, say "I want this, I ask for that"? For I am dust and ashes and full of sin and I am speaking to the living, eternal and the true God.[2]

His own sinfulness returned to haunt him even at the altar, even while offering the sacrifice which redeemed him. Here too he was to find no peace, no assurance of salvation.

What then of Penance, that sacrament for the forgiveness of sins given by a merciful Father? Here surely God would grant assurance of forgiveness, some sense of hope. But this too was to be no source of solace. He fell into the pit of scruples and the sacrament only increased his anxiety and sense of dread. Of the three elements of Penance, confession, contrition and satisfaction, each came to present him with questions he ultimately found unanswerable.[3]

Confession meant to Luther that to be forgiven one must confess one's sins. But how could he be certain he had done this? It became his constantly recurring experience that he would finish a confession, long and carefully prepared, only to remember almost immediately some fault or sin he had forgotten to confess. Little by little the realization dawned on him that his sinfulness lay a lot deeper than this or that transgression. It was embedded in his very nature. And that nature enlisted the aid of its own faculties first to manifest and then to hide its radical corruption.

Will yielded easily, faced by temptation, and then memory conveniently forgot the transgression in order that nature might be spared facing itself. If it were true, Luther reasoned, that the components of his nature allied themselves together in support of his sinfulness, how could he even hope to reveal to his confessor the totality of his corruption, no matter how long and sincerely he searched his conscience? Complete confession thus became more and more an impossibility for him and so the question: How can I be sure of forgiveness for sins I do not confess?—became harder and harder to answer.

Regarding contrition, Luther felt that if God were to forgive, it could only be because one was sorry for having offended God. Any lesser motive for sorrow, like fear, could not possibly hope for forgiveness. And having set the demand thus high, he found he could not scale that height. Was it possible, he asked himself, for a man, whose supreme object of love was himself, to place a genuine act of love of God, the only kind of sorrow that deserved God's mercy? He saw it could not be done. The only acceptable form of contrition became an impossibility.

And, as for making satisfaction for sin, here too he saw that sinful man was not capable of doing that. What man could offer adequate satisfaction for offense against an all-holy God?

Thus did Luther learn, in the crucible of his own personal experience over a period of years, that any reliance on sacramental help to win the favor of God that he so desperately sought was illusory. He came finally to the unavoidable conclusion: he could not find within himself—he knew because he had tried long and hard and had failed—the resources needed to win his way to God. At last he saw that his problem lay not with the means available for salvation but with himself. His nature was not capable of using the means. Bouyer sums up his predicament well when he says:

> He had at his disposal any number of means to sanctification. All of these, however—prayer, fasting, monastic discipline, the Sacraments even, still more his own accumulation of petty devotions—he regarded merely as auxiliaries, or rather, stimulants, to his own will. There, precisely, is the point which he saw too vividly ever to forget—namely, that the powerlessness of the human will, in the matter of salvation, is not merely relative, but absolute. It is not that man lacks resources, even powerful ones, to strengthen his will so as to achieve salvation, it is his will which is purely and simply incapable. A feeble workman may achieve great effects with appropriate tools. In the hands of a dead man the most powerful machines are useless.[4]

There was one last means he attempted to use in his struggle for assurance, the merits of the saints. For the church of his time the cult of the saints occupied a prominent place and it was normal for him to turn in this direction in his search for favor with God. If, as daily experience kept bringing home to him ever more acutely, he was unable, because of his own radical sinfulness, to win merit in God's eyes, then, perhaps, an appeal to the merits of the saints would give him some peace. The saints, in the thinking of his age, had, by the exceptional holiness of their lives, won far more merit than was needed for their own salvation. Devotion to them might earn their intercession before God and win from Him the application of their superfluous merits to oneself. Thus, Luther, unable to reach salvation through his own efforts, might still hope for it through the merits of those who, in the eyes of his church, had led lives of extraordinary perfection. For a time he was able to find some assurance in devotion to the saints and in recourse to that treasury of their superabundant merits which, along with the infinite merits won by Christ, were available to the faithful. By prayers and good works he tried to fulfill the conditions requisite to have these merits applied to himself by the church, custodian of that treasury.

But in the end this resource failed him too. He came, finally, to the conclusion that the all-holy God demanded from each human soul all that a man was capable of giving Him by way of a holy life. The very nature of God and man's relation to Him was such as to render the notion of superabundant merit untenable. No man could do less than give God his best and, this being true, no one could be spoken of as giving God more than He had the right to expect. There was no treasury of the saints' merits for Luther to rely upon.

Thus, in the end, Luther found himself in a completely impossible position, bound to earn his own salvation and yet acutely aware of his own inability to do this. The last stage was, predictably, despair: I am lost. This in its turn led to an awful doubt about God Himself. How can I find it in myself, he wondered, to love a God who can put me in such a position? I do not love Him; I hate Him.

> For however irreproachably I lived as a religious, I felt myself in the presence of God to be a sinner with a most unquiet conscience, nor could I trust that I had pleased Him with my satisfaction. I did not love, nay, rather I hated this just God who punished sinners and if not with "open blasphemy" certainly with huge murmurings I was angry with God, saying: "As though it really were not enough that miserable sinners should be eternally damned with original sin, and have all kinds of calamities laid upon them by the law of the ten commandments, God must go and add sorrow upon sorrow and even through the Gospel itself bring His Justice and His Wrath to bear!"[5]

ITS SOLUTION

At this critical juncture Staupitz, his confessor, intervened. What Luther needed, Staupitz saw, was a work that would turn his energies away from introspection. He put his penitent to the task of earning his doctor's degree in theology and subsequently turned over to him his own chair of Scripture at the University of Wittenberg. Luther set himself to study and began lecturing and preaching on the Scriptures. It was here, in the Word of God, that he found his answer.

His study of the Psalms in preparation for a set of lectures on them in 1513-14 was the first step. It helped somewhat to temper his exceedingly harsh picture of God as Demander and Judge. The agony that Christ suffered as depicted in Psalm 22 ("My God, my God, why hast Thou forsaken me?") led him to see how completely Christ had identified Himself with man up to the very point of sharing the sense of utter separation from God because of sin. It was an alienation that Luther himself knew only too well. He saw too that it was the Father who had put Christ to this task in order that Christ might take upon Himself the guilt and penalty of men and satisfy for it. With this realization the light began to break through for Luther. He had been wrong, he realized, in seeing God primarily as Judge. He was that, certainly, but it was the sending of His Son to save that gave the true insight into who God was. He was above all, Love, Mercy, Forgiveness.

Yet one grave problem still remained: the justice of God. All his training in theology, his piety and devotions, the climate of the age in which he lived, had conditioned Luther to see God as just. He would render to each man according to his works. How, if this was true, was it possible, even with his new vision of God as Love, for Luther to escape the just judgment of God? What grounds for hope in God's love did he have with the acute sense of sinfulness that was his? How could God be all just and avoid condemning him?

It was when Luther turned to preparing his lectures on St. Paul's Epistle to the Romans that he found his answer to these questions. He came to see that the justice of God, as Paul used the term, did not mean what he had been taught it meant. Early in the epistle (Rom. 1: 17-18) he met the expression "the justice of God." What did Paul mean by the expression? How was one to understand the phrase: "it is in the Gospel that the justice of God is revealed"? Luther struggled with the passage long and hard and finally he found the key that opened the lock and solved once and for all his search for some assurance of salvation. His own words tell of his momentous discovery.

> I greatly longed to understand Paul's Epistle to the Romans and nothing stood in the way but that one expression, "the justice of God," because I took it to mean that justice whereby God is just and deals justly in punishing the unjust. My situation was that, although an impeccable monk, I stood before God as a sinner troubled in conscience, and I had no

confidence that my merit would assuage him. Therefore I did not love a just and angry God, but rather hated and murmured against him. Yet I clung to the dear Paul and had a great yearning to know what he meant.

Night and day I pondered until I saw the connection between the justice of God and the statement that "the just shall live by his faith." Then I grasped that the justice of God is that righteousness by which through grace and sheer mercy God justifies us through faith. Thereupon I felt myself to be reborn and to have gone through open doors into paradise. The whole of Scripture took on a new meaning, and whereas before the "justice of God" had filled me with hate, now it became to me inexpressibly sweet in greater love. This passage of Paul became to me a gate of heaven. . . .[6]

In these two phrases of St. Paul: "in the Gospel the justice of God is revealed" and "the just shall live by his faith" and in Luther's understanding of their meaning lies the marrow of his theology, the core of the Reformation, and the continuing living center of Protestantism. All else in his thought is an enlargement upon, a deduction from, or implied in, this fundamental insight.

In the theological tradition wherein Luther had been trained he had learned to think of the justice of God principally in the punitive sense. God, in this view, was preeminently the Judge. He knew man's life in all its detail and demanded strict satisfaction for all his transgressions. His justice was to be served in its fullness by the imposition of the punishment warranted. This conception of God had driven Luther to the brink of despair as he contemplated his own sinfulness and inability to fulfill what God required of him.

Now he became aware that there was another way of understanding what was meant by "the justice of God." In the Gospel God's justice is revealed as something other than Luther had hitherto realized. In simple language the Good News of the Gospel was that God had expended His punitive justice on Christ, that by His death Christ, in fulfillment of His Father's will, took upon Himself the guilt and the debt of man's sins and paid that debt in full. The demands of the just judge were completely met on the cross. There the punitive justice of God was satisfied.

But the cross was more than justice satisfied; it was also love revealed. Precisely because of what Christ did, God treats us differently. In view of Christ He now declares men just, treats them as saved. He communicates to men His own justice (i.e., His own holiness). This is the import of Paul's statement that the justice of God is revealed in the Gospel. His punitive justice is fulfilled and His justice in the sense of His holiness is communicated to men. Both of these are done because of Christ and that is the Gospel message. The New Testament revelation is that, in spite of our sinfulness and inability to merit His forgiveness, God forgives us because of Christ. No merit of ours has earned this; it is a gratuitous act of divine love. God loves and saves us in spite of ourselves. Because of Christ's death God treats us differently than we deserve.

There was one further step in Luther's understanding of Paul. If God has spoken to man, then man should believe Him when He speaks. It is this belief which brings that message to the individual personally, effecting in him that assurance of unmerited salvation of which the Gospel speaks. "The just man lives by faith," Paul had said. It was as simply stated as that. A man's faith makes him just, brings him God's holiness and forgiveness, and enables him henceforth to live in the assurance for which Luther had sought so long. He need not, indeed could not, earn that assurance. But God, knowing this, gave it to him in Christ. Belief in God acting through Christ to save him was all he needed to have.

Out of this understanding of Paul came Luther's doctrine of justified man, as at one and the same time both just and a sinner (*simul justus et peccator*). On the one hand, man is not different once his faith in God's love is expressed. He remains of himself still a sinner, incapable of doing anything which can merit God's favor. But, on the other hand, he is different because now, in faith, there comes the confidence that God is giving him salvation, making him just in and through Christ.

As Luther gave himself to the deeper study of the experience he had gone through, he was able to see that there were three essential elements in it: the principle of gratuity (*sola gratia*—grace alone), the principle of faith (*sola fides*—faith alone), and the principle of God's Word (*sola Scriptura*—scripture alone). For the remainder of his life he was occupied in clarifying, formulating, defending and preaching these three ideas. These are the foundation on which Protestantism rests.

THE PRINCIPLE OF GRATUITY

God gives salvation gratuitously. Herein lies the answer to Luther's problem of uncertainty about salvation. He had been seeking to find an assurance that was based on something he himself did. But the knowledge that his own painful experience had taught him also brought him to despair of any assurance from this source. He had learned only too well both the demands that God made of man (man must be holy as God is holy) and his own powerlessness to meet those demands (the constant sense of sinfulness). As a sincere and loyal member of the Church and a good religious he had tried, intensely and perseveringly, to use the means with which the church provided him. Yet one by one they had failed him.

Now he saw that his focus in approaching the problem of salvation had been wrong. He had erroneously assumed that because it was man's problem, the solution too must be worked out by man. God's part was to reward or punish man for his success or failure in solving the problem.

The answer, of course, which he now realized he should have seen, was that salvation is not in man's hands, but in God's and that in a total and absolute sense. Chapters seven and eight of Romans presented a clear picture of the problem and its solution. In Chapter seven, man (every man) finds himself aware of God's law and equally aware of his own desire to follow that law. Yet he soon becomes aware too of another law in his members dragging him in the direction of violating the very law he approves of. "For I know that in me, that is, in my flesh, no good dwells, because to wish is within my power, but I do not find the strength to accomplish what is good" (Rom. 7: 18). The more man struggles to save himself the more certain he becomes of his incapacity. Finally he is, he must be, like Luther, brought to despair. "Unhappy man that I am! Who will deliver me from the body of this death?" (v. 24). It is only to the man who has come to this despairing awareness that the Word of God can say: Who will save you? "The grace of God through Jesus Christ our Lord" (Rom. 7: 25). And Chapter eight goes on to portray the transformation wrought by the Holy Spirit in the soul of the man who has heard and accepted God's promise. Grace is all. Salvation is completely God's work. To it man makes no contribution whatsoever.

THE PRINCIPLE OF FAITH

But this process of God saving man in spite of himself was not something that happened automatically. God does not simply give salvation. He offers it. Man must make his contribution to the process. He must hear the message and then believe in it as personally applicable to himself. Yet in the very act of insisting that man has a contribution to make to his own salvation, Luther, in another of his paradoxes, denies that man himself can make this contribution. If a man comes to believe, it can only be because

God has priorly decided to give him that faith. Even man's faith is a testimony to the absolute gratuity of salvation.

From the side of God, then, grace alone saves; from the side of man, faith alone. In the dialogue of salvation God speaks and man answers; beyond that there is nothing that need or can be added to the process of salvation. Out of the bitterness of his own experience Luther had come to conclude not that man had need of help in achieving salvation but rather that he had an absolute need to be saved by another. There is nothing we can do but believe in our salvation by God.

Here in this dialogue of *sola gratia* and *sola fides* lies the Lutheran rejection of salvation by faith and good works. There is no sense in which man's works can merit his salvation. It is at this point that Luther first comes into sharp conflict with the medieval church. The posting of his ninety-five theses on indulgences on the church door in 1517 is his first overt move against 'merit theology'. It had always been taught in the medieval church, and in recent centuries more one-sidedly than previously, that man was able and indeed required to earn heaven by his own good works. It was true that initial justification was God's gift, earned in no way. But once justified, it was for man to grow in this life of justice by the performance of good works. These did have merit in God's eyes in winning that final state of blessedness which a man would enjoy.

With this position Luther broke. For him faith and faith alone saved. God did all; man did nothing. Even the justified man was unable to place acts that in any sense deserved a reward from God. Even when justified, man remained a sinner (*simul justus et peccator*), and as a sinner he could never win heaven by his own efforts.

What then was the worth of good works in Luther's eyes? Is it to be concluded that he did not urge their performance? Is he saying all that a man need do is believe and beyond that what he does is of no importance? Is he discarding the need for living a good life and opening the door to doing whatever one wishes? This view has been seriously attributed to Luther by some of his critics. His chance remark to Melanchthon, "Sin strongly, but believe even more strongly," has been seized upon as an accurate summary of his position. But to attribute this view to Luther is to calumniate him. He certainly did not hold that faith released one from the performance of good works. J. S. Whale, in *The Protestant Tradition,* has the following to say on this charge.

> Against the reproach constantly repeated by Catholics that he "forbids good works," Luther defends himself frequently, emphatically and effectively. Did his doctrine of Justification

by Faith encourage men to say: "We will take our ease and do no good works, but be content with faith"? "I answer," said Luther, "not so, ye wicked men, not so. . . . I have not forbidden good works. I have simply declared that just as a tree must be good before it can bring forth good fruit, so man must be made good by God's grace before he can do good." Again: "The Word is given that thou mayest be cleansed; it quickens thee to do good works, not to live at ease." Again: "for God gives no one his grace that he may lie down and do nothing worth while any more." One of his Latin Propositions of 1520 succinctly states the paradox: "Neither faith nor justification comes from works; but works come from faith and justification". . . . One glance at his two famous Catechisms shows the place which he gave to the Commandments of the Law; they have to be fulfilled.[7]

It is false, then, to say that Luther's thesis of salvation by faith alone was understood and taught by him in such a way as to exclude the necessity of good works. But if it be true that he saw the need for works, how does Luther's view on the process of salvation differ from the position of the church he left? For that church the classic formulation was that salvation is attained by faith and good works. For Luther the formula was that man is saved by faith alone, not however, without works. What is the difference?

The beginning of an answer lies in seeing the diverse answers each position would give to the question: what is the value of good works? For the church of the sixteenth century they had value as a means of earning salvation. For Luther they were the inevitable consequence of having been saved by God's grace. He himself puts the difference by saying: "Good works do not make a good man, but a good man does good works."[8] In the one case, works are seen as a cause, along with God's grace, of salvation; in the other, as an effect produced by salvation achieved through faith.

If faith, then, was so important in the salvific process, what did Luther understand by the term? For him it was a compound of belief, confidence, and commitment. Of the three the heart of faith was confidence. In this he differed from the Roman Church which saw belief, the rational assent to the truth of revelation, as the essential element. This is not, however, to say that Luther minimized or dispensed with the need for doctrinal orthodoxy. Quite the contrary, since the whole weight of his writings lay in the direction of clarifying the content of the Christian faith. It is to say that, in effect, he demanded two distinct faiths. One was rational assent to the Christian truth, the other was reliance on God for salvation. The second

tended to be the one on which he put heaviest emphasis. His own torment-
ing experience had taught him that God's message of salvation through
Christ must be heard and answered by faith and so belief is necessary. But
the confidence flowing from this was the most important element. Because
God offers and man accepts, there can be a serene trust that God will be
faithful to what He promises. Man can be confident that God's love once
given will not fail.

Luther saw that this trust was not a once-and-for-all-arrived-at state.
Rather, there always remained the constant need of revitalizing it all
through life, the need too for rejecting any temptation to give it up because of experienced sinfulness. It was to man as sinner that it was first
given; it is to man as sinner that it continues to be given. Man's confidence,
his only hope, is in God's love for him in spite of his sinfulness. This is the
precise Word that God speaks to man in the Gospel.

Arising out of this acceptance of God's love there flows the realization
that one must make every effort to repay that love by loving in return.
One shows one's love by deed, by commitment to God's will, by the
unremitting attempt to live as God wants one to live. It was thus that good
works fitted into Luther's thinking. They are the saved man's spontaneous
response to God's mercy. They do not cause that mercy, nor do they
sustain it. But they are the normal expression of gratitude for the incredi-
ble favor received.

Faith, then, solves the dilemma of the demands of God's law and man's
inability to obey it. It does so by removing not the obligation of the law
but man's lack of capacity to fulfill it. Faith is indeed an emancipation,
not from the law, but from powerlessness in the face of the law and it
effects this release by pointing to where the power to observe the law
comes from, Christ Jesus. In a word, faith, far from releasing man from
obligation, is the only true source of Christian moral conduct. If it does
not imply human activity in response to God's gift of justice, it is not real
faith.

> Faith, however, is something that God effects in us. It changes
> us and we are reborn from God. It puts the old Adam to death
> and makes us quite different men in heart, in mind, and in all
> our powers; and it is accompanied by the Holy Spirit. O, when
> it comes to faith, what a living, creative, active, powerful thing
> it is. It cannot do other than good at all times. It never waits
> to ask whether there is some good work to do. Rather, before
> the question is raised, it has done the deed, and keeps on doing
> it. A man not active in this way is a man without faith.9

One last aspect of Luther's understanding of faith calls for attention, its personalism. The religion of his time tended to be a set of social attitudes and practices. It had become too easy to see Christianity as something into which one was born, in which one lived and died without ever having to face the necessity of making a personal commitment to being a Christian. In this world everyone was Christian and the way to live the Christian life was clearly spelled out. One said these prayers, received these sacraments, performed these works of piety. Christianity was all there as a given, a datum of life. But Luther's own purgatory of doubt and uncertainty had cured him of any tendency to accept this externalism.

Faith for Luther was something that occurred only in a very personal context. God's Word of salvation was not spoken to the group. His grace was not offered in general and purely external terms. Rather His Word had a special message for each man and His grace was given only to the individual. The process begins with God taking a prior interest in the individual. He then evidences this interest by offering His message in personal terms through the Holy Spirit who gives the meaning of this invitation for this individual. God's Word is heard by hearing the Spirit say: This is the meaning of God's offer of salvation for you. Thus faith is always a personal encounter. It calls for an entirely personal decision on the part of each man. All of life is lived in this climate of a personal response to a personal invitation in a personal encounter.

Much of Luther's later thinking was but the logical extension of this personalism. He saw that the all-important need was to establish a situation where the individual might come face to face with God without the interference of intermediaries. Thus when he moved toward eliminating external practices of religion, doing away with many of the sacramental means of grace, removing the ordained priesthood, he was simply implementing this basic conviction. Having learned for himself how these practices had kept him from knowing God as He reveals Himself in His Word, he tended to want to remove as many intermediaries as possible between God and the individual soul. He wanted to restore personal commitment to the heart of the religious experience.

THE PRINCIPLE OF GOD'S WORD

Luther's struggle with the problem of salvation found its resolution in his doctrine of salvation gratuitously given by God to the man of faith.

The instrument he had used to reach this conclusion was the Scripture. He concluded that it was there, and only there, in God's Word to man, that the message of salvation was to be found. The Bible alone has authority in communicating God's revelation to man. All that God wants to speak to man is there.

But to say this much is not to conclude that the Bible is all-important. It is not. What is all-important is God's Word. The Bible and the Word of God are not exactly the same reality. What is necessary for a man struggling with the problem of salvation is that he become aware of God's activity in solving that problem. The Bible is the story of God's saving activity. It is not that activity; rather it tells man of that activity. It calls attention, points in the direction of the living, active God.

Thus for Luther and for subsequent Protestantism the importance of the Bible is not such that one believes in it but rather that one believes in what it bears witness to, God's Word, God at work in Christ saving us. Hence, the act of faith that Luther makes is not in the Book but in the Word it testifies to. Someone has used the image of a window to portray the Bible's function. One does not look at a window; one looks through it. So it is with the Bible; one looks through its words to see God offering salvation and to respond. The constant concern of Protestantism with vernacular renditions of the Bible and with biblical scholarship takes its origin in Luther's concern with rendering the window as transparent as possible.

How, in Luther's view, is one to understand and interpret the message of the Scriptures? Here care must be taken not to mistake for his view either of the two extremes to which certain later forms of Protestantism carried the principle of the supreme authority of Scripture. Some would come to see the actual words of the Bible as inspired and hence to be interpreted in their strict literal meaning. At the other extreme would be those who would see the meaning of Scripture as completely individual. The only norm for determining its meaning would be what each person, under the Spirit, came to decide was its meaning for him. But both of these positions represent deviations from Luther's own view. He clearly saw the Bible and its understanding as set within the context of the Church.

> ... God's word cannot be without God's people, and conversely, God's people cannot be without God's word. Otherwise, who would preach or hear it preached if there were no people of God? And what could or would God's people believe, if there were no word of God?[10]

The Bible belongs to the Church. To her it was given by God; she alone is responsible for preaching it. Hence, its meaning can only be learned within the community of faith. It is not the individual believer who holds final responsibility for its meaning but the community to which it has been entrusted.

In the practical order what does this principle of the supreme authority of Scripture mean? Or, put another way, how does one come to know what he is to believe? Luther's own experience pointed to three elements as constituting the application of the principle: the Bible itself, tradition, and personal experience.

The Bible

In the words of Scripture which have God for their author the Holy Spirit finds the words He needs to speak to the individual. Thus when one reads or hears the Scripture, the Spirit is at work in the individual soul saying, "This message is true for you." For Luther himself it was particularly the study of the Psalms and Paul's Epistles which led him, under the direction of the Holy Spirit, to the understanding of God's Word as applied to him and to his problem. We will see that for Calvin the influential idea in the Scriptures is the notion of the absolute sovereignty of God. This will lead him to a definite way of writing and a definite course of action in Geneva. In different people the Spirit will use different inspirations to personalize for them the meaning of the Word.

The individual then responds and begins to act in accord with the message. He follows the lead of the Spirit. The activity he then produces gives clear testimony to the unique power of the Word from which it flows. His activity is a convincing proof that this is indeed the Word of God.

Tradition

The voice of the church has been speaking the meaning of the Word of God since that Word was first entrusted to her. Luther, Calvin and the other Reformers were well aware that to know only the Scriptures was not sufficient. One had also to know what the great voices in the church's history, men like Augustine, have said is the Bible's meaning. The preacher and the teacher must be aware of this centuries-old voice of tradition in the church as he approaches his own attempt to understand and communicate its meaning. Luther came to his insight into its essential meaning only after having seriously applied himself to discovering how God's Word had been understood by the early Fathers of the church. Awareness of being part of both a community and a continuity played an important role in the shaping of his final interpretations.

Personal Experience

Lastly, there is the strictly personal task of shaping the message to one's own situation and needs. Luther found his own inner experience—the inability to work out his salvation by his own efforts—at variance with the teaching of the contemporary church that it was by using the external means of grace that a man worked out his own salvation. To that variance he felt compelled to testify. Yet even in protest he did not conceive of himself as breaking with tradition. His conviction was rather that, led by the Spirit and his own arduous study of the voices of tradition, he was returning to the authentic interpretation of God's Word. He thought of himself not as innovator but as conservative and traditionalist in the deepest sense of those terms. He felt that protest was in his case called for as a necessary element in his reverence for the Word of God.

R. M. Brown describes the same personal understanding of the Word of God that each man must come to and puts it in contemporary garb when he writes,

> We must obey God rather than men—even the "men" of the Church, if and when obedience to God and men come into conflict, as they may. They came into conflict in Germany in the '30s. They come into conflict in many parts of the South and the North in the '60s. Martin Luther King's "Letter from a Birmingham Jail," written to eight clergymen who disapproved of his action, is a good example of the spirit of authority in Protestantism. Dr. King does not say that he is acting on his own personal whim. He claims to "be standing in the heritage of all those who, in the name of God, protest injustice"; and so he cites Amos and Paul, Aquinas and Augustine, Martin Luther and John Bunyan, along with many others who make clear to Dr. King that on the issue of racial injustice in Alabama in the 1960's, the burden of proof is not on those who are disobeying unjust laws, but on those who are silently acquiescing to them. And since the latter can be found in great

numbers in the church, the church at this point must be called
to account by those who love the church.[11]

These then are Luther's three fundamental principles. It remains now to
show how his thinking on the church, the sacraments and the Christian
vocation is but the logical working out, in specific areas, of the
implications already present in his three fundamental insights, gratuity,
faith, and God's Word.

THE CHURCH

Luther's thinking on the nature of the church is dominated by two of
his fundamental convictions, the necessarily individual response to the
Spirit's invitation to salvation and the essential sinfulness of human nature.
As we have seen, he felt strongly that there should be no intermediary
between the soul and God. The Spirit of Christ has always been at work in
history inviting individual men to accept God's saving activity on their
behalf and by this acceptance to enter his kingdom. This kingdom of
believers in His Word is the only church Christ intended to found. Thus
the one church which exists by the will of Christ is the community of all
those who have heard and accepted His Word. Luther called this the
church of the creed.

Whatever institutional forms this church takes in the course of time,
and it has taken a variety of them, exist not by His will but by human
decision, by the decision of men to band together in a community of
worship and belief for the advantages that such community affords. But it
must never be forgotten that these particular churches are only human
constructs. Because they are, they will always and inevitably show the
sinfulness and corruption of their creators. Hence too, they will always be
subject to the need for reform. There is no such thing as a finally perfect
structure of the church. Despite man's best efforts to build one, every
visible church, because it is a community of sinful men, will always be
relative, fallible, and imperfect in its attempt to proclaim the Word and
live according to God's will.

In the Roman Church's claim to be the one Church of Christ Luther
saw the attempt of sinful man to absolutize the form of the church; this
can never be done. There can never be one and only one externally
manifest way to worship and serve God. Two aspects of Luther's thought
here make clear the controlling function of his initial insight: (1) the

situation of his time offered him the choice of what he saw as two conflicting authorities, his personal conscience or the teaching authority of the church. It was the first alternative he chose, obedience to the Word of God as he saw it. This became for him the primary authority. What form the church took in his subsequent teaching was determined by the authority of conscience directly subject to the Word of God. Hence it was that, given his choice of authority, he was left with no alternative but to build an explanation of the nature of the church which opposed that of the authority he rejected. In place of a single, divinely-founded, infallible church he substituted his notion of multiple, fallible, humanly-founded churches. It was this church he found in Scripture.

(2) The second aspect to be noted is that for Luther what is initially important is the individual and his relation with God. Once one had established this relation he would be drawn to express it in a community of believers. The Roman vision that saw the individual born of the church yielded to the vision of individuals deciding to structure a church.

In the light of his stress on the church of the creed (an invisible church) which so carefully guards the conscience of the individual, there seemed no need for Luther to give a particular form to the church, to construct a visible church. To begin with, then, he was not concerned with organizing his own church. He felt the Word Itself would lead men to do this spontaneously.

But as the Reformation grew and his thinking developed under the impact of contemporary circumstances, Luther moved more and more definitely towards providing a formal structure for the church. There were two reasons particularly that moved him in this direction. First of all, those who joined with him in furthering the Reformation, men like Zwingli in Zurich and Bucer in Strassburg, began to develop notions of the church which stressed the value of an institutional church for preaching the Word and ordering the religious life of the community. He saw the value of peace, of harmony, of stability, that these structures gave to the life of the church.

Secondly, Luther became increasingly aware that his evangelical vision was not of itself enough to guarantee the success and the continuance of the Reform. Radical groups were springing up which were using his interpretation of the Word of God to serve the cause of rebellion against lawful authority and to introduce chaos into the life of the church. It thus became imperative that he should apply himself to building a concrete form of church life, a form which would provide the locus for proper understanding of God's Word and for the proper living out of the evangelical message.

The value of a definite, organized structure for church life became increasingly obvious. It provided organization, discipline, order and was able to formulate statements of credal belief and forms of worship. It gave organized form to the element of community so essential in the religious experience. Luther came to see that God gathers the church, the community of believers. Men then structure that church in viable and visible form. His own organizational principle was quite simple: the church fulfills its basic function if it is so ordered that it proclaims the pure Gospel and administers Christ's sacraments as He intended. Any church order developed to perform this double task was in his eyes a true form of the church.

For Luther, good pastors carefully chosen and trained were at the heart of this organized church. It was for them to conduct the divine worship at the altar and proclaim the Word in its purity from the pulpit. Careful attention was also given to the religious training of the young and for that purpose he developed his two Catechisms, the *Large Catechism* primarily for use by adults and the *Small Catechism* for children. Both incorporated his view of Christianity that we have already seen. To begin with, a discussion of the ten commandments allowed him to detail man's sinfulness under the Law and his consequent need of God's help. The Apostles' Creed then provided the setting for an exposition of the Gospel message of divine forgiveness. Next the Lord's Prayer was explained as the expression of man's confidence in God's gift of salvation. Finally, the two sacraments of Christ were treated, Baptism and the Lord's Supper. These were seen as the two preeminent means by which God confers His justice on men.

The liturgical worship he set up mirrored his belief that the whole Christian people must understand and be part of the worship of God. Hence all of it was performed in the people's native tongue. He translated the whole of the Scripture into German and appropriate selections from it were woven into the service. At that service the high point was reached when the Word of God was proclaimed and explained by the pastor. A simplified communion service followed. The last element introduced was hymn singing. He himself wrote a number of hymns, both words and music, to express the evangelical faith in song; he also made use of hymns and Psalm versifications borrowed from others.

The whole structure of worship as Luther reconstructed it was different in two dramatic aspects from the worship of the medieval church. First of all, emphasis moved away from the centrality of the priest in the Mass toward focusing on the community joined together in divine worship. Secondly, the center of attention moved away from the altar and the sacrifice to the pulpit and the preaching and teaching of the Word of God.

One might finally summarize Luther's thinking on the church by saying that he never lost his initial conviction that religion is essentially the individual and invisible, interior relation of the soul to God. What concern he manifested for the organizing and structuring of a visible church was wrested from him almost reluctantly by the demands of the concrete historical situation. But once the adjustment was forced on him he gave careful attention to the details of church order. In so doing he developed a liturgy and a church life that was very clearly scriptural and instructional in its orientation.

THE SACRAMENTS

In the area of sacramental theology the determining influence for Luther was the supreme authority of God's Word. Out of that Word he formulated his notion of the meaning of a sacrament as an outward sign of invisible grace, instituted by Christ as evidenced by unmistakably clear words in Scripture, and intended exclusively for Christians. Using this criterion he judged five of the seven sacraments of the medieval church as unscriptural. For him there were only two, Baptism and the Lord's Supper.

Marriage had existed from man's beginnings as a universal practice. It was, therefore, not exclusively Christian nor was its institution to be attributed to Christ, but to God. But though it was not a sacrament it did introduce those who were exchanging vows into a life wherein religion should play a major part. That life together should be blessed by the church.

Confirmation, likewise, found no justification in Christ's words. It was a ceremony added later by the church. "But we read nowhere that Christ ever gave a promise concerning confirmation."[12] ". . . it is sufficient to regard confirmation as a certain churchly rite, or sacramental ceremony similar to other ceremonies, such as the blessing of water and the like."[13]

His thinking on *Extreme Unction* is interesting as an example of his use of the principle of scriptural authority. Reference to the anointing of the sick is made in the Epistle of St. James (James 5:14 ff.). This might conceivably serve as scriptural warrant for its sacramental nature. But one of the major themes of this epistle was the necessity of good works for salvation, or, put another way, that salvation comes from faith and good works. This, of course, raises the question of whether or not Luther's view of salvation by faith alone takes adequate account of the complete scriptural message regarding the process of salvation.[14] Luther's view was essentially Pauline in its inspiration, as we have seen, and he tended to regard James' point of view with suspicion. He spoke of the letter of James in one place as an "epistle of straw" and again as "not worthy of the spirit of an apostle." Thus, when it was a question of seeing in the epistle's words an indication of the existence of a sacrament of the sick in apostolic times, Luther set this reference aside as having no probative value. "No apostle has the right on his own authority to institute a sacrament."[15] And as far as any indication of institution by Christ is concerned: "And nowhere do we read in the gospel of the sacrament of extreme unction."[16]

Penance was a rite whose value Luther perceived. About its sacramentality he did not seem quite sure. There was no question in his mind that the need for doing penance was a constant theme in Christ's discourses. He saw, therefore, a definite place in the Christian Church for external acts of sorrow for sin. He was also aware of the consolation and peace that confession to a priest could bring to the individual believer. Thus he approved of Penance and of the use of confession by those for whom it was helpful and he recommended confession of one's sins to a brother. What he did object to, however, was that it be institutionalized, made one of those external good works by which a person might be led to believe that he could place a meritorious act and so win God's favor. He saw confession, looked on as a mandatory form of doing penance, as a contradiction of his doctrine of *sola gratia-sola fides.*

Holy Orders was for Luther one of the prime targets of his reform. As he read the signs of his time, clericalism, the domination of the clergy over many areas of life, could be blamed for much of the venality and abuse found in the church. Privilege had been abused and corruption introduced by the excesses of the clergy. In addition, he felt that no significant change could be effected in God's church as long as the clerical order of distinction and authority remained. Introduced by the church, not by Christ, in his view, the rite of ordination did not confer any invisible grace nor indelible mark that was the foundation of a special status in the church. All were of equal membership in the church. Thus, at a stroke, the basis for the clerical theocracy, which he saw as the great evil of the church, was removed.

The church of God would, of course, continue to need its ministers. Let the community of the faithful choose pastors for themselves, men from their own ranks whom they deemed fit to preach the Word, conduct the service and administer Christ's sacraments. Far more scriptural in its roots, and therefore far more characteristic of Christ's church than an ordained and privileged clergy, was the priesthood of all believers. Man had no need for a mediator between himself and God except God's Word. He was to hear the Spirit's voice speaking to him in that Word and to respond to it for himself. But in his response to that Word each believer became a priest for his brethren, in the sense that a man's total response to God's Word included not only his own commitment to God's will but also the responsibility of carrying the Word to his neighbor. Each man brought the divine message to his fellow men, acting as mediator in proclaiming the message of God's mercy by the example of his Christian life.

Thus five sacraments were set aside as lacking an essential element, institution by Christ. There remained for Luther and for Protestantism in general only the two sacraments of *Baptism* and the *Lord's Supper,* or *Eucharist.*

Before proceeding to a discussion of Luther's views on these two sacraments it will be well to stop and consider his general sacramental thinking. For him there was only one real sacrament and that was the Word of God. It was only in this Word that God gave His grace. Here man met God and was saved. Nothing else could add to what was given in this encounter. Hence the other sacraments were only concrete forms, particular actualizations that the Word took because Christ willed it so. In word and act they made God's offer of grace sensibly present; they rendered His Word perceptibly manifest. By so doing they created an opportunity for a fresh response of faith.

The sacramental rites were not of themselves acts that produced grace. Rather, when the Word of God was made present there always had to be a dialogue if that Word was to have its result. The symbolic word and action was God speaking. In addition there always had to be the personal response of individual faith. When both were present, God gave His grace. This was Luther's reaction to the sacramental theology of the medieval church which had come to put so much emphasis on the sacramental action itself. In the Roman view the sacraments produced their effect of grace if the rite was properly performed by the minister and if it was received by the individual without his placing an obstacle in the way of its effectiveness. This approach to the sacrament seemed, in Luther's eyes, to undervalue the person's part in the encounter, to make him only negatively involved in its efficacy. His own stress on the individuality of the religious experience led him to minimize the objective effect produced by the sacrament itself and to emphasize the influence of the individual's reaction on the effect produced. It should be noted, of course, that even the possibility of the individual's contribution took its origin in God's gift, not in his own power. The response of faith was a gift of grace.

The need for personal response in every sacrament caused Luther a serious problem when he came to discussing the sacrament of *Baptism*. This was the occasion, instituted by Christ, for the external profession of one's interior faith. But, if this were true, what justification could be offered for the Baptism of infants? They could not bring personal faith to the sacrament. Luther's answer to this problem seemed to have varied. At one time he saw this sacrament as the prime example of the absolute gratuity of salvation. God simply decided, because He wanted it so, to give the child His grace without any action on the child's part. At another time he saw the community of believers supplying, by their presence in the sponsors, the faith that needed to be present. This was the one occasion where he allowed faith to be vicariously present. The problem, not solved in Luther's time, would return later to introduce into Protestantism a Fundamental division between those who would allow for the Baptism of children and those who, demanding that Luther's own insistence on the presence of personal faith always be verified, practiced only believer's Baptism.

Luther's thinking on the *Eucharist* began with his rejection of the sacrifice of the Mass. For him it was one of the gravest scandals of the medieval church. He took strong exception both to the manner in which it had come to be celebrated and particularly to the thinking offered to justify it. As a young monk he was sent to Rome in 1510 on business for his monastery and while there he was scandalized at the way the Roman clerics offered Mass. Todd paints this picture of his Roman experience:

> It was only later that his experiences at Rome fused into a kind of horror at what came to seem a radical degradation, as he remembered the almost blasphemy with which the priests had seemed to juggle so casually with the sacraments and remembered the worldly lives of themselves and others; the hurried Masses (he tells of the whispers of a priest at an altar next to him as he finished his Mass when Luther was only a third of the way through his own: "Passa, passa . . . , Hurry up, for goodness sake, there are others waiting. . . ."), and the atmosphere of relaxation and self-satisfaction combined with a putrefying legalism, implying an idea of God far distant from anything to be found in the New Testament, a mess from which others had reacted by instituting one reform or another, but which eventually helped to prompt the whole massive Protestant reaction.[17]

But even more serious than his disgust at seeing priests at the altar distractedly mumbling Latin prayers whose meaning in many instances they did not comprehend was his gradually-arrived-at conclusion that the whole thinking which lay behind and was used to justify the offering of the Mass was a blasphemy. Scripture had taught him that Christ's one offering of his life on the cross was all-sufficient. It totally fulfilled the demands of divine justice for sinful man. How then could one speak of re-offering that one all-sufficient sacrifice? Was this not to imply that Christ's work had not fulfilled all justice? The Mass was a calumny on the redemptive sacrifice of the Savior. The presumptuousness of it became even more evident to him when he realized that here was sinful man presuming he could perform an action which would be meritorious in the sight of God. Man's essential evil precluded any such possibility.

Luther, therefore, moved away from the idea of the Mass as a sacrifice in the direction of seeing it as essentially a Eucharistic celebration and thanksgiving service. For him it had two aspects: (1) By its recall of the sacrifice of the cross which effected man's redemption it afforded the believer an opportunity for renewing his gratitude to God for this great gift; (2) the coming together of the faithful for this commemoration of the Lord's Supper provided the occasion for a strong renewal of Christian fellowship and community. The receiving of communion was a perfect expression of that fellowship in the Lord's Body.

Was the Lord Himself really present in the midst of His people at this Eucharist? For Luther the answer was an unequivocal yes. Christ was really and physically present, not however, in terms of the Roman explanation by transubstantiation which smacked too much of scholastic subtlety. Rather, the Lord, who is always and everywhere present, though normally invisibly, chooses this occasion to reveal that presence in visible form. Christ, hiddenly present, removes the veil of that hiddenness at the words of the minister and stands revealed in visible, bodily presence.

In summary then, Luther's sacramental theology was a compound of a variety of elements. It represented his reaction against what he saw as an overstress on the automatically effective operation of the rites themselves. It also represented the application of his scripturally oriented thinking to a specific area of the divine revelation and the implementation of his stress on the individual's part in the salvific process as that was to be applied in the sacraments.

THE CHRISTIAN VOCATION

One last aspect of Luther's thought remains to be touched on: his conception of the nature of the Christian calling. Here too he had a specifically new interpretation of the idea of vocation. When one spoke of vocation at that time, one meant vocation to the priesthood or religious life. Christianity offered the believer two roads to God, one for the ordinary man, led to salvation by way of observance of the commandments while living in the world. This was the less sure way; it was also the more dangerous one because the world was an evil place and offered many obstacles to living a good life.

By far the safer and more perfect road was to enter religious life. Here, withdrawn from the world's temptations, one could more easily please God and by the sacrifice contained in the life of the vows more assuredly win God's favor. It was the religious who more fully lived the Christian calling. The life of the laity was more or less Christian as it approximated this ideal living of Christianity.

Against this concept of the Christian vocation, Luther spoke out strongly. It was misleading and false to the testimony of Scripture to see the more perfect form of Christianity embodied in a withdrawal from the world. God put man in the world that he might work out his salvation there, that he might find his salvation in being merchant, miner, housewife, farmer. It was in these vocations that the Christian fulfilled the will of God for him. Furthermore, the distinction between commandment and counsel certainly found no basis in the Gospels. Christ intended his entire message for all his followers. Each of them was to strive for the fulfillment of the entire Christian Gospel. Last of all, the religious life represented an element in that cast of mind so characteristic of late medievalism which extolled man's efforts as meriting his reward. Religious life, in other words, was built on the false premise that more strenuous efforts win greater reward. This perspective, as we have seen time and time again, represented a distortion in Luther's view. All was God's in salvation and hence no form of the Christian life was any better or any worse in terms of merit than any other form.

Luther is here striking at the roots of medieval monasticism. His thinking will manifest itself in the practical order in his own leaving of religious life and marrying and it will destroy monastic life in the lands where his reform is adopted. The broader implications of this view that Luther takes on the nature of the Christian vocation are well summarized by Brown in the following words:

> What the Reformers did was to cut through that distinction (between religious and lay) and assert that one's calling could be fulfilled in any kind of occupation and not just in a specifically "sacred" one. As Luther put it, the shoemaker can serve God at his bench just as fully as the priest does at the

altar. . . . Thus the "sacredness of the secular" . . . was reaffirmed. One's response to God in love could be carried out wherever one was. All of life was invested with meaning, and all work was invested with dignity.

This view has had a long and complex history. It has raised difficulties; sometimes *all* kinds of work have been too uncritically sanctified, and sometimes Protestantism has become a little too chummy with the worst forms of capitalist expansion. But as a general principle, granted the need for constant redefinition in the light of differing cultural situations, the emphasis on Christian vocation is an important contribution to the ordering of man's total life under God.[18]

CONCLUSION

By way of a final conclusion, how is Luther's position in the history of Christianity to be assessed? There can be no question that he arrived at a view of Christianity sharply differentiated from the Roman Catholicism of his time. It is likewise true that his estimate of the meaning of the Christian religious experience contained authentic and perenially necessary emphases in that experience. His essential contribution seems to have been the rediscovery and reinsertion into the stream of Christian history of certain emphases which had come to be widely undervalued if not totally disregarded in his age. God is all in the salvific process; man must be personally committed by faith to his own salvation; God's Word must be listened to if man is to know what God is offering and asking from man; all these are of the essence of the Christian message.

But to have said this is not to have said all, because the Christian faith in its fullness says there are other equally essential emphases that must be included if one is to talk with completeness of the relation between God and man and of the way by which man comes to God.

(1) It is certainly true that in salvation God is all. But in the Christian revelation it is of equal certainty that God will not save man without his cooperation. In the dialogue of salvation both partners to the dialogue must be active: God and man, To assert the allness of God is not enough. This must be paradoxically countered by asserting also the role of man. Both are involved and hence neither is sufficient alone. It is a distortion of Christianity to overemphasize either term of the dialogue. To overstress God's part tends to reduce man to nothing and thereby robs him of his

necessary contribution to his own salvation. To overstress man's part is to run the risk of granting him an autonomy in his own destiny which Christianity asserts he does not have. Thus at one and the same time God does and does not alone save man and man does and does not contribute to his salvation. In the Christian revelation only the delicate balancing of these opposite and apparently mutually contradictory truths preserves the totality of the truth.

Luther, in reaction against the contemporary church's tendency to exalt the role of man in salvation, laid heavy emphasis on the role of God. In his anxiety to preserve that absoluteness of God he was led to minimize man's role. The consequence of this imbalance is that his thinking is characterized by an excessively pessimistic view of man. Even after God has justified him man is still not able to make any positive contribution to his salvation. He is before and he remains after justification essentially corrupt. But this is, of course, to limit the power of God; it is to say that man is so evil that even God is not able to cure him.

It is sobering to realize that these two positions still seem to characterize the two forms of Christianity. Roman Catholicism, whose overemphasis on man's part in the process of salvation had led to Luther's initial protest, still tends to lay heavy emphasis on man's ability to merit salvation if he performs a set of externally good works. Protestantism, for its part, still looks at man through overly dark glasses. If the ecumenism that characterizes both positions today is to succeed it will be not by resolving the dilemma, God or man, but by preserving the tension, God-man.

(2) For Luther the involvement of the individual in his own salvation by way of faith is all-important. He is right in so insisting. But this insistence on the personal and subjective element in faith needs to be counterbalanced by the equally essential insistence on the objective element in faith. Man must believe, and no proxy can supply this for him. But he does not create that in which he believes; he accepts it. And in the very act of so accepting he is implicitly acknowledging the need for an external authority to determine the content of faith. If there be no such principle of authority then the personalism of faith can degenerate into the sheerest individualism. Each man then supplies not only his personal act of faith but that also in which he believes.

It is certainly true that the person is all-important; yet paradoxically the object to which his faith is directed is equally all-important. And that importance can only be guaranteed if there is an objectively existent authority able to determine the content of man's act of faith. Faith needs to be both subjective and objective.

Again Luther was both right and wrong in his insistence on the need of personal faith. Faced with the excessive objectivity of the Christianity of his time he reacted strongly in the direction of the subjective. It was not enough for a man to be simply and unquestioningly a part of the given Christian structure of society. Creed, sacramental cult, and moral code had no real value unless subjectively assimilated. In this he was right. The individual must make creed, cult, and code his own. The person is all-important in the religious experience. The danger in Luther's stress on the importance of the subjective comes when such emphasis is allowed to exclude or minimize the equally important need in Christianity for an objective content of revelation to which personal faith subscribes. Without such objectively determined content, personal faith becomes pure subjectivism. Man moves to center stage replacing God there. He not only contributes the act of faith but its content as well. If the necessity of individual faith is not countered with the equally definite necessity of objective revelation then faith is relieved of the need for any support outside itself. Thus the door is opened to the elimination of all content (except what is personally decided upon) from belief and the removal of all visible rites, sacraments and other objective means of grace. Man's belief becomes ultimately belief in himself. Luther himself always remained committed to objective revelation as contained in Scripture. But some later forms of Protestantism tended to lose sight of his commitment to objective revelation in their insistence on the all-importance of personal faith.

As noted in the first paradox, God-man, so too here it is tragic to note that the subsequent history of Protestantism and Roman Catholicism tended to become a confrontation between personal faith and objective content. Subjectivity become subjectivism is Protestantism's perennial temptation. Insistence on the need for an authority to determine the objective content of man's belief tends in Roman Catholicism to move constantly towards an excessive authoritarianism. Again the future of contemporary ecumenism depends on its ability to hold in tension without allowing either to dominate, the subjective individual commitment and the objective content of faith determined by a principle of authority.

(3) Lastly, there is truth and error in Luther's insistence that it is only in hearing and responding to God's Word that man can know God's revelation. God's Word must be all in learning the way He has designed for man to come to Him. Yet it is equally true that Christian revelation speaks not only of an event—the life, death and resurrection of Christ, but also of

the meaning of that event—it is in this that God saves man. The same New Testament that speaks of the event speaks also of leaders who speak with authority, giving the authentic interpretation of the event. The community accepts their role and assents to their interpretation.

Thus the Word of God does not stand alone waiting for the private individual to determine its meaning for himself. This could produce as many meanings as there are men and ultimately no objective meaning at all. Rather It stands within a community where there are those whose task it is to explain Its meaning to the fellowship of believers. Or put more succinctly, to deny authentic interpretation is to deny an essential element of God's Word since that Word has built into It indications of Its own authentic interpretation.

God's Word alone is man's sole criterion for salvation; in this Luther saw rightly. Yet again the paradox and the tension appears. God's Word does not stand alone. It has build into It a guaranteed principle of right interpretation. Only with this principle is It understood rightly.

In the Catholicism of his time Luther came to see the primacy of God's Word overshadowed and lost sight of in the Roman tendency not to serve the Word but to subject It to the Church's own purposes. He reacted by cutting the Scriptures free from the church that he saw corrupting it. Correction was needed; the tragedy was that it introduced an unbridgeable chasm between Word and church. Subsequent history has tended to perpetuate that chasm. The Word of God alone as normative continues to be the Protestant emphasis. That the church to whom the Word was entrusted must continue to be its authoritative interpreter, reflects the dominant Catholic emphasis. There is danger in both emphases taken in isolation. One leads toward fragmentation of Christianity and a gradual evacuation of content from the Christian message. The other leads toward subjection of God's Word to human purposes and is liable to end up in a rigid authoritarianism that stifles the Spirit of God as He attempts to speak that Word to the Christian. The final task of contemporary ecumenism is the healing of this rupture of emphases.

We turn now to the other great Reformer, John Calvin, and the elements that he contributed to the formation of the Protestant Tradition.

FOOTNOTES

1Quoted by Roland H. Bainton in *Here I Stand* (New York & Nashville: Abingdon-Cokesbury Press, 1950), p. 45.

2*Ibid.*, p. 41.

3I am here following Bainton's line of thought in *Here I Stand,* pp. 54-56.

4Louis Bouyer, *The Spirit and Forms of Protestantism* (Westminster, Md.: The Newman Press, 1956), p. 9.

5Quoted by Gordon Rupp in *Luther's Progress to the Diet of Worms,* Torchbook edition, (New York: Harper & Row, 1964), p. 33. Reprinted by permission of SCM Press, London.

6Bainton, *Here I Stand,* p. 65.

7J.S. Whale, *The Protestant Tradition,* paperback edition (London and New York: Cambridge University Press, 1959), pp. 93-94.

8Martin Luther, "The Freedom of a Christian" in *Luther's Works,* vol. XXXI, ed. Harold J. Grimm (Philadelphia: Muhlenberg Press, 1957), p. 361.

9——, "Preface to the Epistle of St. Paul to the Romans," *The Reformation Writings of Martin Luther,* vol. II, *The Spirit of the Protestant Reformation,* trans. and ed. Bertram Lee Wolf (New York: Philosophical Library, 1956), p. 288.

10——, "On the Councils and the Church" *Luther's Works,* vol. XLI, ed. Eric W. Gritsch (Philadelphia: Fortress Press, 1966), p. 150.

11Robert M. Brown, "Protestantism and Authority," *Commonweal,* Oct. 9, 1964, p. 71.

12Luther, "The Babylonian Captivity of the Church" in *Luther's Works,* vol. XXXVI, ed. Abdel Ross Wentz (Philadelphia: Fortress Press, 1959) p. 92.

13*Ibid.*

14For a general discussion of Luther's use of Scripture cf. Joseph Lortz, *The Reformation: A Problem for Today* (Westminster, Md.: The Newman Press, 1964), pp. 228-35.

15Luther, *Babylonian Captivity, p. 118,*

16*Ibid.*

17John M. Todd, *Martin Luther* (Westminster, Md.: The Newman Press, 1964, and A. M. Heath, London), pp. 62-63.

18Robert M. Brown, "Classical Protestantism," in *Patterns of Faith in America Today,* ed. F. Ernest Johnson (New York: Harper & Brothers, 1957), pp. 46-47.

CHAPTER TWO

John Calvin

Besides the Lutheranism which developed principally in Germany, by far the largest section of Protestant Christianity derives from another source, the Reformed church tradition with its roots particularly in the Switzerland of Zurich, Basel, and Geneva. And among the men responsible for this vision of Christianity the name of John Calvin (1509-1564) dominates.

Reformed Protestantism finds its origins rather in a movement than in the personal experience of an individual as was true in Luther's case. The movement was biblical humanism championed at the beginning of the sixteenth century by men like Thomas More and Desiderius Erasmus.

The movement was called biblical because it wished to restore the Bible to the center of Christianity. Its central contention was that Scripture is the unique source of knowledge about divine revelation and contains all one must believe to be saved. The leaders of the movement recognized as clearly as Luther the need for the reform of Christianity by a return to the Scriptural teaching; more radically than he, they wanted to restore Christianity, in its beliefs and practices, to the structure patterned in the New Testament.

It was called humanism because it represented a return to humanistic studies, the study of both the ancient classical languages, Greek, Latin, and Hebrew, and of the early Christian Fathers. Tools were developed for the critical study and interpretation of these languages and texts. The results thus obtained were then put at the service of God's Word in new critical texts of the Bible and in the re-opening to scholarship of the works of men like Augustine and Origen. In a word, return was made to the original expression of Christianity as found in the most ancient and critically authenticated texts. It was out of such a background that men like Ulrich Zwingli, Martin Bucer, and John Calvin came.

One further difference between Lutheranism and Reformed Protestant-ism ought to be noted at the beginning and that is the strong activist strain that characterizes the Reformed churches. Luther's church had no mission-ary thrust built into it. It tended to develop under the patronage of the rulers who adopted his views and made his church the church of their realm. The Reformed tradition, on the other hand, emphasized the obliga-tion that lay on its members of securing God's glory by carrying His message to the nations. Hence, unlike Lutheranism, it was missionary oriented. Once begun in the Swiss cantons it spread widely and rapidly. It spread into France and up into the Low Countries. It was carried across the water to Scotland by John Knox where it soon established itself as the state-fostered religion. The Church of England was also strongly influenced in its theology and church structures by the Reformed tradition. The Marian exiles, who spent the years of Mary's reign in the Reformed Swiss communities, carried their Reformed thinking back to England with them and effected its strong presence in the church built by Elizabeth. From England, Reformed Protestantism passed to the New World where, in America, its Presbyterian and Congregational forms were strongly rooted from the beginning. After the Revolutionary War it became and remained the dominant influence in American Protestantism. Hugenot, Covenanter, Dissenter, Puritan, American Protestantism in its principal forms, all trace their beginnings to the Reformed churches that sprang up under Zwingli in Zurich, Bucer in Strassburg, and, above all, John Calvin in Geneva.

CALVIN'S LIFE

Born in 1509 at Noyon in northern France, John Calvin was early destined for the priesthood and was sent when only 14 to prepare for this career in the University of Paris. By 1528 he had switched to law which he studied first at Orleans and then at Bourges. 1531 marked his decision to give himself to the study of Hebrew and the classical languages that he might better penetrate the meaning of the Scripture. It was most probably in these years (1528-31) that his own personal religious crisis developed and his decision was made to give himself henceforth to the service of the sovereign God he found depicted in the Bible. This meant a break with the medieval Catholic church and what he had come to regard as its idolatry and superstition. He himself describes the process of his conversion in the Preface to his *Commentary on the Psalms.*

> First, when I was too firmly addicted to the papal superstition
> to be drawn easily out of such a deep mire, by a sudden
> conversion, He brought my mind (already more rigid than
> suited my age) to submission [to Him]. I was so inspired by a
> taste of true religion and I burned with such a desire to carry
> my study further, that although I did not drop other subjects I
> had no zeal for them. In less than one year, all who were
> looking for a purer doctrine began to come to learn from me,
> although I was a novice and a beginner.[1]

The most immediate sequel to this decision was a return to Paris for
study and writing. By 1534 his new thinking was manifest enough to lead
to his involvement in the proceedings for heresy brought against Nicholas
Cop, rector of the University of Paris. Calvin was charged with the same
tendency to heresy as Cop because of his friendship with Cop. He had to
flee Paris and his first stop was Strassburg. McNeill summarizes well Calvin's frame of mind at this juncture. Persecution only hardened him in his
resolve.

> Behind the harsh reaction of the Sorbonne he saw the whole
> medieval, papal, hierarchical, and sacramental system sunk
> through long deterioration into a state of corruption and
> superstition, inert in the chains of tradition, negligent of the
> Word of God. Here lay the ultimate hindrance to reform, the
> stronghold of the persecutors of those who sought it. Cost
> what it might, Rome itself must be repudiated; others had paid
> the price. He had known this in an impersonal way for some
> time; but he had resisted the suggestion, having been "stub-
> bornly addicted" to the Papacy and to the system in which
> from boyhood he had expected to participate through his later
> years. Now it was all clear and it was personal. There could be
> no postponement, no rationalized evasion. The hand of God
> was laid upon him.[2]

In Strassburg he had the opportunity to see the reformed community,
which Martin Bucer had set up, with its own ordered communal life and
liturgy. By 1536 he was in Basel where he published his *Institutes of the
Christian Religion.* The remainder of his life would be occupied with revis-
ing and enlarging this, the greatest of his works. It was and remains one of
the monumental statements of Protestant theological thought. With the
Institutes completed, he set out once again for Strassburg. His journey
took him through Geneva where William Farel was at work introducing
reform. Farel confronted him and set the course of his future life by
convincing him that it was the will of God that he should remain and help
build the Reformation in Geneva.

Calvin settled in Geneva, becoming professor of Sacred Letters and assuming the office of pastor in the church of St. Pierre. For two years the work of implementing the reform proceeded slowly because the magistrates and townspeople were not yet ready for the complete submission of the city to God's will that Calvin envisaged. In April of 1538 the contest between Calvin and the General Council for control of the town's spiritual affairs broke out into the open; the issue was the ceremonies of public worship. Calvin and Farel refused to accept the authority of the Council to decide such a directly spiritual matter and they were banished from the city.

Calvin retired to Strassburg and gave himself for three years to working with Bucer for the building up of the Reform there. These years were fruitful ones for him. While there he exercised the pastorate of the congregation of refugees from France. He also took up the task of lecturing and preaching daily. Time was also available for writing and during his stay he published the first of his biblical commentaries, his *Commentary on Romans* (1539). Before the end of his life he would issue commentaries on all of the New Testament and most of the Old. 1540 saw the appearance of his *Little Treatise on the Holy Supper of Our Lord* and his *Reply to Cardinal Sadoleto* (1539) offered his defense for leaving the Roman church.

Last of all, the three years were a valuable experience because they gave Calvin the chance to work with two men from whom he learned much, Sturm and Bucer. John Sturm, the famed humanist, was at the time rector of the school in Strassburg. He would, over the course of the years, make it one of the great humanist schools of Europe. From him Calvin learned much that would be incorporated into his own *collège* in Geneva. From Bucer there was much to learn of church order. He had developed a very close-knit ecclesiastical community where the religious and secular aspects of life flowed together into a harmonious unity wherein the glory of God was sought in all things. Much of the church ordinance Calvin would later set up in Geneva was indebted to Bucer for its inspiration. Thus in many respects the years in Strassburg provided valuable preparation for the life work in Geneva that still lay ahead.

By 1541 the magistrates in Geneva had decided they needed the leadership that only Calvin could supply and a delegation was sent to plead with him to return. With great reluctance, yet under the conviction that God's will called him, Calvin returned to Geneva in September 1541. There he would spend the last twenty-four years of his life building the Holy Commonwealth, God's Kingdom on earth.

n accord with Luther's. He too was
f salvation, the supreme authority of
ong, personal faith. What, however,
was central to an understanding of his
. It was this which distinctly set him
ain focus of our attention.
ation was on man and the problem of
ssentially man-centered. His thinking
ntrism. It is what God does for man
s concentration is the exact opposite.
s radically theocentric. Man fits into
of his relation to God. What is impor-
for the world and, having learned it,
cheme of things. It is not for man that
ue and the supreme act of religion for
himself humbly to the absolute sover-

al theocentrism of Calvin will become
clear if we analyze three of the basic ideas that dominate his theology: The
absolute sovereignty of God, all else exists for God's glory, and the inevitable corollary that flows from both of these principles, his doctrine on
predestination.

The Absolute Sovereignty of God

Man's principal purpose in life is, for Calvin, to know God. The God of
whom he speaks is God as revealed in Scripture. Much of Calvin's vision of
God reflects the Old rather than the New Testament vision of the deity.
God, as he knows Him, is utterly transcendent, beyond any thought that
we might think of Him. He is totally Other, unknowable (except insofar as
He reveals Himself to us and that revelation is more a revelation of His
relation to us than it is of His own nature). Put another way, the most
basic fact God reveals about Himself is His complete mysteriousness, His
absolute hiddenness. To man He is fundamentally incomprehensible. Thus
He is the object, not primarily of our knowledge but rather of our adora-

tion. Once this sense of the complete transcendence of God is grasped, one is able to appreciate how completely this understanding of God dominates Calvin.

In His Word God reveals Himself as majestic, awesome, of infinite power, and complete incomprehensibility. Beyond this He shows Himself as the free and sovereign Lord of all that is and all that happens in creation. He is free because He is bound by nothing save His own will. He is, in consequence, subject in no sense to any limit or condition that might be put upon His will by anything that man might do. He is sovereign in the sense that nothing which happens in the created order escapes His will. What happens in his creation happens because He wills it so.

Such, for Calvin, is the only knowledge of God that has any worth for man, a knowledge that leads man to three basic religious attitudes: humble adoration before the mystery and sovereignty of God, acceptance of man's own significance, and total dedication to manifesting the glory of God.

Some very fundamental attitudes within Calvinism flow out of this way of knowing God. Thus, for example, the acceptance of God as essentially mysterious will prevent man's worst sin, idolatry, the tendency to think of God in human terms and to express Him in man-made forms, to make Him what we think Him to be. But God is not a construct of man's mind or imagination. He is a given, completely apart from man's thinking about Him. He is to be accepted as He presents Himself in His Word, not to be speculated about and gradually made over to man's image and likeness. Here lie the roots of Calvinism's perennial suspicion of a natural knowledge of God and its rejection of a natural theology. Man can know nothing of God except what God tells him. What He tells him is contained in His revelation, His Word.

This awe in the presence of the unknown God will find itself also expressed in the attitude adopted by Calvinism with regard to its churches and the form its worship takes. There is an austerity, almost a barrenness, in the lack of any adornment in its churches. This reflects a rejection of visible idolatry. Any statue, painting, stained glass, that man might use to express his idea of God must be rigorously controlled, if not completely excluded, lest man feel he can express the inexpressible. God cannot be expressed in human terms.

The same stark rejection of sensible appeal runs also through their worship. What alone is necessary is that the individual be brought into undistracted contact with God and His Word. Anything that might impede or distract from this personal encounter is to be eliminated. As it is true that man is liable to speak idolatrously in glass, or stone, or wooden image, so too it is far better to use God's Word in speaking of Him than man's own speech for fear of mental and vocal idolatry. Thus, for example, there is much use made in divine worship of the Psalms for both prayers and hymns. These are God's words and the way that God Himself has provided for man to speak about and pray to Him. In using them man is sure that he speaks of and to God rightly.

One is likewise able to understand in this attitude the feeling approaching horror with which Calvin and his followers regard the statues and images, the candles and vestments, the entire sensible appeal of the Roman Catholic liturgy. They are inclined to read here a violation of God's command: "Thou shalt not make unto thyself graven images." In man's attempt to visualize or otherwise make sensible, God and the things of God, there always lurks the temptation to refuse to accept God as He reveals Himself, essentially mysterious and unknowable, and hence to become idolatrous.

All Things Exist for God's Glory (soli Deo gloria)

This unknown and sovereignly free God enters into a freely chosen relation with created reality. All things that exist come from Him; He is their efficient cause. They have also no other end than Him; He is their final cause. Thus, it is for His own purposes that God acts. The redemption wrought by Christ is directed to man and his salvation but that salvation preeminently manifests the glory of God. This being the purpose of the world and of all in it, man's task is to accept and conform himself to this end. He must come to acknowledge that the only reason for which he exists is to give God glory, to reflect the purpose for which God made him. His end is to attain his salvation. But his salvation is part of the over-arching purpose of the world, to give glory to God.

Yet Calvin, in seeing man's end to be the glory of God, does not thereby intend to crush man but rather to raise him to a sure confidence in God. For God's Word makes it clear that He finds His glory in doing good for man. In the final analysis, God's glory is most surely achieved in His saving of men. Herein lies man's surest reason for absolute confidence in God.

In this doctrine of *soli Deo gloria* two aspects should be particularly noted, (1) Calvin's approach, in his search for assurance of salvation, is different than Luther's, (2) Calvin's view of predestination flows out of this doctrine as a completely logical conclusion.

Luther had rested his confidence that he would be saved on God's promise of gratuitous salvation to sinful man. God will save man despite his unworthiness. Calvin, in his search for the same assurance, came to the conclusion that there is only one absolutely certain, unchanging reality and that is the will of God. Once God decides that His glory is made manifest in the salvation of man then there is nothing that can thwart that will. It is on the will of God that man must come to rely with complete confidence.

Predestination is likewise implicit in this doctrine. God's will is sovereignly free. It is in no way dependent upon or conditioned by any creature. The only condition under which the divine will acts is self-imposed. Its decision is: This creation will give me this particular manifestation of my glory. So it will be. This order of creation will manifest that degree of divine glory that God has predestined it will manifest.

Predestination

It is when this thinking is applied to man that we encounter Calvin's famous doctrine of predestination. As with the rest of created reality, so too with man, all that he does, indeed his final destiny, will be as God has foreordained it would be. God has decided who will be saved and who will be lost in terms of His own will and that decree is irreversible. To suggest that His will is subject to change because of anything man does, whether good or evil, is to blaspheme against His absolute sovereignty.

> We call predestination God's eternal decree by which he determined with himself what he willed to become of each man. For all are not created in equal condition: rather, eternal life is foreordained for some, eternal damnation for others. Therefore, as any man has been created to one or the other of these ends, we speak of him as predestined to life or to death.[4]

One must be careful to qualify Calvin's thinking on this point in two respects. First, he does not claim to do anything in presenting the doctrine of predestination but take into account the clear testimony of God's Word that this is God's plan for men. One need only read, to cite but one of many instances,[5] the ninth chapter of Paul's letter to the Romans to see a description of God choosing whom He will choose and rejecting whom He will reject. "Is not the potter master of his clay, to make from the same mass one vessel for honorable, another for ignoble use?" (Rom. 9:21).

Thus, Calvin is saying, one cannot be selective in reading God's Word. One must read and accept all of that Word and predestination is certainly made explicit in that Word. Secondly, the fact that God predestines is revealed. But beyond that the doctrine is wrapped in mystery. God has not chosen to reveal how the decree is executed, how justice and mercy are served in its execution. Therefore, the only attitude man can adopt that is completely reverent to God's Word is to accept both the fact and the mystery. Any speculation beyond that is idle curiosity about matters that God does not want man to know.

In Calvin's eyes, asking why God acts as He does regarding the salvation of some men and the loss of others is presumptuous. For him it is enough to know that God wills it so.

> For his will is and rightly ought to be the cause of all things that are. For if it has any cause, something must precede it, to which it is, as it were, bound. This is unlawful to imagine. For God's will is so much the highest rule of righteousness that whatever he wills, by the very fact that he wills it, must be considered righteous. When, therefore, one asks why God has so done, we must reply: because he has willed it. But if you proceed further to ask why he so willed, you are seeking something greater and higher than God's will, which cannot be found.[6]

Is it possible for a man to come to know what is God's decision in his own regard? Or, put another way, can a man come to that unshakable assurance that only conviction of predestination to glory can give him? Calvin's answer to this is to describe the process by which a man comes to salvation.

Deep-rooted in every human nature he finds the desire to be master of its own fate, determiner of its own destiny. This is human pride, the conviction each man has that his actions do make a difference in his final destiny. It is the tendency that each one has to play God for himself. It is this universal human urge that is sharply challenged when one comes face to face with the Word of God revealing that He alone determines human destiny.

Once this awareness is reached it demands a response from man. He either accepts the fact that God is all-determining in human destiny or he does not. If he bends in adoring humility before the fact of the divine absoluteness he is at the same time acknowledging his own nothingness and is thus surrendering himself to the will of God. He is equivalently saying: "So be it; for better or worse I submit myself to God's design."

This, for Calvin, is the heart of the act of faith. It is this humble acceptance which gives rise to the absolutely certain conviction that one is destined to glory, is of the number of the elect. God's Spirit rewards man's creaturely surrender with the conviction of salvation. Man comes to believe, to be convinced, that he is saved.

Thus, for the believer the decree of predestination, far from being a source of terror and anxiety, becomes the surest foundation for a serene and unwavering confidence. His conviction of salvation is rooted in the divine will and that is unchangeable. Even though life in its passage may bring frequent doubt, sin, failure, or temptation, these can always be countered and overcome by the recollection of the divine changelessness, God's fidelity to His decree of election. He does not choose on the basis of what a man does; so too He will not change His choice because of what a man does. One may rest secure in the divine fidelity to His own will.

Here in this unshakable confidence lie the deepest roots of that activism so characteristic of Calvinism referred to at the beginning of this chapter. The man of faith is released by that faith from any further self-concern. He is assured of salvation. No further energy need be diverted to worrying about himself. Now the elect is free to direct his energies elsewhere.

At this juncture Calvin makes the point that predestination is not so much to privilege as it is to responsibility. The elect are intended by God to give themselves unceasingly to His service. By election He has forged Himself an instrument for the manifestation of His glory. It becomes the solemn obligation of the elect to work toward the establishment of God's kingdom on earth. For this were they chosen. God has a plan for this world and it is their task to become involved in this world in order to impress God's plan on society.

Of boundless energy in God's cause and supremely fitted to withstand danger, misfortune, opposition, and failure because of his unshakable reliance upon the divine faithfulness, such is Calvin's man of faith. If God is for him, who or what can be against him? The image most readily evoked in the American mind by this description is that of the early American settlers. It was the faith of Calvin that supported them in their harsh environment. Hudson speaks of the role that Calvinism played on the early American scene.

> From a theological point of view, it was the stamp of Geneva which left the deepest mark upon American Protestantism during this early period, when it was being shaped to a common pattern. This is not surprising . . . when one remembers that

Calvinism was well adapted to the needs of men struggling to tame a wilderness. Sturdy virtues were demanded by the hard conditions of life in the New World, and these virtues were supplied by a religious faith which spoke to men in terms of stern imperatives and high destiny and expressed itself most characteristically in terms of restless energy, unfaltering confidence, and unblinking acceptance of the harsh facts of life.[7]

The Church

Calvin himself saw that the task imposed upon him by the divine call to service in Geneva was precisely of this kind, to dedicate himself with every energy and in spite of whatever opposition to the establishment there of the Holy Commonwealth. One might summarize his life and work in Geneva (1541-64) by saying that he spent these years giving form and structure to Reformed Protestantism. This he did in two ways: By his writing he gave order and systematic treatment to its theology; by his activity he developed a thorough, well organized church order.

What Calvin set out to do was build a church patterned on the church as he found it described in the Word of God. There is, he saw first of all, an invisible church,

> ... the society of all the saints, a society which spread over the whole world, and existing in all ages, yet bound together by the one doctrine, and the one Spirit of Christ, cultivates and observes unity of faith and brotherly concord.[8]

For Calvin the members of this church are all those throughout human history who have been the object of the divine election to glory. At this point Calvin's thinking on the church should be clarified by Zwingli's thinking on the notion of covenant. Covenant theology has been central to Reformed Protestantism's thinking on the church from its very beginnings.

The divine purpose in the creation of the world was that it become the theatre of His glory. That it might become so, God, at the beginning, entered into a covenant with man, a covenant of works. Man was in a state of justice and so he had both the ability and the responsibility for obeying God in all things. By his complete obedience man was to manifest the glory of God and by so doing merit his salvation. Thus, before the fall the divine plan was that salvation would be based on the merit of man's good works. The fall shattered this covenant once and for all. No longer was man able to keep the covenant.

God did not, however, abandon man. He decided rather to enter into another covenant, this time a covenant of grace. He chose Israel as His elect that, through her, He might still realize His purpose in creation. With His grace, promised to her if she was faithful to Him, she would be the instrument through which glory would be given to Him. But Israel also failed.

It was then that Christ was sent, He fulfilled the covenant of works perfectly. His life was a total mirroring of the divine glory because it was a complete obedience to the divine will. Thus did He fulfill the covenant of works for men and thereby did He lay the foundation for the covenant of grace of both the Old and the New Testament. Through Him the church comes into being as the new embodiment of the covenant of grace. To her is given the mission and the power to express fully in her life the absolute sovereignty of God. To this church there belong only the elect. She is the society of the faithful whom God has predestined to eternal life. Thus Calvin sees the church as both invisible and visible and he finds that Scripture itself talks of the church in both senses.

> For we have said that Holy Scripture speaks of the church in two ways. Sometimes by the term "church" it means that which is actually in God's presence, into which no persons are received but those who are children of God by grace of adoption and true members of Christ by sanctification of the Holy Spirit. Then, indeed, the church includes not only the saints presently living on earth, but all the elect from the beginning of the world. Often, however, the name "church" designates the whole multitude of men spread over the earth who profess to worship one God and Christ. By baptism we are initiated into faith in him; by partaking in the Lord's Supper we attest our unity in true doctrine and love; in the Word of the Lord we have agreement, and for preaching of the Word the ministry instituted by Christ is preserved. In this church are mingled many hypocrites who have nothing of Christ but the name and outward appearance. There are very many ambitious, greedy, envious persons, evil speakers, and some of quite unclean life. Such are tolerated for a time either because they cannot be convicted by a competent tribunal or because a vigorous discipline does not always flourish as it ought.[9]

Turning attention to the visible church which Calvin saw it to be his task to build in Geneva, the basic premise on which all his thinking regarding the church rests is that Christ Himself indicated what elements He wanted in His church. If, then, the church is to fulfill the glory of God it must structure itself as Christ wills. Put another way, Calvin was convinced that the divine will for all areas of human society was clearly spelled out in God's Word and that it was therefore his obligation to exert every effort to set up a society in Geneva which reflected God's purpose in its least detail.

It was the first function of the church to preach the pure Word of God and to administer Christ's sacraments. But beyond that the church was also responsible for discovering the will of God for human society and for setting up the structures which would ensure that society would manifest the divine glory by obedience to the divine will in all of its activities. His view of the nature and function of the church stands out clearly when compared with the other two views of the church characteristic of early Protestantism.

Luther, as we have seen, was not overly interested in the external and organizational aspects of the church. He felt she fulfilled her purpose if she preached God's Word and administered Christ's sacraments. Beyond that basic function, Scripture itself and the needs of the local community would suggest what church order seemed best. Luther's church was a People's church. To it belonged all the people of a given area. Membership in the church was coterminous with membership in the state. For Luther the church and the state were essentially distinct in their spheres of operation. The first three of the Lord's commandments were the concern of the church. The last seven were the concern of the state. Thus there were two clearly delineated areas of responsibility. Church and state existed side by side, each with its own set of responsibilities.

Anabaptism lay at the other end of the spectrum in its view of the nature of the church. Perfection was attainable in this life and membership in the church was restricted to those who freely chose to give their lives to the pursuit of perfection. The Anabaptist church was, therefore, a separated and a holy church. It was a gathered church of strict believers only and it lived its life in complete separation from the sinful world. The state in the Anabaptist view existed only to control sin and it was meant therefore only for sinners. Believers were to have as little as possible to do with the state. Theirs was a doctrine of absolute separation between church and state. Life for the saints of God was controlled in all its details by the church.

Calvin's view lies midway between the Lutheran and the Anabaptist view. For him all the people of Geneva were to belong to the church. They belonged because they had come to the conviction of election and were eager to live out the full implication of that election. Those not so convinced were not welcome in Geneva. The purpose of the Genevan community was to discover and then live the divine plan. By so doing, it would meet the responsibility implied in election, the manifestation of the divine glory. The function of the state in this view tended to be one of service to the church. The church discovered and promulgated the divine will; it was the task of the state to enforce that will and punish the offender.

Calvin, in a word, took Luther's People's church and transformed it into the Gathered church of Anabaptism without, however, adopting the separatism of Anabaptism. His church included all the community and was, therefore, a People's church; yet all in the church were treated as gathered (willing to live a life directed in all its details by the church).

Calvin's church and each member of it had a triple ideal to strive for, the glorification of God, the service of God and the sanctification of life. The church would embody her quest for that ideal in four characteristic marks: doctrine—the preaching of the pure Word of God; discipline—the subjecting of all of life to the divine will; sacraments—the administering of Christ's sacraments as He instituted them, and ceremonies—the developing of a liturgy and a set of pious exercises for the membership.

When it came to the practical implementation of his ideas on what the church should be, Calvin was precise and specific in his blueprint for church order. His *Ecclesiastical Ordinances of the Church of Geneva* spell out in detail the manner of constructing a society that would be dedicated in all aspects of its life to the service and glory of God. A brief look at its contents will show how specific Calvin was in working out the practical implementation of his theological principles.[10]

Calvin finds that Scripture makes provision for four offices of government in the church: pastors, doctors, elders, and deacons. A pastor is to be chosen with great care. Only after the good habit and conduct of his life has been proven and his good and holy knowledge of the Scripture tested, is he to be admitted to the ministry. In that office it will be his function to proclaim the Word of God, to instruct, admonish, exhort, and censure, to administer the sacraments, and to enjoin brotherly correction.

Doctors will have as their main task the instruction of the faithful in true doctrine. At its highest level this office will call for lectures in biblical theology. But care must also be taken that the young are instructed in languages, humanities, and religion. That this office may be well fulfilled, a school for boys and one for girls is to be established in Geneva.

Elders are to be the overseers of the life of the community. They are to admonish and offer fraternal correction to those whom they find leading a disordered life. Lastly, deacons are to be appointed. They will be of two kinds, those who are to receive and dispense alms for the poor and those charged with caring for the sick. A public hospital is to be maintained as one chief way to care for the poor and the sick.

Following the description of the ministries, careful attention is directed to the sacramental practice. Baptism is to be conferred near the pulpit that all may hear and is to be administered at the time of the sermon, a focal point of the divine service, chosen to underline the sacrament's importance. Calvin's own desire was for the administration of the Lord's Supper at least once a month but the final decision of the Council was four times a year, Easter, Christmas, Pentecost, and the first Sunday of September. The minister is to distribute the bread and the deacons are to assist him in giving the chalice. Specific instructions are then given for Marriage, burial, visitation of the sick and prisoners, and catechetical instruction for the children.

Next there comes a detailed instruction on how to deal with those guilty of infractions of God's law: those holding unorthodox doctrine, those remiss in church-going, those guilty of notorious and public vices. The penalties range in severity from admonition, through exclusion from the Lord's Supper to excommunication.

The records of the Council of the time make evident the great range of human activity that fell under supervision and was punished: dancing, cardplaying, gambling, obscenity, drunkenness, wife-beating, adultery, nonattendance at church. Thus, Calvin's Geneva was an austere theocracy where God's will was spelled out in great detail and strictly enforced. Both the ecclesiastical and secular authorities were called upon to point out and demand observance of what was the will of God for His people. It was felt that by such supervision and vigilance God's glory would be most securely safeguarded.

To those who then or now would find his control of life too detailed and excessively harsh Calvin would reply: For the truly elect the joy they find in the divine election will urge them to search out in all of life the ways and means by which they can give expression to that joy in glad service for the glory of Him who has chosen them.

The Sacraments

One last area of Calvin's thought should be touched on, his sacramental thinking. Here as in all other facets of his thought Calvin turned to the Word of God for his inspiration. There he finds that

> The sacraments themselves were also diverse, in keeping with
> the times, according to the dispensation by which the Lord

was pleased to reveal himself in various ways to men. For circumcision was enjoined upon Abraham and his descendants (Gen. 17:10). To it were afterwards added purifications (Lev. chs. 11 to 15), sacrifices, and other rites (Lev. chs. 1 to 10), from the law of Moses. These were the sacraments of the Jews until the coming of Christ.[11]

With the coming of Christ the sacraments of the Old Law were abrogated. In their place Christ gave His church two sacraments: Baptism and the Lord's Supper. Both of these are outward signs,

> . . . by which the Lord seals on our consciences the promises of his good will toward us, in order to sustain the weakness of our faith. And we in turn attest our piety toward him in the presence of the Lord and of his angels and before men.[12]

For Calvin the sacraments fulfill a double function. They serve as sensible signs to constantly reassure men of God's love for them. Christ is the supreme sign of that love and so the purpose of the sacraments is ". . . the same office as the Word of God; to offer and set forth Christ to us, and in him the treasures of heavenly grace."[13]

Their second function is to present men with occasions for the exercise and increase of their faith. Indeed "they avail and profit nothing unless received in faith."[14] Each sacramental encounter with Christ offers the believer an opportunity to reaffirm his acceptance of the salvation God has given him in Christ.

Baptism is, for Calvin, the "sign of the initiation by which we are received into the society of the church."[15] It does not deliver a man ". . . from original sin, and from the corruption which has descended from Adam to all his posterity; . . . ."[16] Rather,

> . . . the Lord promises us by this sign that full and complete remission has been made, both of the guilt that should have been imputed to us, and of the punishment that we ought to have undergone because of the guilt. They also lay hold on righteousness, but such righteousness as the people of God can obtain in this life, that is, by imputation only, since the Lord of his own mercy considers them righteous and innocent.[17]

Calvin is thus at one with Luther in declaring that, when a man is justified, he remains *simul justus et peccator*, a sinner and yet just because in Christ God imputes justice to him.

Infants are to receive Baptism because it (like circumcision before it) is the sign and seal of admission into the covenant of grace. The children of believers have by that fact a right to enter the covenant.

> ... the children of believers are baptized not in order that they who were previously strangers to the church may then for the first time become children of God, but rather that, because by the blessing of the promise they already belonged to the body of Christ, they are received into the church with this solemn sign.[18]

Baptism is then the sign of belonging to the covenant. It commits the one baptized to living out the glory of God in all of life and for the child it points forward to God conferring upon him the conviction of his election to glory.

Regarding the *Eucharist,* Calvin concurs with Luther in rejecting its sacrificial character and in his refusal to accept the Roman doctrine of transubstantiation as a satisfactory explanation of the nature of Christ's presence in the sacrament. His own theory of how Christ is present tries to steer a middle course between what he considers to be the extreme of Luther's explanation on the one hand and that of Zwingli on the other.

Luther, as we have seen, held for a real and physical presence of the body and blood of Christ in the sacrament. For him the bread and wine are the body and blood of Christ insofar as they are united with that body and blood. Both substances are really and physically present. Zwingli, on the other hand, bases his interpretation on the doctrine of the Ascension. Christ has ascended into heaven and is with the Father. Hence there can be no question of the real, physical presence of Christ's body in the sacrament. The sacrament is a sign or symbol of the covenant between God and man. The Lord's Supper is a memorial and thanksgiving for this covenant. It is not a means of grace in itself. Thus the words "This is my body" are to be understood as meaning "this signifies or is a sign of my body." There is no physical presence and hence the believer does not receive Christ's body. The Supper is a faith sign. The spiritual gift of Christ's redemption is recalled and received in faith.

Calvin is uneasy with Luther's notion of the local, physical presence of Christ's body. For him this opens the way to adoration of the sacrament and thus a created, material object would come to be adored instead of God. He is in agreement with Zwingli in holding that Christ's body is in heaven.

On the other hand, he is unhappy with the Zwinglian position because it seems to evacuate the sacrament of much of its meaning. Calvin himself felt that the sacrament did have an objective content, that what occurred was not merely a spiritual communion in faith with Christ. The key to his understanding seems to lie in his conception of the nature of a sign.

A sign, first of all, points to something else, draws attention to it. The bread and wine turn us to the contemplation in faith of Christ's humanity and what it does for us.

> ... from the physical things set forth in the Sacrament we are led by a sort of analogy to spiritual things. Thus when bread is given as a symbol of Christ's body we must at once grasp this comparison: as bread nourishes, sustains and keeps the life of our body, so Christ's body is the only food to invigorate and enliven our soul.[19]

But a sign is more than just a pointer in this case; it partakes of the reality toward which it points.

> ... if the Lord truly represents the participation in his body through the breaking of bread, there ought not to be the least doubt that he truly presents and shows his body.
>
> ... when we have received the symbol of the body, let us no less surely trust that the body itself is also given to us.[20]

In the Eucharist Christ really gives the believer what He promised to give, his body and blood.

Care must be taken, however, to clearly differentiate the bread and wine from the body and blood. Both are received; yet sign and reality are distinct. The reality of the body and blood is not identified with the bread and wine yet that reality is really received at the time when the believer eats and drinks the bread and wine.

In summary, Calvin's position would seem to agree with Luther's in stressing the reality of the presence as over against Zwingli's merely symbolic presence. On the other hand, he would seem to approach Zwingli in insisting that the presence is rather spiritual than physical (as Luther would seem to hold).

CONCLUSION

An overall evaluation of Calvin's thinking may follow the same principle that we used in assessing Luther's contribution, namely that Christianity, in its entirety, is the holding in balanced tension of what appear to be mutually exclusive opposites. In reaction against what he saw to be the superstition and idolatry of the Roman church, Calvin, like Luther, returned to the Scriptures to probe again for the authentic voice of Christianity. What he found there was an overpowering sense of the majesty, mystery and transcendence of God. This became the strongly emphasized core of his thinking. That God and His glory be restored to the primacy accorded them in the Scripture is the essential thrust of his thought. Drawn, as he so strongly was, to this idea of God as central, it was inevitable that he should lay almost exclusive stress on this aspect of the Christian message and in the process underplay the also scripturally authenticated role of the human in Christianity.

Rome had moved a good distance toward overasserting that human role and thereby tended to distort the total Christian vision. Devotion to the saints had grown dangerously close to the superstition that by formulas of prayer one could engage their power in controlling the will of God. Indulgences tended to take on the appearance of magic rites whereby one placated an angry tribal God. Thus Calvin was right in putting his finger on the perennial temptation that humans face of wanting to conform God and His will to their own pattern and desire. Man stands always in need of being reminded that the Creator is sovereign and the creature subject. In Calvin's time Christianity, in its strong insistence on the value of external good works and its fostering of devotion to the saints and indulgences, seemed to be giving man a degree of autonomy in working out his salvation that was a distortion of Christianity. Men needed to be reminded strongly that God is the sovereign Lord of all things. This, Calvin did; by so doing he served well the cause of Christianity.

But as with Rome, so with Calvin, stress tended to overstress. Restoring the balance between God and man in the salvific process is not accomplished by overemphasizing the role of either. Calvin's flaw lay precisely here. For one overemphasis, man, he substituted another, God.

Scripture does not see the sovereignty of God as absolutely unconditioned. By his own choice God conditions His will and its execution by the responsible action of man. God does not save or damn a human in spite of what he does. To say that God is all in determining human destiny is a fundamental Christian theme. Equally fundamental is the assertion that man himself is involved in determining his own destiny. One does not portray complete Christianity by excluding or undervaluing either member of the God-man tension.

Robert M. Brown, a contemporary expositor of the Calvinist tradition,

points up the values that must be part of a total picture of the sovereignty
of God.

> It is important to defend . . . the stress upon the initiatory
> activity of God, the recognition upon the part of the believer
> that his salvation is a gift, and not something he has produced
> through his own resources.

> The integrity of human freedom must not be jeop-
> ardized . . . We must retain for the individual his right, if he so
> chooses, to say "no" to God.

> But we must also allow for a limitless love on God's part which
> can reach out to those desolate of his love or even of the desire
> for his love, recognizing the possibility that he may have ways
> beyond our understanding for bringing men to free acceptance
> of him.[21]

God's prior activity, freedom, love, these are the components of the
balanced Christian view of the sovereignty of God.

One further comment should be made on Calvin's tendency to exclude
all that is human from man's worship of God—that all that is human (save
sin) is the object of God's love and Christ's redemptive activity and all of it
is intended to be directed back to God and His glory. Certainly one of the
most constant and noble elements in the Christian tradition has been the
enduring quest of the Christian spirit to express in sensible form its adoration of God. One thinks of the stained glass of Chartres, Michelangelo's
Sistine Chapel, Handel's Messiah. There is always danger of distortion and
many a church in its architecture and interior furnishings bears witness to
how far astray man can go in his attempt to give sensible expression to his
reverence for God and the things of God. But excess and the recurring
tendency to distort are not the norms by which one judges the worth of
man's attempts to worship God with all in him that is human. The perennial danger of idolatry and superstition points to the need, not for inhibit-
ing the human spirit's urge to dedicate its creative activity to the worship
and glory of God, but for tempering that expression by the constant
reminder that God is ultimately inexpressible in human terms.

Calvin, then, reemphasized always valid elements in the Christian revelation. God is the sovereign Lord of all creation and that creation does exist
to serve and glorify Him. But he was a child of his age as all men are and so
his vision of the nature of the Christian vision was inevitably myopic in
some areas. Succeeding ages have tried to balance and thereby complete

his thought. Yet even today ecumenical theologians are still engaged in trying to reconcile the apparent opposites that Calvin struggled with. Natural and revealed knowledge of God, the sacraments as signs and symbols and yet as realities of the Lord's presence, the nature of Christ's church and the manner of belonging to it, these and other areas are, as they were in Calvin's time, elements in the Christian revelation which still resist our efforts to penetrate the mystery inherent in them. Yet we have come to recognize, perhaps more sharply today than in many generations, what Calvin always saw quite clearly, that our reflections on these mysteries must always take their origin in God's Word.

Luther is the original, bold and creative thinker. Calvin is more the logician and systematician. Together they are the principal architects of the Protestant Reform. The remainder of Protestant history that we will attempt to trace in its main lines takes on its meaning in terms of a continuation of, or reaction to, the five basic insights of these two men. That history will serve too, to highlight the strength that inheres in these principles when they are sincerely lived. The same history will point up the extreme lengths to which these principles can be pushed, extremes which deserve the name Christian only by stretching that term to its furthest limit of inclusiveness. Finally, by manifesting these extremes, history bears witness to the need for complementing and counterbalancing these essential Christian ideas by other equally authentic Christian values.

FOOTNOTES

[1]From *Calvin: Commentaries,* Library of Christian Classics vol. XXIII, p. 52, translated and edited by Joseph Haroutunian and Louise Pettibone Smith. Published in the U.S.A. by the Westminster Press, 1958. Used by permission.

[2]John T. McNeill, *The History and Character of Calvinism,* 2nd printing with corrections (New York: Oxford University Press, 1957), pp. 114-15.

[3]On this difference between Luther and Calvin cf. Louis Bouyer, *The Spirit and Forms of Protestantism* (Westminster Md.: The Newman Press, 1956.), pp. 59-60.

[4]From *Calvin, Institutes of the Christian Religion,* II. LCC vol. XXI, p. 926, edited by John T. McNeill, and translated by Ford Lewis Battles. The Westminster Press. Copyright 1960, W.L. Jenkins. Used by permission.

[5]J. S. Whale, *The Protestant Tradition,* (London and New York: Cambridge University Press, 1959), p. 142 provides other scriptural evidence of election and reprobation.

6Calvin, *Institutes,* III, 23, 2, LCC, XXI, p. 949.

7Winthrop S. Hudson, *American Protestantism,* paperback edition (Chicago: University of Chicago Press, 1961), pp. 22-23.

8Calvin, *Reply to Sadoleto* in *Tracts and Treatises on the Reformation of the Church,* trans. Henry Beveridge, vol I (Grand Rapids, Mich.: Wm. B. Eerdmans Publishing Co., reprinted in 1958), p. 37. Used by permission of the publisher.

9Calvin, *Institutes,* IV, 1, 7, LCC, XXI, pp. 1021-22.

10The "Draft of the Ecclesiastical Ordinances of the Church of Geneva" may be found in Calvin: *Theological Treatises,* LCC, vol. XXII ed. Rev. J.K.S. Reid (Philadelphia: Westminster Press, 1954), pp. 56-72.

11Calvin, *Institutes,* IV, 14, 20, LCC, XXI, p. 1296.

12*Ibid.,* IV, 14, 1, LCC, XXI, p. 1277.

13*Ibid.,* IV, 14, 17, LCC, XXI, p. 1292.

14*Ibid.*

15*Ibid.,* IV, 15, 1, LCC, XXI, p. 1303.

16*Ibid.,* IV, 15, 10, LCC, XXI, p. 1311.

17*Ibid.*

18Calvin, *Institutes,* IV, 15, 22, LCC, XXI, p. 1323.

19*Ibid.,* IV, 17a, 3, LCC, XXI, p. 1363.

20*Ibid.,* IV, 17, 10, LCC, XXI, p. 1371.

21Robert M. Brown, "Classical Protestantism," in *Patterns of Faith in America Today,* ed. F. Ernest Johnson (New York: Harper & Brothers, 1957), pp. 23-24.

CHAPTER THREE

Anabaptism

Very soon after the Protestant Reform began there started to appear small groups of those who felt that its insistence on the need to return to the Scriptures in order to recover the authentic meaning of Christianity was the all-important key to any real reformation. They accepted Luther's *sola Scriptura* principle but felt that he and the other Reformers had not gone half far enough in their application of this principle to sixteenth century Christian belief and life. They were convinced that so drastic a renewal of Christianity was called for by any serious reading of God's Word that reformation, as Luther and his associates conceived it, was totally inadequate. What was needed, they felt, was a restitution of Christianity without any compromise to the form portrayed in the New Testament. Thus was born the radical Reformation, the reformers of the Reformation, sometimes called the left wing of the Reformation, or more popularly, the Anabaptists (Rebaptizers) so-called because of their practice of rebaptizing all who joined their movement.

The beginnings of Anabaptism (1519-23) were rooted in small groups of earnest, Bible-reading Christians in the Swiss cantons, especially around Zurich. Their reading and discussion of the Bible brought them to see that a return to biblical Christianity in the strictest sense of that word was the only true path to reformation. In accordance with their conviction that the Word of God spoke to them of a church radically different from any Christian church then existing whether Reformed, Lutheran or Roman Catholic, they began to separate themselves from the established churches of the time in order to rebuild the primitive church of which the New Testament spoke.

To begin with, the movement was a quiet and peaceful separation from the world. All that was asked of society and the churches was the right to separate and develop communities modeled on that of the early church. They were sober and pious folk who wanted only to withdraw from the world they saw as sinful and from the churches they viewed as corruptions that they might live together the warm, communal, and totally dedicated kind of life described in the Acts of the Apostles.

Their attempt met unyielding opposition and bitter persecution from society and churches alike. Thousands were exiled or unmercifully destroyed by fire or drowning during the early years and for a time the leadership passed into the hands of revolutionaries who felt sword should be met with sword, persecution by active resistance. There was a brief flurry of revolutionary activity within the movement typified by men like Thomas Muntzer[1] and the infamous Munster incident.[2] But these were temporary aberrations brought on by the fierceness of the persecution. Within a quarter of a century the violence died and the quiet, separated form of Anabaptism reasserted itself as the main line of the movement. In this form the radical Reformation has continued to exist to this day in the rural and out of the way places of the world.

What were the elements of Anabaptism's view of Christianity? Why did that vision set them so radically apart from the rest of Christianity? The answer to these questions lies in understanding the seriousness with which Anabaptism took the principle of Scripture alone and the view of the nature of the church that flowed out of this insistence on Scripture as alone normative in determining what Christianity meant.

ANABAPTIST VISION OF THE CHURCH

The key to grasping Anabaptism is to know their thinking on the nature of the church. And to know that thinking it is necessary to recognize that they took the picture of the church painted in the New Testament as the only licit form of church life. The church must be what she is described as being in the New Testament. That set of documents made it clear to the Anabaptists that the church was meant to be a disciplined community composed only of voluntary believers whose faith determined the pattern of all of life. Only those who saw the total demands that Christianity made on its followers and, seeing, freely accepted these demands in a personally meaningful act of faith, made up the church of apostolic times. In contrast with this kind of church the Anabaptists saw that Christianity, as it existed in the sixteenth century, had come to an almost total identification of church and society. One was born simultaneously into both. Thus, for

Anabaptism, the fundamental reason for the corrupt state of Christianity that he saw all around him was the indiscriminate admission of all into the church.

The same point can be made by contrasting Anabaptism with the position of mainline Protestantism on the nature of salvation. Luther, Calvin and their associates put the essence of the Gospel message in justification by faith. For them confidence that God is at work in Christ saving me is the required Christian response to God's saving offer. Anabaptism would rather see Christianity as rooted fundamentally in the presence and transforming action of the Holy Spirit in the heart of the believer. As they read the Gospel it was not consciousness of justification but commitment to a way of life that was central. For the one tradition, the lives of the early Christians are typical of the way in which a Christian should reply to God's gift of redemption in Christ. For the other, the New Testament pattern of life is not typical of Christian life; it is normative for that life.

These two basic attitudes regarding what it means to be Christian also account for the different approach that the two traditions take in their understanding of the Scripture. Classical Protestantism thought it essential to understand the meaning of justification, of sacrament, of predestination and the like. Theological speculation or intellectual penetration of the Scripture was important if one was to grasp rightly the Christian vision. Faith, in this view, needed to seek understanding of that in which it believed. Anabaptism saw the Gospel rather as a book of life, portraying the life that the saints of God must lead. What was important for them was adhesion to the New Testament form of life, not comprehending what Paul meant by the justice of God. Theologizing on God's Word could produce a sterile formalism in the living of Christianity. One needed rather to read the Book and then live according to the model It proposed.

Once convinced of the corruption of Christianity the Anabaptist moved against the situation first of all by denying the validity of infant baptism and by refusing either to recognize or to practice it. Admission to the church could be only through a process of conversion and infants were not capable of such a process. Only after a man had heard the Word of God, recognized the totality of Its claim on his life, and freely accepted It for himself, could he be baptized. Baptism when conferred was not the cause of one's regeneration. The conversion experience produced that rebirth. Baptism merely confirmed, or better manifested, that state in a public ceremony.

> ... outward baptism avails nothing so long as we are not inwardly renewed. regenerated, and baptized with the heavenly

> fire and the Holy Ghost of God . . . . In the spiritual strength
> which we have received, we henceforth bind ourselves by the
> outward sign of the covenant in water which is enjoined on all
> believers by Christ. . . .[3]

The New Testament also made it clear that when one entered into the
church he entered a separated community. Christ designed His church as a
place to which He called His true followers out of the sinful world. In the
Anabaptist view the world had always been a place of sin and those who
lived in it could not but be sinners. Civil society existed for but one
purpose: to control the world's sinfulness by law and power. Because the
world was such, the saints of God, dedicated as they were to the total
living of Christianity, could not live in it. Theirs must be a separated
existence. Total separation was demanded between the church and the
world.

As Anabaptism moved to the implementation of this conviction, it
demanded of its membership a refusal to participate in any of the world's
activities. Thus, for example, a believer could not hold any official position in society. Likewise he was not to have recourse to society's legal
system for settlement of disputes. Mutual love among the brethren would
provide the norm for settling their own differences. If called into court by
a nonbeliever, one went but one refused the swearing of any oaths. Such
was forbidden to Christians.

Anabaptism was, of course, realistic enough to recognize the necessity
of civil authority if society was to have any order. His normal attitude was,
in consequence, to live in peaceful obedience to the civil law as long as it
did not command anything which conflicted with what Christianity
demanded of him. But at the point where this occurred his only recourse
was passive resistance to the law, which implied, on the one hand, a refusal
to obey and, on the other, the willing acceptance of whatever penalties
such refusal incurred, fine, imprisonment, confiscation of property, exile,
even death itself.

The life of the church was not only one of separation from the world;
it was also one of opposition to the world. Here again their reading of the
New Testament convinced the Anabaptists of the rightness of this view.
Early Christianity had known only God's cause. In the spread of His
Kingdom its only weapon had been the staff and the Scriptures. The first
Christians had traveled everywhere spreading the Word as persuasively as
they could but always by peaceful means. Therefore, the sixteenth century
believer could live in no other way and call himself Christian. He must be
dedicated to peace and to the peaceful spreading of God's Word. In con-

trast with such a way the state had always used force, war, persecution, violence, and the sword, for the enforcement and spread of its own will. Such a way of life was foreign to Christianity and must be resisted.

> The government magistracy is according to the flesh, but the Christians' is according to the Spirit. Their houses and dwelling remain in this world, but the Christians' are in heaven; their citizenship is in this world, but the Christians' citizenship is in heaven; the weapons of their conflict and war are carnal and against the flesh only, but the Christians' weapons are spiritual, against the fortifications of the devil. The worldlings are armed with steel and iron, but the Christians are armed with the armor of God, with truth, righteousness, peace, faith, salvation and the Word of God. In brief, as is the mind of Christ toward us, so shall the mind of the members of the body of Christ be through Him in all things, that there may be no schism in the body through which it would be destroyed.[4]

The Anabaptist resistance in this matter took a double form. In the first place he was unalterably opposed to war in any form. No true Christian could bear arms in the service of the state. Pacifism was the only possible Christian stance. Only uncompromising resistance, whatever the cost, could be offered to the state's attempt to make one bear arms. In the second place, it was the practice of the state to put its power at the disposal of the church for the enforcement of religious conformity. Protestant and Catholic alike looked on the toleration of religious heterodoxy as a serious social weakness. Error, especially in religion, was a grave danger to the common good and was to be stamped out wherever found. Anabaptism, on the other hand, felt that one had to be free to form and follow his own conscience in the light of God's Word. Force could never be used in support of religious assent. The Anabaptists were convinced they had no choice but to follow the Scriptures as they read them even though the choice brought them into conflict with the established Christian churches and their generally accepted interpretation of the meaning of Christianity. It was inevitable that this insistence on religious liberty would bring down on Anabaptism the wrath of church and state alike. Persecution, suffering, martyrdom for their religious beliefs became their courageously accepted lot. But the persecution served only to strengthen them in their view. For, did not the pages of the New Testament speak of this as the lot of the early Christians? Not only had the primitive church separated from the state, but, in standing apart, she had questioned and opposed the state. This stance had brought persecution, rejection, opposition from the state. The church of the apostles had, in consequence, been a church of martyrs, men willing to bear testimony to the truth with their lives; and that price had been frequently demanded of them. The lesson from this was clear: the church of Christ will always be recognizable by her willingness to suffer. Suffering will always be an essential part of her life. Indeed, it cannot but be that where there is a true church and real Christian witness, opposition will spring up against it. The world is of its nature evil and always will be. The Christian has no choice but to withdraw from it and protest against it. One true mark of Christ's church will always be persecution. If ever the church comes to be accepted and well thought of by the world, it can only mean that the church has abandoned her witness. The community of grace must always stand over against the community of sin. There can be no compromise. So the inevitable lot of the Christian must be exile, persecution and martyrdom. But the testimony of this suffering is one of the surest signs to the believer that he is keeping alive the message and the church of Christ.

INTERNAL STRUCTURE OF THE CHURCH

His separation from the world created for the Anabaptist the need to develop a community of his own to replace that of the world he left and to provide him with the support he needed to live his separated existence. Many of them met the need, as did the Hutterites in Moravia, for example, by setting up completely self-contained and self-supported communities where all was shared in common in accord with what they took to be the mandate of the New Testament. Within this communal structure each plied his own trade for the support of the group. Together in community the brethren lived, worked and worshipped in a life of shared dedication to the living out of God's Will as they found that will expressed in His Word. Whatever form their communal life took, its aim was a life of complete holiness to be achieved through a total commitment to the way of life of the early Christians. To ensure that this end was achieved Anabaptism developed two characteristic instruments, the consensus and the ban.

Consensus

When a man entered Anabaptism it was understood that he did so because, by conscious choice he wanted to seek and follow God's will in living with his brethren. This searching out of the divine will was seen as the constantly recurring responsibility of the entire community. And that will was always to be found in the application of God's Word to whatever the present situation might be. Thus, a major concern for Anabaptism became the creating of circumstances which would allow the entire community, through prayer, reading, and open discussion, to find the meaning of Scripture that applied to this present problem. The meaning of the Word of God was not for them a static, once and for all given; it was rather a living reality and its current application was to be discovered by the group. The Word would find its concrete explication for current circumstances in openness of discussion among the brethren. Because the Spirit of God would be present in these discussions leading each member towards the truth it was to be expected that a consensus would ultimately be reached which would be a commonly agreed upon interpretation. All recognized that each, under the Spirit, bore responsibility for all the others and that only together could they discover what the Spirit wanted them to know and do.

Thus, in its interpretation of the Word of God, Anabaptism tended to take a middle position between those who believed that the authoritative interpretation of the Word of God was the province of the leadership in the church and those who believed that only the individual under the direction of the Spirit could come to the meaning of God's Word for himself. For Anabaptists it was consensus that shaped conscience. The setting was communal prayer and discussion. The end was a commonly achieved interpretation of the Word of God as applied to this situation.

The Ban

Because decisions were communally arrived at, conformity to these decisions was the normal result. But Anabaptism was not unaware of the sinful proclivities of human nature and it developed another instrument to complement the consensus and ensure observance. This was the ban. Should a member of the group manifest a consistent tendency to turn his back on his commitment to holiness, it became the responsibility of the community to banish him from the church. Here again the early church's practice of excommunication was invoked to justify the practice. The well-being of the church demanded that constant vigilance should be exercised over the lives of the members lest sin should find its way into God's church.

> For as a city without walls and gates, or a field without
> trenches and fences, and a house without walls and doors, so is
> also a church which has not the true apostolic exclusion or
> ban. For it stands wide open to every seductive spirit, to all
> abominations and for proud despisers, to all idolatrous and
> wilfully wicked sinners, yes, to all lewd, unchaste wretches,
> sodomites, harlots, and knaves, as may be seen in all the large
> sects of the world (which, however, pose improperly as the
> Church of Christ). Why talk at length? According to my opin-
> ion, it is the distinguished usage, honor, and prosperity of a
> sincere church if it with Christian discretion teaches the true
> apostolic separation, and observes it carefully in solicitous
> love, according to the ordinance of the holy, sacred Scrip-
> tures.[5]

Two other features were also characteristic of the internal life of the
Anabaptist communities, the priesthood of all believers and the seriousness
with which the Lord's mandate to missionary activity was taken.

Priesthood of all Believers

Whereas Roman Catholicism had a clergy set apart for ministry by the
sacrament of Ordination, Lutheran and Reformed Protestantism, though it
still retained a selected and trained ministry, believed in the priesthood of
all believers in the sense that all believers had the responsibility to minister
the Word to his neighbor. Anabaptism carried the notion of universal
priesthood one further step, again relying on the New Testament testimony to the full participation of all members of the apostolic church both
in the life of the church and in the evangelization of the unbeliever.
Conversion, it was held, conferred full priesthood on all Christians. This
meant that every Christian was empowered to preach, to teach, to conduct
divine worship service, to evangelize. No grade or rank of any kind was
permitted within the Anabaptist church. All were equal and equally capable of ministry. More than any other of the Christian churches, Anabaptism gave the fullness of priesthood to all the brethren.

The Great Commission

Nowhere is the Anabaptist's insistence on the right and responsibility of
every Christian to engage in ministry made clearer than in the seriousness

with which he took the admonition of Christ to preach to all nations. "Go, therefore, make disciples of all nations," was the Great Commission, a command imposed without distinction on every believing Christian. "He sent out His messengers preaching this peace, His apostles who spread this grace abroad through the whole world, who shone as bright, burning torches before all men, so that they might lead me and all erring sinners into the right way, O Lord, not unto me, but unto Thee be praise and honor. Their words I love, their practices I follow."[6]

In the beginning of the movement the execution of this command put wandering preachers and missionaries on all the roads of Europe. But as the movement grew and organized itself, each community came to choose those who would be its representatives in missionary endeavor. The communal living adopted by so many of the congregations provided the possibility of caring for the families of the missionaries while they were away preaching the Word. Yet, though the mission task came to be organized, the Great Commission continued to be seen as binding on all Christians and in the ceremony of admission for new converts each new brother was required to promise to go wherever sent.

Thus did its reading of Scripture bring the radical Reformation to a life of separation and opposition to the world, to communal living, and to voluntary, disciplined fellowship wherein all bore equally the responsibility for holiness and for witness. One last feature of Anabaptism calls for attention, their interpretation of the meaning of History.

MEANING OF HISTORY

Faced as they were with the grim prospect of an unending and almost hopeless struggle against the state and the established churches of Christianity, it became imperative for the Anabaptists, if they were to preserve any sense of their destiny and any assurance of their final victory, to develop a view of history which saw its meaning and purpose as centered not in the great state churches but in their own small conventicles. So they came to their notion of the periodization of history. History was to be read as a series of periods in the execution of the divine plan for mankind. Each period taught its own lesson and made its own contribution to the final meaning of the total process. In each period God was at work in His chosen ones effecting through them His own mysterious purposes. The elect carried the meaning of history; through them He would bring it to its final consummation.

The church of the apostles and early martyrs was the Golden Age of the church's life. It was the age of heroes when believers gladly gave whole-hearted commitment to the living of the Christian life. Using only the weapons of the Lord: meekness, long-suffering, simplicity, single-mindedness, missionary preaching of the Word, charity toward all, the primitive church had grown and conquered the world in spite of almost total opposition by the world and against unceasing persecution and martyrdom. Thus were God's mysterious ways vindicated; His choice of the weak ones of the world to confound the strong validated.

But, in the very hour of victory and again in accord with God's inscrutable purposes, the church fell from righteousness. For most Anabaptists this fall coincided with the reign of Constantine. It was then that Christianity became the official religion of the state. Then was born the Constantinian church, wedded to the power of the state, open to privileged status within the state, subject to all of its corruptive influences. This union of the church and state was and remained the mark of the fallen church. In its wake the union brought infant baptism, mass conversion, and the forced imposition of Christianity on whole peoples. Temporal power became the church's weapon for witness and evangelization of the nonbeliever rather than the sword of the Spirit. Thus did the church lose her initial form as a community of voluntary believers. Membership in her now came to depend not on personal decision but rather on the accident of birth in a Christian land. With that loss, all the corruption and evil that has characterized her life for thirteen hundred years began to be introduced. The church of the Word became the church of the land and in so becoming she ceased to be the true church of Christ.

This state of affairs continued until the sixteenth century with only small, scattered groups of the faithful keeping the church alive during the intervening centuries. Now, in their age, the Anabaptists saw the providence of God beginning again to choose out the small, separated remnant that through them He might start again the restoration of His true church.

It was through Anabaptism, then, and not through Catholicism or Protestantism that the God of history was at work. Their task became what had been the task of His primitive church, to begin again living the life to which Christ called His followers. They were to separate themselves from the state and the corrupt churches, oppose the use of force as a weapon in support of religion, build a strong, communal life with a vigorous, internal discipline. Thereby they would present to the sinful world the true picture of the church of Christ. For this they would be persecuted as His true church had always been.

But all of this was the beginning of the Last Age; they were themselves the instruments chosen by God to inaugurate the end time. He would complete their work by ushering in the final Kingdom of God through a miraculous display of His power. The Day was not far distant when the Lord would appear in might and majesty. Meanwhile His people had their task: the restitution of His church through witness and suffering.

By such a vision of final, triumphant success was Anabaptism able to steel itself against despair. In the sixteenth century the vision and the demanding life it called for captured only a very small percentage of the Reformation movement. The absoluteness of the demands it made on its membership, the life of total separation from the world that was expected and the certainty of relentless persecution, all guaranteed that the movement would remain small. Down through the centuries Anabaptism has continued to remain a minority community within Christianity. Even today the lineal descendants of the radical reformers are relatively few. The most vigorous of those descendants would be the Mennonites and they number only about half a million around the world. There are about one hundred and seventy thousand of them in the United States centered mainly in the Pennsylvania Dutch country and in Virginia, Indians, and Iowa. The remainder are scattered in small groups principally in the Netherlands, Canada, Russia, India, the Congo, and Germany. The other branch that continues the tradition is the Hutterites. They are far smaller than the Mennonites numbering only about eleven thousand in the western provinces of Canada and about forty-five hundred in South Dakota, Montana, and Minnesota. Both these remnants of sixteenth century Anabaptism remain to this day small, highly disciplined, and rigidly separated communities whose life is still very much patterned on the life of the New Testament apostolic church.

CONCLUSION

The decision of Anabaptism that Christianity meant separation from a corrupt world points up the recurrent problem that has faced Christianity all through her history. What does the Gospel say the church should be? Is she to be a hedged vineyard protecting her membership for eternal life or a leaven present in the world and working to bring men to God through the attractiveness of her witness and the completeness of her service?

Anabaptism chose the first as her understanding of what the church means. The followers of that tradition to this day tend to be found in the byway places of the world. They have preserved their witness but only at the price of remaining a small, minority group. In terms of their dedication to the Great Commission it may be asked: how can a separatist testimony to the Gospel be taken as a preaching of that Gospel to all creatures? It is true that the other choice, witness in the world, has often led to overidentification with the world and consequent corruption of the Word of God. But to say this is only to lead to the further question: need the choice, indeed should the choice, be only between the two extremes? It would seem that Anabaptism's strengths, community and discipline learned in community, are essential. It would seem equally true that such strength is only really Christian strength when it is seen as preparing for witness to the world. Separation from the world and witness in it are the two poles back and forth between which a creative Christian tension must run.

It is interesting to see one of this tradition's most sympathetic contemporary interpreters, Franklin Littell, urging the Mennonite churches to give serious thought to how their separated witness can best focus its spiritual power for good in contemporary America. He suggests the inner city as the best place for their witness. He is, in effect, arguing that the leaven must be in the mass, not apart; the light must shine in the darkness, not high on a separated hill, if it is to fulfill its witnessing purpose.

> It seems to me that, as strange as it sounds in an address to a people that has been traditionally rural in orientation, the inner city is precisely the area which calls for the kind of community witness for which the sons and daughters of Menno are justly noted. In the world which we are moving toward, for some time to come the group witness to purity of life, Scriptural simplicity, non-violence, sharing, spiritual government, the "house church" as a community of brethren, etc., will be desperately needed. For generations the Mennonites have moved into the desert places and through faithfulness, mutual aid, and plain hard work turned prairies and jungles into garden places. What would be the impact if the Mennonites would tackle the most desperate deserts and jungles of America, the inner cities from which the prevailing forms of culture-religion are fleeing?[7]

From a negative point of view, then, the Anabaptist tradition tends to blunt the impact of its Christian witness by its insistence on separatism. From a more positive point of view, the continuing value of Anabaptism's witness lies, as O'Hanlon notes,[8] in her ability, through the form of life she leads, to provide the Christian churches with sorely needed freshness of vision. Her accent on the need for a faith that is responsibly arrived at and lived in its fullness suggests that Christianity needs to move away from both a leadership and a membership that is content with formal membership and routine observance. Along the same lines, her strong criticism of a Constantinian church raises the serious question of just how far Christianity can accommodate itself to the culture in which it lives and still retain the freedom it needs to be critical of that culture in the light of the Gospel.

Last of all, Anabaptism evidences a strong emphasis on the local church. For her ". . . the church is not just an automatic ongoing *institution* but an *event* that happens again and again in the worship and life of the local congregation."[9] A renewed Christianity will find her renewal at the local level in churches open to forms of worship that meet the community's felt needs and in churches that make demands on their membership in terms of service to the needs of the surrounding community. Anabaptism can, in a word, offer the Christian churches much light on the meaning of Christian life, worship, and witness.

FOOTNOTES

[1]Muntzer first appeared in history at Zwickau in 1528 where his name was linked with the Zwickau prophets in their opposition to infant baptism and their insistence that the only real method for interpreting the Scriptures was through the work of the Spirit in the heart of the believer. He soon moved to the organization of a secret band of revolutionaries pledged to initiate the kingdom of God on earth by force of arms. In this kingdom all sinners were to be exterminated and the true believers were to live in a community where all possessions were shared in common. It was Muntzer's conviction that the peasants were so misused, their lot so miserable, that little energy or leisure was left to them to attend to the reading of God's Word or developing their faith through prayer. For him, therefore, there could be no real religious reformation without social revolution and so he threw in his lot with the cause of establishing the kingdom by the sword. When the Peasants' war broke out in 1524 he took up the "sword of the saint" to wage war on the godless. By the summer of 1525 he was dead, beheaded by Philip of Hesse after the frightful slaughter of his followers.

[2]In 1534 two Dutch Anabaptists Jan Mathijs and Jan van Leiden came to the north German city of Münster proclaiming that the time of patience with the wickedness of the world was at an end. The saints of God who, until then, had accepted persecution quietly were to rise against the godless and destroy them. A kingdom was proclaimed, the New Jerusalem; herein the millenium would be realized. The town council was ousted and those refusing to accept rebaptism were forced to leave the town. Now began the reign of the saints. All property was made common. Churches and monasteries were plundered. Polygamy was introduced after the example of the

Old Testament patriarchs. At this juncture the local bishop, who was also the lord of the town, laid Münster under siege. The revolutionaries managed to hold out for over a year but finally on June 25, 1535, the episcopal troops took the city. Most of the inhabitants were slaughtered. The bodies of the leaders, after death by torture, were suspended in iron cages from the steeple of a local church.

[3]*The Complete Works of Menno Simons,* trans. Leonard Verduin, ed. John Christian Wenger, with a biography by Harold S. Bender (Scottdale, Pa.: The Herald Press, 1956), p. 125.

[4]John C. Wenger, "The Schleitheim Confession of Faith," *The Mennonite Quarterly Review,* XIX, No. 4 (1945), 247-52.

[5]*The Complete Works of Menno Simons,* p. 962.

[6]*Ibid.,* p. 71.

[7]Franklin H. Littell, *A Tribute to Menno Simons* (Scottdale, Pa.: Herald Press, 1961), p. 50.

[8]Daniel O'Hanlon, S.J., "What Can Catholics Learn from the Free Churches," in *Concilium,* vol. XIV, *Do We Know the Others?* (Glen Rock, N.J.: Paulist Press, 1966) pp. 94-103.

[9]*Ibid.,* p. 99.

Anglicanism

It was only a few years after the Reformation was launched in continental Europe that its influence began to be felt in England. The point in history at which this impact is focused is the reign of Henry VIII (1509-47). Having petitioned the pope for an annulment of his marriage to Catherine of Aragon that he might, by marrying again, provide the throne and England with a male heir, and having been refused his petition, Henry decided to set up in England a national church independent of Rome and subject to himself as its supreme head.

But this single set of events is not of itself the sufficient explanation of how the Reformation came to England. Rather, Henry's petition, the refusal, and the consequent separation from Rome turned out to be the occasion which set free and allowed to begin working far more openly than ever before, forces which had been present in England long before Henry but which had been, until his schism, prevented from producing too drastic a change in the religious and ecclesiastical life of the nation. Henry opened the door to schism and thereby, beyond his own intent, to the Reformation. He introduced change but it was only the prelude to what would follow. Those who counseled him and his successors for the next fifty years would build a reformed church far beyond Henry's own plan.

ANTECEDENTS

Of the forces already at work well before Henry's time the first was a bitter anticlericalism. Ecclesiastical ownership of property was widespread. One estimate would put their holdings at one-third of all the land in

England. Such ownership gave power and real abuse had developed in the exercise of that power. The clergy monopolized both government and administration. At one level, many of the common people had come to hate the clergy for their venality and immorality. At another, the more educated despised the parish clergy for their ignorance and superstition and feared and hated the higher clergy for their wealth and power. Thus, the suppression of the monasteries, the appropriation and redistribution of their lands, and the break with the Roman church which the clergy served were, when they came, welcomed or at least accepted without much resistance by most Englishmen.

In process, too, since the late Middle Ages had been the gradual hardening of popular piety into superstition. Christianity's central beliefs, the Trinity, Incarnation, and Redemption, tended more and more to lose the attention and devotion of the common people. They were replaced in popular preaching and piety by an overexaggerated emphasis on hell and purgatory, their horrors, and how it was possible to escape them. The cult of Mary and the saints with its long procession of easily abused practices: relics, pilgrimages, alleged miracles and apparitions, indulgences, became the core of much of England's Christian belief and practice.

This tendency toward distortion and superstition had gone largely unchecked because, along with it, there had grown up a serious decline in clerical learning. The parish clergy tended to be largely uneducated and so threw up no strong wall against the rising tide of superstition. More serious in its consequences was the fact that the tradition of learning had dimmed in the great monasteries of England and very little was the light they shed on the darkness of the country surrounding them.

By the sixteenth century two further factors had developed: a growing lay literacy and the advent of books, especially the Bible. It now became possible for more and more people to see the grotesque deformations in the understanding of Christianity that had grown up among them. It was thus not too long a step to move from Henry's break with the Roman Church, which had permitted such aberrations to exist, to the acceptance of the doctrinal reforms in that church's teaching which were proposed by the continental Reformers.

A preview of what was to come had already been given to England two centuries previously in the person of John Wycliffe (c. 1328-1384). Wycliffe had seen and opposed the abuses that, even then, were rampant in the English church. He decried the rich, powerful and worldly clerics, condemned monasticism, called for a return to the Bible as the sole source of Christian belief and rejected transubstantiation in favor of a spiritual presence of Christ in the Eucharist. In a word, he developed many of the positions that would be adopted by the Reformers two hundred years later. But the forces needed to effect the reforms he sought were not yet strong enough in England. What he did accomplish, though, was to bequeath a legacy of dissent to the English church which continued for the next two centuries. When Henry was ready to move against Rome, the tradition of Wycliffe, perpetuated among the Lollards, had produced two effects which would contribute substantially to making Henry's break with Rome far more than a juridical separation. Dickens summarizes these effects.

> By 1530 they had already accomplished their two main services to the Reformation. In the first place fifteenth-century Lollardy helped to exclude the possibility of Catholic reforms by hardening the minds of the English bishops and their officials into a sterile, negative and rigid attitude toward all criticism and toward the English Scriptures. . . . The second and more important function of the Lollards in English history lay in the fact that they provided a springboard of critical dissent from which the Protestant Reformation could overleap the walls of orthodoxy.[1]

IMPLEMENTATION OF THE REFORM

By Henry's reign the time was ripe. His marital problem and the solution he found to it allowed all these factors greater freedom and sharper focus than they had ever had in the past. Now he led England to jurisdictional separation and these forces led her to doctrinal separation from Rome. Henry initiated the revolt from Rome, broke the power of the medieval church in England, and asserted his own supremacy in both church and state. But reformation in the teaching of the church was not in his plans. He remained to his death an orthodox believer in the teachings of Rome and that meant that the English church remained so too.

While Henry lived, the implementation of the Reform in England proceeded very slowly. Henry was more concerned with establishing and extending the royal supremacy than with doctrinal innovation. The latter, on the rare occasions when it occurred, took place because it served the former. But two developments during his reign did lay the groundwork for the future.

First, there was the new availability of the Scriptures in English. Englishmen abroad began producing English translations of the Scriptures. In 1525, for example, William Tyndale brought out an English New Testament in Holland. Copies of it were soon being brought over from Holland in increasing numbers by the English merchants. Along with the other vernacular versions of the Bible now starting to appear, it helped to provide the basis for a growing concern among the English that Christianity be based solely on the Word of God. Thus did Luther's principle of *sola Scriptura* make its way to England.

Secondly, Thomas Cranmer (1489-1556) was created Archbishop of Canterbury by Henry in 1533. By the time of his appointment Cranmer was already a convinced Protestant. He had converted to Lutheranism while on the king's business in Europe. By tradition, doctrine and worship in England were the responsibility of Canterbury's archbishop. Thus, Cranmer found himself in the position of being able to influence strongly what the future course of England's belief and worship would be. In that position, during the reign of Henry and especially of Edward, he was to become the chief architect of liturgical and doctrinal reform in the church in England.

With the accession to the throne of Henry's young son, Edward VI (1547-53), the reform began in earnest. Edward's two Protectors, first Somerset and then Northumberland, were Protestant in their sympathies and thus the power of the state came down on the side of reform. Cranmer, now that he had a freer hand, moved toward reform in liturgy and church life. These were the years during which relics and images were removed from the churches; fasting was abolished; clerical marriage was approved; communion under both kinds was introduced; the practice of private confession was done away with and transubstantiation as an explanation of Christ's presence in the Eucharist was abandoned. A new book for the conduct of liturgical worship was also issued by Cranmer in two versions, the first in 1549 reflecting Luther's views, the second in 1552 rather Zwinglian and Calvinist in its leanings. With this *Book of Common Prayer,* Cranmer was building the future liturgical practice of the English church.

Perhaps the most significant doctrinal reform under Edward was the appearance, under Cranmer's authority, of the *Book of Homilies.* This was a collection of twelve sermons, one of which was to be read each week at Sunday worship service in all the churches of England. Cranmer himself authored three of these sermons, those which dealt with the doctrine of justification. The approach adopted in explaining justification moved toward Luther's position of faith alone as the source of salvation. As Ridley puts it in his life of Cranmer:

> [Cranmer's] doctrine fell a good way short of the new Protestant theology of justification by faith in its Lutheran and Calvinist form. Cranmer went to St. Hilary and St. Ambrose for the plain statements that 'faith alone justifieth' and that 'he which believeth in Christ should be saved without works, by faith alone', and commented: 'What can be spoken more plainly than to say that freely, without works, by faith only, we obtain remission of our sins?' But he immediately qualified this position by explaining that the faith which was necessary for salvation was a true and lively faith, which manifested itself in good living and good works.[2]

The *Book of Homilies* meant that the people of England would hear, at every Sunday worship service, the principal articles of the Christian faith explained in terms that were beginning to reflect the interpretation given those articles by the continental Reformers. These were the years, finally, when the *Forty Two Articles of Belief* were issued. They embodied a definite commitment to the Lutheran *Augsburg Confession* and the writings of Luther and Melanchthon.

Thus, by the end of Edward's short six-year reign, all the changes needed for a Reformed church in England had been promulgated and their enactment begun. But the time was not yet at hand for their final acceptance by the people of England. The Catholic reaction under Queen Mary would go a long way toward assuring that acceptance; and when Elizabeth came to the throne, the Church of England would at last be ready to settle into its definitive form.

Mary, daughter of Catherine of Aragon, was herself a staunch Catholic and her five-year reign (1553-58) was marked by a determined effort to restore Roman Catholicism to England. But five years was too short a time to undo what had been done and achieve her purpose. Indeed, by making almost every mistake she could have made, she deepened England's hostility to Rome and strengthened the English people's receptivity to the Reformation. Her burning and exiling of heretics, her marriage to Philip of Spain, her attempted restoration of church lands and property, her intransigent resistance to all things Protestant, all these alienated her people and doomed her cause. When she was succeeded by Elizabeth (1558-1603) the English were ready for a period of peace and an end to religious division and persecution.

THE ELIZABETHAN SETTLEMENT

What her people wanted, Elizabeth provided, a stable government and a church that was so structured as to serve England's political and social well-being. Together with her bishops, she built a church and a religious life in England that served the cause of peace, order, and stability.

The definitive form of the Church of England, the so-called Elizabethan Settlement, was the produce of a variety of influences and was constructed by men whose Protestantism was representative of most of the major forms of the continental Reform. There were the Marian exiles, many of them clergy and theologians, whose return from five years of banishment in the Rhineland and the cities of Switzerland meant that a strong Reformed influence would be at work in the building of the Church of England. There was also regular correspondence between the English bishops and the German Reformers which guaranteed a Lutheran presence in the English church. Cranmer's liturgy was at hand and it reflected elements of the medieval Catholic liturgy, modified considerably under the influence of the thought of Luther, Calvin and Zwingli. Lastly, the *Forty Two Articles* were in force, providing a statement of belief which was an adaptation to the English scene of German and Swiss doctrinal views.

To these foreign imports, specifically English ingredients were added, the royal supremacy in all matters of religion, and a strong sense of tradition embodied particularly in the preservation of the order of bishops as the cornerstone on which the structure and continuity of the church would rest. Out of all these elements the Church of England was built and built so firmly that four centuries of history have effected only minor modifications in its structure, practice, and belief.

ELEMENTS OF THE ENGLISH REFORM

The continental Reformation, as embodied in the Lutheran and Reformed churches, was fundamentally a theological reform. It inevitably developed and expressed itself in the context of political and social situations. But it was in essence a doctrinal movement. The English Reform, however, did not express itself principally in a doctrinal form. The Church of England as Elizabeth and her bishops built it was a composite of three components: government, belief, and worship. But, as these elements took shape in England they manifested a characteristically English mode of understanding and living Christianity. Thus, the form that government took in the Church of England testified to England's strong reverence for tradition, the belief that what has always been in the church is to be retained because it has proven itself of value. What was enshrined in that Church's book of divine worship, *the Book of Common Prayer,* was not just a set of ceremonies, prayers, and Scripture readings but represented the studied conviction that the worship of God must be as stately, as ordered, as majestic, as human language could make it and biblical to its core. And the English church's expression of doctrinal belief, the *Thirty Nine Articles,* mirrors the English sentiment that articles of faith should be as few and as simple as possible, that how a man lives is of more ultimate consequence than the intellectual expression of his beliefs.

One must understand this blend and interplay of universal Christian themes and English national characteristics if one is to appreciate the spirit of Anglicanism. The Church of England is the paradigm of a *national* church, not so much because the monarch is its supreme head but because Christianity as it is believed and lived in this church is thoroughly English in its expression. In no other church is this blend of universal Christianity and national identity so strikingly present as in the Church of England.

Church Government—Esteem for Tradition

Paramount in the thinking of those who built the Church of England was the belief that they were constructing not a new church but one that preserved strong bonds of unity with the church as it had always been in England. The sign above all others of that continuity was the episcopacy. The episcopal structure of the church stretched back to the beginnings of Christianity and it had its roots in the clear testimony of Scripture. "It is evident unto all men diligently reading Holy Scripture and ancient authors, that from the Apostles' time there have been these orders of Ministers in Christ's Church, Bishops, priests and deacons."[3] Indeed, it was in order that the bishops might be the living embodiment of Christian belief through the ages that Christ had given this form of government to His church. It was the continuous line of bishops from apostolic times that had preserved the faith in unbroken continuity through the centuries, Christian belief owed its preservation and transmission to the episcopacy. That was the bishops' primary task.

Richard Hooker (1553-1600), the greatest of the theologians of Elizabeth's reign, laid out the sense and value of the bishops' role in the church in his *Ecclesiastical Polity.* As he saw it one could formulate several arguments for an episcopal order of church government. The first of these was scriptural. The New Testament bore ample witness to the presence of bishops in the apostolic church. To this one could add the overwhelming testimony of Christian tradition. East and West, for sixteen hundred years, the church had been ruled and taught by bishops. Last of all, it could be argued, and tellingly, that episcopal government had given the church order and stability and continuity. In a word, it worked.

So the Church of England remained what it had always been, an episcopal church. Thus did Elizabeth's advisers stress the continuity of their church with the Catholic church as it had always existed. Their acceptance of the Reformation in doctrinal matters did not, they felt, justify or denote a break in the continuity of the church in England. That church was to be kept in its traditional form while at the same time the effort was to be made to remove the deformations which had crept into that church over the centuries.

On the one hand, then, the Church of England set itself apart from most continental forms of the Reformation which tended to minimize if not abolish the episcopacy because they found little or no justification for it in the Word of God. By so deciding, Anglicanism manifested a much sharper awareness of its identity with the traditional church catholic than the Lutheran and Calvinist Reformers did. These tended rather to look to the apostolic church for their identity, setting aside the church of the intervening centuries.

On the other hand, the English church broke sharply with the Roman Catholic church and its insistence on the centrality and the supremacy of the pope. The order of bishops became, in place of the Supreme Pontiff in the Roman church, the final ruling and teaching body within the church.

This sense of tradition in reformation was in Elizabeth's time and continues to be today, one of the primary elements in Anglicanism's understanding of itself, the conscious attempt to maintain, through its preservation of the episcopacy, continuity with the belief and practice of the church of all the preceding centuries of Christianity. The episcopal order is the embodiment of Anglicanism's accent on the value of tradition in the church.

So strongly does the Church of England feel about the episcopacy as the form of government which Christ Himself gave to His church that she makes it an absolutely necessary element in any proposed reunion of the Christian churches. The Church of England accepts the other Reformation churches as true churches of Christ, authentic preachers of His Word and valid administrators of His sacraments. But a distinction is made in Anglicanism between the being (*esse*) of the church and her well-being (*bene esse*). The first has to do with the essential reality of the church. That reality is had so long as the church is structured to preach Christ's Word of salvation and administer His sacraments. The other Protestant churches are seen as having this essential reality and, therefore, theirs is a saving ministry.

How the church is structured belongs to her well-being, and it is the Anglican position that Christ's will is an episcopally structured church. Grace and salvation do not depend for their presence on the episcopal structure but in terms of any future unity with other Christian churches, Anglicanism insists that only in an episcopally ordered church will the church order be achieved which Christ gave His apostles and intended for His church.

The order of bishops is, in sum, one of the foundation stones on which the Church of England rests her conviction that she has always remained throughout the centuries, in living contact with the church Christ founded.

Doctrine—A Spirit of Comprehensiveness

What the doctrinal commitment of Anglicanism is, how she understands the Christian faith and what is the assent of faith she asks of her membership, are questions that call for varying answers depending upon what expression of Christianity is under consideration.

First of all, to the Christian faith as it is set forth in Scripture the Church of England gives her unqualified assent. Her faith is a biblical faith which she shares with the other Reformation churches. The Bible is the sole rule of faith. Only what is contained in the Scripture must be believed for salvation.

> Holy Scripture containeth all things necessary to salvation; so that whatsoever is not read therein, nor may be proved thereby, is not to be required of any man, that it should be believed as an article of the Faith, or be thought requisite or necessary to salvation.[4]

Secondly, in addition to the authority of Scripture, the Church of England also recognizes what the tradition of the universal church has done, especially in the early centuries, to clarify and develop the understanding of that initial deposit of faith. She, therefore, pays great reverence to the creeds (Apostles', Nicene, and Athanasian) and the teaching of the early Fathers and Councils of the church as embodying the common teaching of Christianity.

The words of James I in his *Premonition to All Most Mighty Monarchs* (1609) epitomize this typical English regard for the doctrinal formulations of the church of the first four centuries.

> I am such a Catholic Christian as believeth the three Creeds, that of the Apostles, that of the Council of Nice, and that of Athanasius, the two latter being paraphrases to the former. And I believe them in that sense as the ancient Fathers and Councils that made them did understand them, to which three Creeds all the ministers of England do subscribe at their Ordination. . . . I admit the Four First General Councils as Catholic and Orthodox. And the said Four General Councils are acknowledged by our Acts of Parliament, and received for orthodox by our Church.[5]

Thirdly, to these expressions of the Christian faith, the sixteenth century church in England felt called upon to add its own set of credal affirmations, the *Thirty Nine Articles*. Yet, in so doing, the bishops did not intend to produce a doctrinal statement demanding the same quality of assent as the Scriptures, Creeds, and early Councils. Their statement was meant, rather, to be a relative statement, relative in the sense that the *Articles* may be characterized as the doctrinal stance adopted by the Church in England at a particular moment in its history in relation to the doctrinal positions being expressed by the other Christian churches at the time. When the *Articles* are read in this light, it is clear that in them Anglicanism is expressing its understanding of the Christian faith in com parison with the understanding of that faith being held and taught by the other three Western Christian churches of the time: the Protestantism of Luther and Calvin, Roman Catholicism, and Anabaptism.

(1) With regard to Lutheranism and the Reformed churches, a series of articles make it evident that the Church of England is in fundamental agreement with their understanding of Christianity. It is, in a word, a Protestant church. Assent is given to Luther's three basic principles: Scripture alone is the source of saving knowledge: faith is central to the attainment of justice; God alone saves, yet in justifying man He produces in him a state from which good works inevitably flow. Calvin's thought is most obviously present in the *Articles'* adoption of his teaching on predestination. The adoption is done, however, in very cautious words that speak only of God's predestination of the elect to glory, saying nothing of those who are lost.

> Predestination to life, is the everlasting purpose of God, where-
> by (before the foundations of the world were laid) he hath

constantly decreed by his councel secret to us, to deliver from
curse and damnation, those whom he hath chosen in Christ
out of mankind. As the godly consideration of predestination,
and our election in Christ, is full of sweet, pleasant and
unspeakable comfort to godly persons, so, for curious and
carnal persons to have continually before their eyes the sen-
tence of God's predestination is a most dangerous downfall.[6]

The church, too, is described as the continental Reformation would
describe it as "a congregation of faithful men, in the which the Pure Word
of God is preached, and the Sacraments be duly administered according to
Christ's ordinance."[7] Again, in accord with Reformation thinking, only
Baptism and the Lord's Supper are seen as sacraments "ordained of Christ
our Lord in the Gospel." The other five Roman sacraments do not have
"like nature of sacraments" with them. Thus, it is clear that the positive
thrust of the *Articles* is Protestant in its understanding of the Christian
faith.

2) The radical Reformation is uncompromisingly rejected by the
Church of England in a series of articles which defend the swearing of
oaths, assert the right of private property over against the Anabaptist
tendency to endorse communal possession of property, and insist that it is
lawful for citizens to obey civil authority when it commands what is just.
Finally, Anabaptism's insistence on religious liberty, that a man must be
free to form and follow his own conscience, is rejected in *Article 18* with
its condemnation of the proposition that "every man shall be saved by the
Law or Sect which he professeth, so that he be diligent to frame his life
according to that law and the light of nature."[8]

(3) The *Articles* are also explicit in their rejection of what the bishops
considered to be abuses in belief and practice within late medieval Catholicism. *Article 23* speaks out against belief in Purgatory, the superstitious
veneration of images and relics and the invocation of saints. Devotion to
the Blessed Sacrament is reprehended in *Article 25*. *Article 28* repudiates
transubstantiation as an acceptable explanation of the Real Presence of
Christ in the Eucharist. Preferred, rather, is the formula, allowing of either
a Zwinglian or Calvinist interpretation, that "the Body of Christ is given,
taken and eaten in the Supper, only after an heavenly and spiritual manner. And the means whereby the Body of Christ is received and eaten in
the Supper is Faith."[9] Lastly, *Article 31* condemns the Roman emphasis
on the sacrificial aspect of the mass, insisting that Christ's sacrifice on the
cross was all-sufficient.

The doctrinal position taken in the *Articles* is, then, a mediate one, mediate between the extremism of late medieval Catholicism, on the one hand, and the radical expression of the Reformation embodied in the Anabaptist or Puritan view of Christianity, on the other. It is in this sense that Anglicanism may be called the *via media* (middle way). There is, however, no doubt that this is a Reformation document. It represents a clear commitment to all the basic principles of the Reformation.

This mediate stance in doctrinal matters is, like the episcopal structure, another expression of a typically English characteristic, reasonableness or moderation. Anglicanism has always believed that what constitutes a man a Christian is his acceptance of the Gospel message. The spelling out of that message in precise doctrinal statements and exact rational terms represents man's attempt to put God's revelation into human language. Because such formulations are human language, they ought not to be made into necessary objects of faith. God's revelation, not man's words, are what a Christian should believe and live by. Thus it is that within Anglicanism there has never been a strong insistence that theologically correct, and carefully reasoned expressions of the Christian faith must be assented to by its membership. It prefers, rather, to stress the essentially simple message of the Christian Scriptures, leaving to the individual the task and the right to understand that message in ways that are personally meaningful. Thus, for example, the Church of England recognizes that the New Testament account of the institution of the Eucharist speaks of Christ as really present in that sacrament. The true Christian believes in that presence. Attempts to explain the manner of that real presence are human attempts and the Christian may or may not choose to accept such explanations insofar as they seem helpful to him.

Such an attitude towards doctrine has always meant the presence within Anglicanism of a great flexibility and comprehensiveness in its possession of the Christian faith. The act of faith takes as its object the Scripture message. Beyond that, reasonableness takes over and an extremely broad latitude is granted in interpreting that message. Put another way, what is primarily important in Christianity is not so much what a man gives intellectual assent to as how he lives his life.

Liturgy—Tradition Within Reformation

One central place in Anglicanism is given to episcopal government. The other equally central position is occupied by the liturgical worship of God. Cranmer's *Book of Common Prayer* is the official liturgical book of Anglicanism. For the Church of England, it replaces Rome's four liturgical books: the monk's book of daily prayer, the priest's mass book, the ritual for the conferral of the sacraments, and the bishop's book for ordinations.

Evident in each of the book's four parts is the conviction that controlled its composition, the determination to join together the best of tradition with the best of reformation. This meant that Cranmer was always careful to preserve the ancient liturgical forms, yet always conscious that the liturgy should reflect the Reformation's understanding of the Christian faith.

Thus, he retained the structure of the Roman mass in order to preserve what he felt was tradition's well-proven form of divine worship. But he made it into a communion service, stripping it of its sacrificial emphasis in line with the Reformation conviction that Christ's sacrifice was all-sufficient.

He recognized, too, the soundness of the principle that the church should offer daily prayer of petition, praise and thanks to God and he retained, therefore, the practice of the divine office. But he rewrote the office once prayed by monks, simplifying its format, putting it into the language of the people and moving its recitation to the public churches that the people themselves might understand and participate in it. He saw to it, too, that each of the two daily services of prayer included readings from the Old and New Testaments that the congregation might be fed on the Word of God and, thereby, have the lived experience of the all-sufficiency of God's Word in Christianity.

Yet again, he agreed with the Reformers that the sacraments of Christ were only two in number and he provided the manner of their celebration. But he was traditionalist enough to realize also that the other "commonly called sacraments" had a long and treasured place in the church's life and so the ritual for their conferral was also included.

The Roman tendency in liturgy at the time was to put chief emphasis on the worship of God. The Reformation tendency was to accent the participation and instruction of the congregation. Cranmer's liturgy blends the two, expressing in stately and reverent language, coupled with magnificent orderliness and sober restraint, both the Word and Sacrament aspect of the liturgy. Ample attention was given to both. In no other Christian church is such sustained and serious attention paid to the reading of the Word of God in public worship. Yet, equal place is given to the praising and glorifying of God in sacramental celebration and daily prayer service. Pulpit for preaching and altar for worship, both have their honored place in the *Book of Common Prayer.*

And again, as in episcopal government and in doctrinal commitment, the English character comes through. English piety avoids unseemly display of emotion and shuns sentimentality. It tends rather to be restrained and measured in its expression, quiet rather than ostentatious in its public forms. Cranmer's prayerbook captures that national spirit and expresses it magnificently. The *Book of Common Prayer* stands alongside Luther's *Treatises* and Calvin's *Institutes* as one of the great masterpieces of the Reformation. It makes clear, too, that Anglicanism always has been far more a liturgical than a doctrinal church.

CONCLUSION

The contribution of Anglicanism to the Reformation does not lie primarily in the field of theology as is true in the case of Lutheranism and the Reformed movement, which is not, however, to deny that there has been, since the sixteenth century, a distinguished line of theologians and biblical scholars in the Church of England. It is, rather, to say that she has a particularly strong sense of how man ought to worship God and a unique facility for expressing that worship in appropriate forms and language. The Church of England's other major influence on the history of Protestant Christianity lies in her retention of the episcopal order and through that, her preservation of a much deeper sense of tradition in the church than is true of the other Reformation churches.

As the Christian churches begin working toward reunion more seriously than they have since their separation, there are many who see how well Anglicanism, especially in her worship, her episcopacy, and her reverence for tradition, has kept elements that must be central values to be preserved in any reunited church. Her middle way of moderation between extremes, likewise, offers hope to many as a pattern and a goal for the future of ecumenism. Of the Christian churches she embodies, most obviously, the principle of unity in diversity.

Yet, like most values, her moderation has been bought at a price. That price has meant a growing doctrinal comprehensiveness over the centuries. To preserve Anglicanism's bond of unity has demanded an almost unlimited willingness to tolerate within that unity any and every shade of Christian belief. In consequence, it has grown increasingly difficult to find in Anglicanism any strong sense of a teaching authority to guarantee her continuing possession of the essential elements of Christian fiath.

Mediation and moderation will be key factors for the future of Christianity. Anglicanism, in her history, exemplifies one way in which these values can be embodied in a Christian church. At the same time, her history poses in sharp terms the dilemma that Christianity faces when it tries to house unity and diversity under a single roof.

The problem, faced but not adequately solved by Anglicanism, grows increasingly critical for Christianity in the contemporary pluralistic world. How are the Christian churches to become the one church Christ willed His church to be, while, at the same time, preserving diverse understandings of the Christian faith and varying modes of Christian worship?

FOOTNOTES

[1] A.G. Dickens, *The English Reformation* (London: B.T. Batsford Ltd., and New York: Schocken Books, Inc., 1964), p. 36.

[2] Jasper Ridley, *Thomas Cranmer*, paperback edition (Oxford: University Press, 1966), p. 266. Used by permission of The Clarendon Press, Oxford, England.

[3] From the introduction to the section on the rite of ordination in the *Book of Common Prayer*.

[4] Article 6 of the *Thirty Nine Articles*.

[5] The text is quoted in J. W. C. Wand, *Anglicanism in History and Today* (New York & Toronto: Thomas Nelson and Sons, 1962), p. 52.

[6] Article 17 of the *Thirty Nine Articles*.

[7] Article 19 of the *Thirty Nine Articles*.

[8] Article 18 of the *Thirty Nine Articles*.

[9] Article 28 of the *Thirty Nine Articles*.

Puritanism

The England that Elizabeth found upon her accession to the throne had known nothing but religious differences, bloody persecutions, and one government succeeding another for almost twenty years. Sick of religious warfare and confused by the constant shift of governments, the nation wanted nothing so much as peace in religion and stability in the state. Elizabeth read the signs of the times and made it the aim of her reign to provide what was longed for. She would settle the religious situation and give her kingdom a measure of stability in government.

But the problem of religion was not open to easy solution by Elizabeth because her subjects themselves did not agree upon its solution. There was general agreement that there was but one true religion and that the power of the state should lend itself to the support of that religion. But beyond this consensus there was disagreement in answering the question: which is the true religion? The Catholics, by now in the minority, held one view on what was the true religion. The Protestant majority, of course, disagreed. Even among them there was divided opinion on what form religion should take in England.

Elizabeth recognized the difficulty and proposed to solve it by a judicious blend of imposed conformity and broad tolerance. She chose to retain the episcopal form of church as the official framework for the church in England. Bishops were chosen she could depend on and they were given the task of implementing her authority and theirs in terms of a national church with its own system of worship and code of belief. Outward conformity to this church was imposed on the nation. Beyond this each man was free to believe and practice what he wished. It was only when that belief or practice took the form of a disobedience which threatened the peace and stability of the realm that repressive measures were adopted.

THE PURITAN PARTY

For the generality of Englishmen the policy was perfectly acceptable. But one group among her subjects, the Puritans, was unhappy with her policy. It was their conviction, learned during an exile spent in Switzerland imbibing Calvin's view of the church, that Elizabeth's church was an abomination in the sight of the Almighty. This was so because it did not conform to the pure Word of God as the church of Geneva did. For the Puritan, Scripture was the sole authority both for what the church believed and also for what she did. Anything not explicitly authorized in Scripture did not belong in the church. Following this norm they found much in the Elizabethan church clearly at odds with what the Word of God said His Church should be.

For the Anglican theologians, on the other hand, who defended the structure and practice of the Church of England, the answer to the question: what is the authority of Scripture in determining the creed and cult of the church, was different. For them its authority in what was to be believed was absolute. What Scripture taught and only what Scripture taught must be believed. The Word of God was the final word in matters of belief. But in the area of church life and worship, Scripture did not provide complete, specific directions as to what was to be done. The church had always recognized this fact and had, throughout her history, developed forms of worship and norms for living which were best suited to the needs of the age. Thus had Tradition developed, as human reason in the service of the church tried to embody the Scriptural message in appropriate forms. In this field the authority of Scripture was principally negative. Nothing could be instituted in life or worship which was contrary to the teaching of Scripture.

The Puritans, however, would have none of this distinction. Elizabeth's church in terms of what Scripture demanded was a church scarcely reformed at all. It was then their bounden duty, faced with the disparity between the English church and the church that God willed in Scripture, to use all the means at hand to effect the radical purification of their national church. Thus was the party of opposition to Elizabeth's religious policy born, the Puritans, bent on purifying her church of its corruptions. In their view the church had need of a more Scriptural and therefore purer form of government, a purer form of worship, purification of doctrinal beliefs, and a stronger insistence on a holier way of life for the people of England.

For the Puritans, Elizabeth's policy of moderation was at once a frustration and an opportunity. It was a frustration because she would not tolerate their extremism. What were halfway measures for them were peace-keeping policies for her. So long as she lived she would not let them seize power in her church. But it was for the Puritans an opportunity, too, because, provided they did not unduly disturb the peace with their preaching and pamphleteering, she would not crush them completely. So they gained time to unite and to develop their strategy for bringing the church under the control of their vision of what a church should be.

With the passage of time the general lines of their strategy became apparent. Their key idea was organization, the enlistment of the support of those elements of English society which could best ensure the spread and general acceptance of their view of the church. This meant especially the cultivation of the university and the press and the winning to their cause of as many Englishmen as possible, especially the tradesmen, artisans, and merchants of the rising middle class.

The universities, most especially Cambridge, were the cradle of the movement and that in a double sense. From this base the leaders of Puritanism could launch their tracts, pamphlets, and sermons aimed at condemning in the strongest possible language the corruption of the established religion. Along with condemnation, they spoke, too, of the kind of church that God's will, clearly expressed in Scripture, demanded.

In addition to providing the intellectual leadership for the movement, Cambridge also became the source whence flowed a steady stream of preachers prepared to take over, wherever possible, the pulpits of England. Thoroughly committed to the vision of Geneva, these ministers were well equipped with the plain and sober language and the intense earnestness of personal conviction needed to win to their cause the solid middle class merchants and lawyers of the city and the small landholders of the country. It was on this class of society that the full force of their persuasiveness was concentrated.

The press and the rising literacy among the people offered another useful instrument for propaganda; the country began to be filled with Puritan literature. As the years passed, a mounting tide of diaries, autobiographies and biographies, tracts, histories of God's People, programs for the building of the Holy Commonwealth and for living God's will, spread the vision of a church fully reformed and completely purified in accord with the divine will.

THE PURITANS IN POWER

By 1640 the strategy had produced its desired effect. The Long Parliament which began its sessions that year was predominantly Puritan in its outlook which meant that it saw the need for reform of the church as a pressing national problem. During the next ten years it moved to the enactment of that reform. But even as reform began the full effect of Elizabeth's policy, which was continued by her successors, James I (1603-25) and Charles I (1625-49), came to fruition and defeated that reform.

The first effect of that policy was that over the years many of the Puritans gave up hope of ever being able to reform the Church of England. They sought, in voluntary exile, the freedom that God's saints needed to build their purified church. For those who chose America, their holy commonwealth lasted for several generations but faded when the descendants lost the vision of their forebears. The groups that sought refuge in Holland were never large and when they returned to England under the policy of religious toleration in 1688, their impact on the religious life of the nation was minimal. Thus, for a significant segment of Puritanism, Elizabeth's policy produced frustration which led in turn to the choice of exile. Ultimately the exile dissipated the force of their influence.

But by far the most significant effect of Elizabeth's firm restraint was produced among the majority of Puritans who chose to remain in England and suffer through the period of waiting until power fell into their hands. For them her policy provided ample time for differences of opinion to develop regarding the true nature of God's church. These differences produced, in their turn, a splintering of Puritanism into a variety of visions of what the church should be. William Haller puts the matter well.

> Elizabethan policy waiving consistency and ignoring variations of opinion when politically harmless, gave scope for all sorts of men to search the scriptures, to fall in love with their own strange ideas, to espouse fantastic dreams, to collect bands of earnest souls, in short to go and eat forbidden fruit so long as they did not try to upset the apple cart. . . . Thus English Puritanism, denied opportunity to reform the established Church, wreaked its energy during a half century and more upon preaching, and under the impetus of the pulpit, upon unchecked experiment in religious expression and social behavior.[1]

In the Parliament of 1640 which marked the culmination of the Puritan drive to power in the English church two policies came to simultaneous fruition, Elizabeth's religious policy and the Puritan strategy of power. The first, through the fragmentation it produced, guaranteed that the second, once achieved, could not but fail in its attempt to implement its vision of what the church should be. So it turned out. The twenty years until the restoration of the monarchy in 1660 was time enough to prove that the Puritans did not have the unity of vision and power necessary to reform the Church of England according to their own design. Puritanism faded as a significant religious influence in the Church of England.

ELEMENTS OF THE PURITAN VISION

What were the elements of the Puritan vision that produced such passionate, even fanatic dedication among its followers? At the heart of that vision stood Calvin's doctrine of election. The Puritan came through personal conversion to a sense of his own election and a conviction that he was responsible for bringing God's will to his own life, his church and his nation. Three roads, therefore, led out from that center, one to the individual believer and his life, one to the church and its government, belief, and worship, and one to society in general. And all three roads by varying routes reached the same destination, the glory of God. Or put another way, Puritanism could be summarized as Simpson does, in these words:

> The Puritans were elect spirits, segregated from the mass of mankind by an experience of conversion, fired by the sense that God was using them to revolutionize human history and committed to the execution of His will.[2]

The Individual

To enter into the Puritan vision one had first to pass through the door of a personal conversion. In Puritanism one found that door in God's Word and the way above all others for learning God's Word was through the sermons of His godly ministers. The sermon, then, was the key initial experience for the Puritan. The preachers, aware of its crucial importance, directed all the skill of their education to developing a style of preaching

remained generally accepted that God spoke through them and in that sense they were inspired books but they were also a set of humanly written documents and as such contained error and contradiction, legend and myth, along with historical facts. Perhaps the most radical result of the movement was the dramatic change effected by the critics in the traditional view of Jesus Christ. The Jesus discovered by the biblical critics was quite different from the Jesus that tradition had known until then.

Biblical criticism applied to the Bible the type of literary analysis to which the other literary productions of the past were being subjected. The critics were convinced that a thorough application of the methods of historical and literary criticism to the Scripture would yield a much more accurate understanding of the Bible than had thus far been achieved. The task of biblical study was conceived to be not so much a study of the text itself as an attempt to get behind the text, to discover what the text was really saying, to separate the text into its various components: fact and fiction, history and legend, ideas intended as distinct from literary forms used to express them.

To achieve this end of a deeper understanding of the text's meaning, the scholars began to ask critical questions regarding the Bible: When were these books written, were the authors really those traditionally accepted to be such, what did the authors really intend to say, what was the effect of history on the thought of the books of the Bible, what relation can be determined between the various books, can a common stock of religious ideas account for the likenesses between the Scripture and the other documents of the ancient Near East?

When applied to the Old Testament this historico-critical method yielded a number of new and startling conclusions. The first five books of the Old Testament were not, as had previously been believed, written by Moses. Different styles, vocabularies, literary forms pointed to a number of authors. Isaiah too was not singly authored but manifested at least two, possibly three or four, different hands in its composition. The creation story in Genesis was not a single unified account, but two distinct traditions had been woven together to give the impression of one account. Many passages previously understood as foretelling the future were now seen to have been written after the event foretold. As the evidence mounted for such views, the traditional position that Scripture was literally true in all that it recorded was gradually undermined.

The major focus of attention of the biblical critics, however, was the New Testament. Specifically their studies concentrated on the person of Jesus or, as Schweitzer later characterized the movement, the work of the scholars became a "guest of the historical Jesus." The task of New Testament study was conceived as involving an attempt to distinguish the words and deeds of the historical Jesus of Nazareth from the interpretations which the Church, in writing the New Testament, added to this basically simple historical portrait. Careful study was needed to separate fact from interpretation of fact or myth in the case of Jesus so that the historical Jesus might be disengaged from the nonhistorical elements that the Church added at a later date. David Strauss' *Life of Jesus* published in 1835-36 will serve as a typical example of the way in which the problem was handled.

David Strauss

To begin with, Strauss (1808-1874), acknowledged that there had been before him two different kinds of attempts to interpret the meaning of Jesus. The orthodox or supernatural approach started with the premise that all the Scripture contained was true, its supernatural (e.g., miracles and prophecies) as well as its natural elements. From this starting point it explained the meaning of the various books, coping as best it could with whatever apparent contradictions it met. The natural or rational approach began with the opposite premise: Only what was historical or rationally explicable could possibly be true. Hence only those passages allowing of rational explanation were to be considered as true. All else was to be eliminated. Strauss found both approaches unsatisfactory and he proposed, in typically Hegelian style, a third method of interpretation, the mythological one, which would achieve a synthesis of the acceptable elements of the two prior types of explanation. The supernatural interpretation was seen as the thesis; the rational as the antithesis and the mythological as the synthesis.

Myth for Strauss means ". . . the clothing in historic form of religious ideas, shaped by the unconsciously inventive power of legend, and embodied in a historic personality."[7] Jesus of Nazareth was a historical person who, in the course of his life and under the influence of the spirit of the age, especially the strong strain of Messianic expectation that characterized the Jewish religious thought of the time, came to believe that he was the Messiah whom the Jews expected. The admiration and reverence he evoked in his followers was so strong that after his death they proceeded, unconsciously, to invest him with legendary and mythical attributes. Their myth-making tendencies were encouraged by the strong Messianic expectations of the contemporary Jews.

All the Messianic allusions of the Old Testament, its references to traits that the future Messiah would have, could quite naturally be absorbed into their increasingly idealized picture of Jesus. The final stage of their mythologizing was the attribution to him of divine qualities. He became for them the Son of God. The Jesus of Scripture is then a combination of historical fact and Christian imagination fashioning a historical figure into a divine person through the process of mythologizing that figure.

A look at the way in which Strauss works out some of the elements of this thesis will clarify his thinking and at the same time provide a typical example of a biblical critic at work.

Jesus of Nazareth

For Strauss, Jesus at some time before his death had come to the conviction that he was the Messiah. The probability was that this was a gradually dawning consciousness. We need not, however, believe that Jesus was a fanatic because he came to this conclusion. He too was, like most of his contemporaries, subject to the suggestive power that myth-making exercised on the men of his time.

Once convinced of his Messiahship, it is easy to conceive how that conviction could have led Jesus to see his own suffering and death as an inevitable consequence of his acceptance of that role. The Old Testament had spoken much of a suffering Messiah, especially Isaiah. The further conclusion that death willingly accepted would possess an atoning power and would exert a powerful spiritual influence on the lives of his followers was also quite understandable. Following this line of thought Strauss could conclude that the death of Jesus was indeed a historical fact but the implications that Christians have found in that death were in large part put there by Jesus, himself a human person, who was formed in his thought patterns by the religious climate of his times.

His Followers

Another strong influence at work in the shaping of the final form of the New Testament was the impact that Jesus' powerful personality had on his apostles and disciples. Much of the detail about him, his healing power, his resurrection, his divinity, is due to their reaction to the strength and attractiveness of his personality. Intimations of his messianic consciousness, for example, would be given to his followers and once the seed was planted their reverence for him would quite naturally lead them to link his deeds and words with the Old Testament descriptions of the future Messiah.

Such a tendency would, for example, explain how the stories of his healings, his prophecies, and his miraculous raisings from the dead made their way into the story of his life. They would be the product of his followers' conviction that the Messiah must surely equal and even surpass the deeds done by the prophets of the Old Testament. Thus the prophet Eliseus had cured Naaman the Syrian of his leprosy; and the same prophet had restored to life the son of the Sunamite woman (*IV Kings:* Chaps. 4-5). Or, again, the transfiguration of the face of Moses after his conversation with God on Sinai would offer obvious background material for the story of the Transfiguration. Such thinking introduced the miraculous stories into the New Testament and led finally to the conclusion that, since he was greater than the prophets of the Old Law, not only did he raise others to life but his own superior power effected his own resurrection.

St. John's Gospel provided Strauss with the last link in his chain of mythological interpretation of the Scripture. Here the person of Jesus moved from the possession of extraordinary power to the status of divinity. By the time John came to write his Gospel he had acquired a familiarity with Greek philosophical thought. That thinking provided him with a series of thought categories: divine sonship, the Logos concept, the notion of preexistence. He came to see all of these as ideal concepts for expressing his own and his fellow Christians' ever deepening reverence for the person of Jesus. When he came to write his life of Jesus these ideas were worked into the fabric of the narrative in such a way that later readers would see them as integral parts of the story of Jesus' life rather than as products of a long period of reflection which had resulted in the weaving together into a single account both historical fact and John's introduction of mythical and philosophical elements into the narrating of these facts.

CONCLUSION

In consequence of Strauss' work and that of the other nineteenth century Protestant biblical scholars a dramatic revolution in the interpretation of Scripture entered the mainstream of Protestant thought. Later scholars would tend to be much less drastic in their application of the new method and Schweitzer's observation at the end of the century that

Strauss' search for myth had led him to underestimate the amount of history in the Gospels was an estimate shared by most scholars.

> . . . he overestimates the importance of the Old Testament motives in reference to the creative activity of the legend. He does not see that while in many cases he has shown clearly enough the source of the *form* of the narrative in question, this does not suffice to explain its *origin*. Doubtless, there is mythical material in the story of the feeding of the multitude. But the existence of the story is not explained by reference to the manna in the desert, or the miraculous feeding of a multitude by Elisha. The story in the Gospel has far too much individuality for that, and stands, moreover, in much too closely articulated an historical connexion. It must have as its basis some historical fact. It is not a myth, though there is myth in it.[8]

Yet allowing for all the moderating influence that such criticism has exercised, the historico-critical method of scriptural interpretation still holds the field as the dominant influence in the contemporary study of the Bible. Indeed, the manner of understanding the Word of God not as text but as event which occurs when God speaks to the individual, the meaning and usage of mythological and symbolic language as a vehicle of religious truth, the recurrence of the birth, life, death and rising theme in the literature of most of the world's religion, the historical dimensions of God's dealing with His people, these are the major themes in today's scriptural studies. All of them trace their lineage back to nineteenth century biblical criticism and beyond that back to Luther's principle of *sola Scriptura.*

ALBERT RITSCHL

The third major influence operative in nineteenth century Protestantism was the work of Albert Ritschl (1822-1889). Schleiermacher was a response to romanticism and rationalism. Biblical criticism was Christianity's attempt to come to terms with the new learning and contemporary methods of scholarship. Ritschl represents Christian theology's confrontation with the philosophy of Immanuel Kant. Ritschl's theology was strongly influenced by Kant's thought particularly at two points: the rejection of metaphysics or theoretical speculation as a source of valid knowledge about God; and a strong insistence on religious thought as essentially practical and moral.

Kant, in dealing with the nature of human thought, concluded that man could not know things as they are in themselves. All that could be known were phenomena, things as they presented themselves to the senses, the appearance of things. This being so, it followed that a knowledge of God as He is in Himself (a metaphysical or philosophical knowledge of God) was not a possibility.

But for Kant there was another type of human knowledge. That was the field of moral consciousness, the sphere of man's practical reason. Man is aware of moral obligations that bind him, a series of thou shalts and thou shalt nots. When analyzed out, this moral sense pointed to the existence of One responsible for the existence of this moral imperative in all men. God exists as the necessary postulate to explain man's moral sense and religion is man's recognition that the laws that bind him are commands given by God.

Ritschl accepted this Kantian analysis of the nature of human knowledge and on its basis worked out his interpretation of the meaning of Christianity. His basic premise is that religion and therefore Christianity must be separated from theoretical knowledge. God is apprehended through the moral sense; He is not known rationally. The Christian faith was not, therefore, metaphysical. It was rather moral and ethical. Its primary concern was concrete and practical rather than intellectual and philosophical. Put another way, the object of the Christian message is not concern about the nature of God or Christ but the answer to the question: How is man saved?

Building on this fundamental notion of the practicality of religion Ritschl viewed Christianity as based on value judgments. Man is initially conscious that, though he is part of nature like the other things that surround him, he is unlike the rest of nature in that he sees himself as having a worth and an independence over against nature. Religion offers man an explanation of this consciousness of himself. It provides him with . . . "a solution of the contradiction in which man finds himself, as both a part of the world of nature and a spiritual personality claiming to dominate nature."[9]

The solution that it gives man is

> . . . faith in superhuman spiritual powers, by whose help the power which man possesses of himself is in some way supplemented and elevated into a unity of its own kind which is a match for the pressure of the natural world. The idea of gods, or Divine powers, everywhere includes belief in their spiritual personality, for the support to be received from above can

only be reckoned on in virtue of an affinity between God and men.[10]

Ritschl is here saying that man makes a value judgment regarding his own worth. He is conscious of a stature above and beyond that of the rest of nature. Implicit in that judgment is the awareness of a Person who is responsible for man's conviction of his own worth and who collaborates with him in his practical assertion of that worth. God is then part and parcel of man's consciousness of his own worth just as for Schleiermacher He is implicit in man's awareness of his dependent state. Thus knowledge of God arises out of a value judgment.

In relation to the objects around him, man judges them as supporting or detracting from his sense of his own worth. They give rise in man to value judgments, feelings of pleasure or pain, happiness or sorrow, guilt or peace, worthwhileness or worthlessness. They are seen as good or bad in terms of whether they help or hinder a man in realizing his own worth.

It should be noted that in this analysis of the nature of religion the feelings and the will play a far more important role than the intellect. For the religious man what is important is the set of values to which he commits himself, not what he knows about the nature of God.

Human history is the place where man has discovered his values and worked out their implementation. For it is in history that movements have grown up dedicated to the pursuit of those values which make life meaningful. It should be concluded then that it is not in nature but in history that God has revealed Himself to man, giving him a sense of his own worth, creating in him a sense of real values and implanting in him the desire to pursue what is worthwhile for human existence.

Jesus Christ and his life are the supreme historical instance of God at work. In him God is revealing Himself as love and at the same time offering this value to man as his supreme ideal. In the life of Jesus man is presented with the paradigm of a total dedication to the highest ideals and their perfect attainment. In Jesus God reveals that love is the highest value to which man can give himself. Therefore what matters for man in the case of Christ is the impact that his moral personality makes on man. Jesus may be called divine because like God he presents man with the highest values and ideals. His divinity is, in Ritschl's words, "the worth to be put on those human achievements of his which suffice for our salvation."[11] Man's faith in Jesus then is at base a value judgment, the conclusion that there is no higher set of aspirations to which man can dedicate himself than those exemplified in Jesus.

But the presentation of an ideal is not his only nor is it his most important work. That lies rather in the reconciliation and justification that he effects in a man. Left to himself man tends to make self-regard and self-concern his principal value. But confrontation with Jesus presents him with love as the highest of human values, love of God and love of neighbor. Belief in Jesus and dedication to his sense of values carries with it the power to make man free from himself and his selfishness and from the alienation from his true self which proceeds from this self regard. Belief in Jesus makes love man's supreme value and brings with it also the power to insert that value into all of life.

It should be clear from this description of Jesus and his work that redemption is understood by Ritschl not so much in terms of an emphasis on Jesus as atoning for the sins of men. He preferred rather to view it in terms of Christ restoring man to his true self and to a true sense of values wherein love holds the primacy. Thus the prime end of the redemption is to bring man to a life based on love and to be redeemed means to accept the values for which Christ gave his life.

The place wherein the redeemed carry on their common pursuit of love also owes its origin to Jesus. He left behind him the value-creating community which is the Church. She serves as the focal point of human aspiration and human endeavor because in her the value system of Jesus is preserved, nourished and preached. In her men can together find and follow the value that God reveals to man through Christ. She is the community of those who have accepted redemption through Christ.

But redemption of the individual and his incorporation into the Church is not the final purpose of the divine plan for history. That purpose is the establishment of the kingdom of God; redemption and church exist to serve that end. The kingdom is to be "the organization of humanity through action inspired by love." It is the divine intention to bring mankind into a universal moral community whose task will be concern for the moral and social needs of the world. Thus the task of the redeemed and of the church is to give themselves to a life of selfless dedication in serving humanity. This life lived out of the motivation of love will contribute to the gradual acceptance of this way of life by other men and thus bring about the inauguration of the kingdom of God on earth.

It is clear then that Christianity, as Ritschl conceives it, is a commitment to moral and ethical value judgments and their implementation in society. But if these judgments are to escape subjectivism, i.e., the individual judgment determining what is right or wrong, good or bad, they must be based not on what the individual might conceive Christianity to be but on what objective, historical investigation establishes as factual in the life and work of Jesus Christ, the founder of Christianity. Like

Schleiermacher, then, Ritschl welcomed biblical criticism because he saw in it the attempt to discover the facts relating to the life of Jesus. This could only help Christianity because in determining who Christ was, what he said and did, this critical investigation would help to provide ever more perfectly the facts in the life of Jesus on which the Church could continue her existence as a value-generating and preserving community.

Ritschl himself was confident that the Scriptures did provide a trustworthy testimony to the life and deeds of Christ yet he was willing to have the biblical critic evaluate that testimony. Whatever might be the outcome of historical investigation, he himself did not feel that Christian faith was evoked by the facts of Jesus' historical existence. It came rather from Jesus as God made him personally present and meaningful in the life of the believer. From Jesus thus presented to the Christian there comes the power of acceptance and the commitment to the values Jesus stands for; there comes also the capability of being free from self-assertion and of dedication to the pursuit, with other men, of the goals of God's kingdom.

It should also be observed that by his insistence on the need for possessing objective facts before making value judgments Ritschl makes clear the distinction between religion and science and the province and competence of both. He saw that the two are needed for the fully human life. It is for science to search out the facts of reality; it is not, however, competent to pass judgment on the human meaning of these facts. This is the task of religion which is competent to attach value meaning to facts. Confusion and conflict occur whenever either strays into the province of the other. Science, for example, should give itself to careful study of the theory of evolution, to the discovery of the facts relating to man's evolving from lower animals. It exceeds its competence, however, if it forms value judgments on these facts.

Religion, on the other hand, needs to listen to science for its factual data; it cannot, for example, speak of man's span on earth as beginning in a garden four thousand years ago if evidence is available indicating that man's presence on earth is of a considerably longer span. But once the facts of man's existence are determined, it is for religion to determine the values which give that life meaning. Both need to respect the competency of the other and rely on the other to fulfill its function.

CONCLUSION

With Ritschl, accent on the practical, ethical, and social implications of Christianity entered the main stream of modern Protestant thought. It has

been a central preoccupation of that thought ever since, in the Social
Gospel movement with its concentration on the reformation of the social
order, in Reinhold Niebuhr's lifelong analysis of the relation between
Christianity and society, especially in its political dimension, and last of all
in the present attempts of Christian thinkers to bring the Christian faith to
bear on the great social issues of race, poverty, war, and international
community.

Along with Schleiermacher, Ritschl is also responsible for a line of
Christian thought running from his day to the present which is strongly
anthropocentric. The starting point for any thought about religion must be
man, his experience, his needs, his problems. Karl Barth's thinking will
represent the twentieth century's response to this trend in his emphatically
theocentric interpretation of Christianity. But the experiential, man-
centered approach to thinking about religion is still a dominant trend
within Protestantism.

There are those who would hold Ritschl responsible for robbing Christianity of its sense of mystery and its awe in the presence of the transcendent God. He had little patience with mystical experience, pietism, or any
approach to Christian faith which did not address itself to the problem of
living in and affecting society. Practicality was for him central to authentic
religion. Perhaps the best final estimate would be to say that confronted
with the two poles between which any true interpretation of the Christian
message must steer a middle path: the biblical message and the human
situation, Ritschl's emphasis lay on the latter pole. This gives his interpretation all the strength and all the weakness that such a position entails.

FOOTNOTES

1Friedrich Schleiermacher, *On Religion, Speeches to Its Cultured Despisers,* trans.
John Oman, Torchbook edition (New York: Harper & Row, 1958), p. 36.

2Michael Novak in *Commonweal,* April 2, 1965, p. 57.

3Richard R. Niebuhr, "Friedrich Schleiermacher," in *A Handbook of Christian
Theologians,* ed. by Martin E. Marty and Dean B. Peerman, Meridian Book edition
(Cleveland & New York: The World Publishing Co., 1967), p. 31.

4Paul Tillich, *Systematic Theology,* 3 vols. (Chicago: University of Chicago Press,
1951), I, p. 60.

5Bernard Lonergan, S.J., "Theology in Its New Context," in *Theology of
Renewal,* ed. L.K. Shook, C.S.B., 2 vols. (New York: Herder and Herder, 1968), I,
44-45.

[6]Karl Barth, *The Word of God and the Word of Man,* Torchbook edition (New York: Harper & Row, 1957), p. 43.

[7]Albert Schweitzer, *The Quest of the Historical Jesus,* Paperback edition (London: A. & C. Block Ltd.; New York: The Macmillan Co. 1966), p. 79.

[8]*Ibid.,* p. 84.

[9]Albert Ritschl, *The Christian Doctrine of Justification and Reconciliation,* trans. J.S. Black, ed. H.R. Mackintosh and A.B. Macaulay, 2nd. ed. (Edinburgh: T. & T. Clark, 1902), p. 199.

[10]*Ibid.*

[11]*Ibid.,* p. 438.

CHAPTER EIGHT

Karl Barth

To say Karl Barth (1886-1968) is to name the giant of twentieth century Protestant theology. His influence on the thinking of all the Christian churches has been enormous and his productivity is unparalleled in this century. There are those who would say that he has done for this age what Luther and Calvin did for theirs and what Aquinas and Augustine had done before them.

Born in Basel in Switzerland in 1886 he did his early training in the great German centers of liberal theology, Berlin, Tübingen, Marburg. At that point in Christian history theology had turned in the direction of a religious anthropology. Man and his religious experience rather than God and his revelation were the characteristic starting point for Christian thought. To that emphasis, liberalism joined a somewhat uncritical optimism about man's innate goodness and perfectibility as well as a great trust in his capacity to build an ever better future for his world.

It was this vision that Barth learned from his masters, from Harnack an understanding of Christianity wherein Jesus, the supreme teacher and revealer of God, but himself a man, was the central focus, from Herrmann that Christian faith and morality flowed from the individual's personal relationship with the person of Jesus, from Gunkel and Schlatter, the latest methods of historical criticism of the Bible.

Thus when he decided to enter the pastoral ministry first for two years at Geneva (1909-11) and then for ten years at Safenwil (1911-21), he was thoroughly committed to liberalism's view of Christianity. But those twelve years of pastoral experience produced a gradually growing disillusionment with liberalism. His first major work, *The Epistle to the Romans,* a commentary on that Pauline letter, reflected this disenchantment. It was the occasion too for his passing from the parish to the university ministry.

Göttingen invited him in 1921 to accept its chair in systematic theology. A brief stay there was followed by periods of teaching at Münster, Bonn, and finally Basel where he taught until his retirement in 1960. During all those years his thinking moved more and more definitively away from liberalism and toward a theology based exclusively on the Word of God.

Barth's rejection of liberalism stemmed from two main causes, the world events occurring during his twelve years as pastor, and his study of the Scriptures. World War I and its aftermath produced mounting evidence that the optimism which liberal theology had developed regarding man, and its projection of a future that would grow increasingly better, needed serious examination and reevaluation. He found his congregation during those years looking to him for answers to the grave problems that the times were forcing upon them and he came to find that the only answers liberalism could provide were the vague and inadequate generalities of a conventional bourgeois morality and a Christianity that had been emasculated by its conformity to the surrounding culture. It had little to say to the irrationality and meaninglessness of the war; nor did it seem able to deal realistically with what events were making more and more clear, that there was a dark side of man, that sin was very much part of him.

Along with his growing uneasiness with liberalism there went a constant study of the Scripture. As he read and pondered he was led to see how different the message of the Bible was from what liberalism had made of it. Asking himself in later years what it was that altered his view of the meaning of Scripture, he wrote

> Was it . . . the discovery that the theme of the Bible, contrary to the critical and to the orthodox exegesis which we inherited, certainly could not be man's religion and religious morality and certainly not his own secret divinity? The stone wall we first ran up against was that the theme of the Bible is the deity of *God,* more exactly God's *deity*—God's independence and particular character, not only in relation to the natural but also to the spiritual cosmos; God's absolutely unique existence, might, and initiative, above all, in His relation to man. Only in this manner were we able to understand the voice of the Old and New Testaments. Only with this perspective did we feel we could henceforth be theologians and in particular, preachers—ministers of the divine Word.[1]

He came, in other words, to see that the Bible has as its primary focus not man but God. It aimed to speak first of God, His transcendence and His sovereign freedom and only then of His judgment on man and His gracious forgiveness of man in spite of that judgment. It concerned itself with

> not the history of man but the history of God! Not the virtues of men but the virtues of him who hath called us out of darkness into his marvelous light! Not the human standpoint but the standpoint of God![2]

In consequence of this newly discovered view of the meaning of Scripture his thinking turned away from the anthropocentrism of liberal theology towards a strict theocentrism. Two stages mark the development of his thought from this point on.

FIRST STAGE

In the first phase his thinking is characterized as a theology of crisis or again as a dialectical theology. In the second phase it becomes a theology of the Word. The term "theology of crisis" is used to describe his earlier thought because the expression sums up the method he used to describe the central message of Scripture at this period.

His thought begins and continues as a protest against the official Christianity of his day. The protest was made in the name of God's Word. That Word did not picture man as innately good; quite the contrary, it saw him as radically and inescapably a sinner, "a sinner through and through." As such, man was incapable of right thinking about God. He had "no point of contact" for relating to God and in consequence all his thought about who God is and what is His relation to men will be in error.

But this is not the only message that Scripture has for man, that he is a sinner. It also constantly accentuates the absolute difference between man and God. God is the "totally Other," the absolutely Transcendent. Between Him and man there is an "infinite qualitative distinction." Liberal theology was wrong then in thinking that man could reach God through his own experience or his own reasoning. The gulf that separated him from God was unbridgeable from man's side. Therefore no attempt on man's part to find God can succeed. The only God that man can possibly know of himself will always be an idol of his own construction. Because God is completely transcendent He is beyond the possibility of man conceiving a correct notion of Him. Such does Scripture say is man's position *vis-à-vis* God.

But the chasm, uncrossable from man's side, can be and has been crossed from God's side. That is the message of Christian revelation, that God has spoken to man. He has revealed Himself to man in Jesus Christ, His Word. Man cannot speak of God; therefore if he is to know God he must listen as God speaks to him.

It is at this point that Barth's thought becomes a crisis theology. God's message to man, when it is spoken to and heard by him, provokes a crisis situation in man's life. He finds himself confronted by a choice, either a refusal to hear the Word which characterizes him a sinner, and the choice to continue on the path of self-reliance, or an openness to that Word, an acceptance of one's state as sinner and the choice of reliance on God as the sole source of salvation. This is the crisis with which God's Word confronts man.

> [Barth] . . . laid great emphasis upon the fact that men could not hear the Word of God without being thrust into a situation where the whole basis of their existence was imperiled—where their lives were at a crisis and where they were judged by God—and where their only hope was in the leap of faith.[3]

From another point of view this stage of Barth's thought is also called a dialectical theology. Such an approach sees the Word of God as God speaking a divine No and a divine Yes to man. It interprets revelation as a series of contrasts set off against each other, each accenting the other: God's holiness and man's sinfulness, God's judgment of man and yet his forgiveness of man, God as creator, man as creature. God is forever saying 'no' to man's sinfulness and to his pretensions to be what he is not. Yet in spite of this he is also forever saying 'yes' to man, lifting him out of his sin and accepting him in spite of his unworthiness. Or, put another way, God deals with man not in terms of a natural 'therefore' but in terms of a divine 'nevertheless'. The message of revelation is not that man is unworthy and therefore God rejects him but rather that man is unworthy and nevertheless God saves him.[4]

All these themes of Barth are summed up in his discussion of the meaning of the cross. Here are all the contrasts between Holy God and sinful man; here meet the divine Yes and the divine No; here finally faith encounters religion. In Christ on the cross God has spoken His Word in condemnation of human sinfulness and in forgiveness of human sin. Here God offers friendship and thereby reveals the meaning of human life. Here finally He asks man to accept Him as He reveals Himself to be. On the cross that Word meets human rejection; Jesus the Word is killed by sinful man. Yet the final message of the cross is not human rejection. That message is rather the divine love and forgiveness which is offered and which persists as God's attitude toward man.

It is here at the cross that faith and religion confront each other. Those responsible for the death of Jesus were the religious men of that time. They are representative of all those who know who God is and how He is to be worshipped, who have built a religion with its holy places, its theological systems, its liturgy and its detailed law of conduct. They are the ones who have domesticated God, made Him over into a god, or more correctly an idol, of their own creation. It is their religion that has made it impossible for them to recognize God when he presents Himself to them in a form or under circumstances other than what they will allow. Religion is the very thing that keeps them from God and makes them sinners. In Barth's words, "religion is the enemy of faith."

Faith, on the other hand, is the opposite of religion. Where religion is man's attempt to relate to God on man's terms, faith is open to accepting God's Word on Who He is and who man is. The man of faith sees the crucifixion as God's Word on human sinfulness and on divine forgiveness. And he sees Jesus Christ as the embodiment of who God is, as His revelation of Himself. He recognizes religion for what it is, man-made forms and structures, human beliefs and attitudes, all that complex of human pride and pretension that leads man to believe he can know God of himself.

From this brief summary of Barth's early method of theologizing, it is evident that two notions stand out strongly in his thinking at this state, the divine transcendence and its corollary, the necessity of revelation.

The Divine Transcendence

Nineteenth century liberalism had, in Barth's mind, reversed the real meaning of revelation. Revelation, as he understood it, was not man's knowledge or experience of God nor was Scripture given to man that he might find in it confirmation of his own idea and his own experience of God. In their eagerness to render Christianity acceptable to their contemporaries, the liberals had moved towards destroying God's transcendence, had brought Him so close that men felt more and more free to make Him over into what their philosophy, their science, and their historical method told them He ought to be. Barth moved to release God from man's notion of who He is by pointing to Scripture's recurring insistence that God is completely other than man and thus can be known only as He reveals Himself.

Because the notion of divine transcendence is at the heart of Barth's thought it is important to be quite clear what he means by it. Transcendence for him is not to be conceived in spatial terms as if by saying God is wholly Other one means He is other-worldly, that He exists somewhere outside this world and its history. Rather transcendence for Barth means God's complete freedom from human attempts to express who He is, where He is to be found, how man relates to Him. He is free of man's holy places and holy times; He is not capturable in metaphysical speculations. He escapes our attempts at a natural theology, a knowledge of Him arrived at by unaided human thought. All we can know of Him, Barth might say, is that we cannot know Him. He comes to man in His own time and place and way. He reveals Himself to man when and how He wishes. As Colin Williams sums up the notion,

> God's transcendence, in the theology of Barth, is the transcendence of our 'other' who meets us in the midst of life as our Lord; it is the transcendence of a Lord who resists all our attempts to control him; but it is not the transcendence of one whose home is in a separate sphere outside our world.[5]

God, in sum, is beyond man's capacity to grasp and know Him. Yet in another sense He is not beyond him but very much present to man by His own choice, in His own way, at His own time and place as revelation makes clear.

Revelation

Transcendence and revelation are correlative ideas. Transcendence makes clear that man's way of knowing God and his expression of that understanding in his religion, his morality, his piety and his culture is all idolatry. Not only is all of this idolatry but also, since man bases his idea and his pursuit of salvation on this erroneous concept of God, he mistakenly believes that he is the fashioner of his own destiny. Thus he is wrong both in his notion of God and in his idea of salvation. From this error he can be rescued only by revelation, by God telling man who He is and what is the road that leads to Him. So we come to revelation.

If God transcends man's power of knowing Him this can only mean man cannot know Him unless He reveals Himself. Transcendence requires revelation if any relationship is to exist between God and man. God has made such a revelation of Himself in Jesus Christ. The whole process of man's relating with God begins when man believes that Jesus Christ is the revelation of God, His Word to men. That revelation, when it is heard, strips man of all his self-reliance, his belief in self-redemption and lays open to him the miracle of God's grace, that he does not save himself; he cannot. God saves him in Christ.

> For the Word of God is not an abstract general idea conceived by the human mind but a particular fact, namely the particular fact of God's actual revelation of Himself and of His will for man in and through the concrete person and work of Jesus Christ, who is Himself the incarnate Word of God, the Lord (Son of God) who became a servant and the servant (the royal man) who became Lord. Hence, the Word of God is a particular event, or rather a series of particular events constituting the *Heilsgeschichte,* particular events which not only happened in the past but continue to happen in this world, in the course of the history of mankind.[6]

SECOND STAGE

By the end of the twenties Barth realized that he was not yet making the Word of God the sole source and criterion of his thinking. Rather he was still strongly wedded to certain philosophical thought forms, especially existentialism as employed by Kierkegaard, as instruments for the presentation and interpretation of the Word of God.

The publication of the first volume of his *Church Dogmatics* in 1932 represents his definitive break with all such reliance on human instruments to explain the Word of God. From now on his thinking attempts to be solely concerned with the exposition of God's revelation of Himself as that revelation is contained in His own Word. He wants to remove any reliance on philosophical, cultural, or anthropological elements as the basis for his exposition of God's Word. Existentialism in particular was to be set aside because it was only another form of liberalism's anthropocentric approach to Christianity.

Now it became his intention to work only with faith-knowledge. He begins with the premise that he has accepted in faith, that God has spoken to man in Christ and it becomes his task to "explicate this self-revelation of God in faithful obedience to His Word." Faith, once it is possessed of God's truth, naturally seeks understanding of that truth.

To one who would ask him: why should I have such faith, what reason is there for accepting as God's Word what you simply assert as such, Barth offers no apologetic, no defense of Christian revelation as truly from God. He replies simply that if Christian theology is rightly grasped, it will prove itself to be true. Revelation is self-authenticating.

His work since then, especially his multi-volumed *Church Dogmatics* is done in careful reliance on that premise of faithful exposition of the Word of God. A thorough treatment of that work is beyond our present purpose. Our discussion will be limited to a treatment of some of the key notions that form the fundamental structure of his thought. We will deal in turn with his notion of revelation, then his thinking on Jesus Christ, the Word of God, and finally say something about the ethical dimension of his thought.

Revelation

Barth's understanding of the meaning of revelation does not begin with a definition of what he means by the term. He begins rather with the concrete reality of revelation. That reality is the event of God's intervention in human history. God reveals by acting. Thus revelation begins not with man and his seeking God. The initiative lies with God. He decides the time and the place and the circumstances of the encounter between Himself and man. Thus the first note Barth strikes is the divine sovereignty and freedom. Were He not to take the initiative, there would be no human knowledge of God. Revelation depends totally on God's decision to reveal. But, having strongly accented the absoluteness of the divine role in revelation, Barth is equally careful to insist on the activity of the human role in responding to revelation. Man's part is not that of passive acceptance. Confronted with God speaking, it is for him to respond in responsible human freedom. There are two partners to the dialogue: He who speaks and he who hears. Man bears the responsibility of a free human act of acceptance. That act is man's faith, his decision to hear and respond in obedience to God's Word.

Next Barth explores the nature of God's revelation, again as that nature manifests itself in human history. God's Word is not a set of propositions to be accepted as true. He does not reveal ideas to be believed. It is not a question of data about God to which one assents intellectually. It is in act that God reveals Himself. His revelation is a series not of words, but of events. He is concerned with showing men who He is, not in communicating truths about Himself. He does not reveal His nature. He reveals Himself in acts done for man.

The same notion may be approached from another perspective by say-ing that God's revelation is forever active. He did not once and for all speak what He wished man to know about Him. Rather it is true that throughout history He is continually in the process of revealing Himself to men and when that self-disclosure is responded to by faith and obedience His act has become His Word, His revelation of Himself to this man.

There is a sense in which revelation may be viewed as an objective fact. In that sense there is only one revelation that God has made of Himself and that is the event of the life of Jesus Christ. Christ is God's revelation of who He is and his life and work is a set of objective happenings in history. Much of Barth's attention is given to exploring the implications of those events since they are God speaking of Himself in His relations to men. In them man can read the story of God's judgment on man and yet His final graciousness in dealing with man. The life, death, and resurrection of Jesus must always remain the primary, indeed the only, revelation that God makes of Himself.

Yet, this said, revelation is always in the final sense, subjective. The subject, man, to whom it is addressed must accept it before it becomes revelation for him, since the Word has not really been spoken until it has been heard. God has not, therefore, really revealed Himself until He has, through the action of the Spirit, brought a man to the free decision of faith.

> ... the content of the Christian message is neither a subjective nor an objective element in isolation, neither man in isolation, nor God in isolation, but God and man in their encounter and communion, God's dealings with the Christian and the Chris-tian's dealings with God.[7]

Finally in his treatment of revelation Barth turns back to where he started, to God. His last word on the subject is precisely that, an insistence on the subject of revelation. All through the events by which God speaks to man, it is He who speaks that is all-important. It is not as an object that God reveals Himself. He reveals Himself as Subject, as Person. He wants to give Himself, not knowledge about Himself. What is important in revela-tion then is not that which is revealed but He who in all His dealings with men is present revealing Himself. God does not, through revelation, indi-cate that He judges, teaches, forgives, or loves man. He is rather present in revelation revealing Himself as He who judges, He who forgives and He who loves man. In paradoxical terms, there is no object of divine revela-tion; there is only the Subject who reveals Himself.

Jesus Christ, the Word of God

When Barth turns to a discussion of Jesus as the Word of God he has not really left his central notion of revelation. He is merely approaching it from yet another point of view. The essential affirmation of Christian revelation is that Jesus Christ is the Word of God. That means that in Him is contained God's sole revelation of Himself. He who would know God must know Jesus. It is to be expected then that all of Barth's thought has a "Christological concentration" about it. He sees nothing except in terms of Christ. What Christ is and does is revelation. Or put perhaps more accurately, there is nothing man can know of God except in and through Christ.

One of the sharpest criticisms of Barth's earlier thought was that his insistence on the otherness and transcendence of God was so strong that he seemed to allow little place for any real relationship between God and man. His stress seemed to underline the distance separating them, whereas the Christian faith emphasized, rather, God's closeness to man. Barth's answer to the criticism was that his initial accent on the divine transcendence was a reaction evoked by liberal theology's tendency to rob God of any otherness, to make Him almost wholly immanent in man's experience and his culture.

> Evangelical theology almost all along the line, certainly in all its representative forms and tendencies, had become *religionistic, anthropocentric,* and in this sense, *humanistic.* . . . There is no question about it: here man was made great at the cost of God. . . .[8]

When he felt the point had been made strongly enough that God was completely other than man, he then turned his attention to the "humanity of God," to God turning toward man, to His being with man in the person of Jesus Christ. He himself acknowledged the one-sidedness of his prior view, pointing out that the full Christian vision gives its attention to God being with men and for them. In doing this, however, Christian revelation also brings out clearly that, though God is with man, He is there in sovereign freedom and so He remains even in that being-with, quite other than man.

> But did it not appear to escape us by quite a distance that the *deity* of the *living* God—and we certainly wanted to deal with Him—found its meaning and its power only in the context of

His history and of His dialogue with *man,* and thus in His
togetherness with man? Indeed—and this is the point back of
which we cannot go—it is a matter of *God's* sovereign togetherness with man, a togetherness grounded in Him and determined, delimited, and ordered through Him alone. Only in
this way and in this context can it take place and be recognized. It is a matter, however, of God's *togetherness* with
man. Who God is and what He is in His deity He proves and
reveals not in a vacuum as a divine being-for-Himself, but
precisely and authentically in the fact that He exists, speaks
and acts as the *partner* of man, though of course as the absolutely superior *partner.* He who does *that* is the living God.
And the freedom in which He does *that* is His deity. It is the
deity which as such also has the character of humanity. . . . It
is precisely God's *deity* which, rightly understood, includes His
humanity. 9

Thus in his later teaching Barth restores balance to his thought. God
is the totally Other; yet He chooses to be with man. It is true that He is
different from man and the world. But in Christ He affirms man and his
world. Though transcendent, He is by His own choice radically present in
the world of men.

For Barth the Word of God like revelation does not allow of an *a priori*
definition. One comes to understand it by exposure to the person who is
the Word of God, Jesus Christ. What is involved is an encounter between
two persons in which the one reveals himself and by so doing reveals who
God is and what is the nature of the relation He has freely chosen to enter
into with man. The Word is a person (Jesus) who acts. In that act God
speaks not to men in general but to this particular man. As this man listens
God tells him what He has done for him.

Like revelation, the Word of God has also its objective and subjective
aspect. Barth's study of the Scripture provides him with the objective
content or meaning of that Word. Its subjective aspect is the individual
Christian's appropriation of that meaning, an appropriation which is
accomplished by the Holy Spirit bringing the individual to faith in, and
obedience to, the Word of God. Barth uses the term in a triple sense: The
Word is primarily the person of Jesus, but it is also, in a subordinate sense,
the witness of Scripture and the preaching of the Church. All three are the
Word only when they are heard and responded to.

To be noted also is that the human appropriation of the Word of God is
not a once-and-for-all occurrence. God's Word is not a datum or a set of
propositions given once and to be assented to at that time. It is that series
of acts by which God through Jesus Christ enters into relation with man.
Thus it is not a question of having received the Word of God; it is rather a

question of being continually in the process of hearing God as He speaks His Word and responding to It.

In Jesus then God speaks, and there are three elements in that speaking, who God is, who man is, and Jesus as the only one in whom God reaches man and man reaches God. The story of Jesus, His life, death and resurrection, speaks of God as one who knows man for what he is, a sinner, but one who, in Christ, judges him, punishes him, and then forgives and saves him. Thus God, as Jesus' life speaks of Him is ultimately the God who loves.

Regarding who man is, Jesus reveals him to himself as at once sinner and forgiven, prideful and yet called to obedience, condemned and yet in Christ elected by God, fallen and yet meant for eternal life with God. He is, in sum, created and sinful, yet saved by grace.

Finally, Jesus Christ speaks of both authoritatively precisely because He is both, God and man. Sharing the nature of both He mirrors, in what He says and is and does, the nature of both. He is the Lord God become Servant, lowering Himself to man's lowliness; He is at the same time Servant as Lord, man raised to God's level. He is the true man; all others are by contrast false to what it means to be a man. He is also 'very' God; in Him the divine plan expresses itself; the divine attributes manifest themselves and God is known for what He truly is, God for man, God with man. In sum, Jesus Christ, at one and the same time, reveals who God is and determines what man ought to be.

THE ETHICAL DIMENSION OF HIS THOUGHT

We have spoken of the first reason that turned Barth away from liberalism, that it was false to the biblical witness. There was another reason closely related to this one, though it lay at a more practical level. Liberalism had also proved itself valueless in providing norms for human action in times of crisis. The first world war and its sequel made all too clear to Barth the inadequacy of human answers to the problems of the world. He realized that, in making revelation man-centered rather than God-centered, liberalism had robbed man of the norms he needed to judge the world and its contemporary situation. No ability to criticize or power to resist inadequate human solutions was left to man if the otherness of God's way of thinking, acting, and judging human events was taken from him. It was only if the man of faith could rely on God's Word to supply him with the answers for human problems that he could exercise his prophetic function of criticizing society. If man's answers alone are available and they do not work, what then is to be done?

Out of this impasse Barth believed man could be led only by the Word of God. That Word spoke of God's way with men. It spoke too of what God expected would be man's way with God and with other men. Revelation speaks not only of what God wants man to know about Him; it speaks too of how man is to act in consequence of that knowledge. He is to act as God Himself has acted, in the humble giving of Himself for the sake of man.

Thus for Barth in his rejection of liberalism two principles became of primary importance, first the acceptance of the Word of God as the only reliable source of human knowledge about the divine, and second, the adoption of the divine solution to the problems that plague man.

The second of these principles led Barth to a deep involvement in many of the great social issues of his lifetime. The resistance of the Confessing Church in Germany to Nazism had him as one of its most outspoken leaders. He was spokesman too for defeated Germany, urging the Allies, soon after the war, to restore to the Germans their political freedom that they might once again begin to develop a sense of responsible political action. Communism knew him as a continuous critic, yet he felt that a good deal of the appeal of Communism was due to the Christian churches and their failure to become involved in the solution to pressing social problems. It was this inertia that made Communism much more attractive as a world-view than Christianity. He was likewise adamant in his opposition to the proliferation of atomic weapons or their use no matter what the provocation.

In summary Barth saw the Christian's task not as withdrawal or noninvolvement in political life but rather as an insistently urgent responsibility to be concerned with the application of God's Word to all areas of life. The responsibility is rooted in man's nature which is a nature shared by all men.

> The minimal definition of our humanity, of humanity generally, must be that it is the being of man in encounter and in this sense the determination of man as being with the other man. [We cannot accept that] man can be a man without the fellow man, an I without the Thou.[10]

CONCLUSION

Barth dominated the theological scene for almost thirty years. But the signs are now multiplying that his influence is on the wane. True to his own deepest convictions he would want it so. He would not want his own theological thinking to become a new system, a new "religion" to be studied and followed slavishly. This could only lead men to yet another idolatry, the belief that they had found a way to speak truly and well of God. Barth himself would want that the only legacy of his thought should be his insistence on the Word of God as the sole source of man's knowledge of God.

But in the eyes of many contemporary theologians Barth's insistence on the transcendence of God is the reason they ultimately find his thought unacceptable. They would agree that at the time when Barth began to write, his insistence on the radical transcendence of God was a needed antidote to the man-centered Christianity that liberalism had developed. Needed too, they would admit, was his striking out at the false optimism that liberal theology had developed in respect to man's own ability to lead a good life, solve his own problems, and build his own future. But yesterday's problems are not today's. For the contemporary theologian the central problem is that of faith, the possibility of belief in God. Allied with that is the other concern for building the best possible world for all men out of the technology that is developing so rapidly. Faith and the construction of a human society are today's concerns and latter-day thinkers tend to fault Barth's way of thinking on both counts.

First of all, his wholly other God does not speak to today's man. So wide and deep is the gulf he has opened between God and man that it does not seem possible or indeed worthwhile to try spanning it. Today's man is a this-worldly man and to speak to him of a God who transcends this world is to speak of what he neither comprehends nor is interested in. Eugene Borowitz summarizes this reason for the present feeling that we have gone beyond Barth.

> Barth's explanation of modern man's failings and hope in what Christ has done for him rests on a radically transcendent sense of God. But contemporary man lives and thinks only in terms of this world, so the vision of a wholly other God who sends salvation like a stone thrown from heaven does not move him.[11]

It is evident from our treatment of what Barth means by transcendence that this objection to Barth is based, at least partially, on a misconception of what transcendence means to him. Yet his language does, in much of his earlier writing, lend itself to such an interpretation. In any case it is clear that, in making God transcendent, Barth has made Him contemporaneously unacceptable. Thus he does not have a contribution to make to the present problem of faith.

A further indictment of Barth's position flows out of the first one. His relegation of God to another world and man's inability to speak of God in any meaningful sense provides one of the foundation stones on which the present death-of-God movement is built. It is but a short step from a wholly other God of whom human language can say nothing intelligible to the conclusion that the reason why man cannot speak of God is because He is not there to be spoken of. At best He may represent man's projections of his hopes and fears, his ideals and his values. Objectively He does not exist; He is only a subjective creation of man. Thus present thinkers would say, not only does Barth not have anything to say to the problem of belief as it is currently experienced; but he also contributes to man's disbelief.

With regard to the other contemporary concern, the building of a better world for all men, and hence total involvement in the city of man and its needs, Barth is also criticized by those who come after him. For Barth the meaning of every event, every movement, every society is always ambiguous. It may speak of God and His will; it may speak only of man and his sinfulness. God is always hidden in His manifestations of Himself in human history. Hence to see any society as reflecting God's presence in the world is to run the risk of idolatry. It is, therefore, extremely difficult to find God present, to say that what one is presently doing to serve the needs of men is clearly God's will. Barth's God, in other words, is so hidden in events that it is well-nigh impossible to discover what is His will in that event. The consequence is that Barth's God provides little by way of specific direction in the building of the better world. As Colin Williams puts it,

> By warning so strongly against the danger of domesticating God in particular religious structures and by insisting so strongly on God's judgment against all our idolatrous attempts to say 'Lo here,' 'Lo there,' Barth fails to give us the help we need in making the dangerous but necessary decisions as to how Christ is calling us to be his servants in the secular events of our time.[12]

To offer this kind of criticism is to say no more than that Barth, like all theologians, theologizes in history. What he or any thinker says is the produce of his time and its needs.

Finally, in this matter of speaking to one's time, it is instructive to note that the history of the past one hundred years has been an example of the very process of dialectic that was so much part of Barth's own method of thought. One could write a history of that period of Christian thought in terms of three stages of development. Liberalism highlighted man's part in the God-man dialogue. The accent was on the immanent, this-worldly character of Christianity. Barth was the worthy champion of the transcendent dimension of Christianity, emphasizing God's primary role in the God-man relation. We are at present in the process of swinging back again to a concentration on the here-and-nowness of religion. If it has meaning then that meaning must be immanent in this world. No other world exists in any significant sense for the men of the sixties.

Once this process is understood, Barth's place in the history of Christian thought is seen as a secure one. He saw and spoke to the needs of his time and in the speaking he towered over most of his contemporaries.

FOOTNOTES

[1] Karl Barth, *The Humanity of God* (Richmond, Va.: John Knox Press, 1966), p. 41.

[2] ——*The Word of God and the Word of Man*, Torchbook ed. (New York: Harper & Row, 1957), p. 45.

[3] Daniel Jenkins, "Karl Barth," in *A Handbook of Christian Theologians*, ed. Martin E. Marty and Dean G. Peerman, Meridian Book ed. (Cleveland & New York: The World Publishing Co., 1967), p. 403.

[4] Georges Casalis, *Portrait of Karl Barth*, trans. and with an introduction by Robert M. Brown, Anchor Book (Garden City, N.Y.: Doubleday & Co., Inc., 1964). The reference is to Brown's paraphrase of Barth's words in the Introduction, p. xxviii.

[5] Colin Williams, *Faith in A Secular Age*, Chapelbook ed. (New York: Harper & Row, 1966), p. 50.

[6] Herbert Hartwell, *The Theology of Karl Barth* (Philadelphia: The Westminster Press, 1964), pp. 22-23. Used by permission.

[7] Barth, *Church Dogmatics*, IV/3, ed. G.W. Bromiley and T. F. Torrance, (Edinburgh: T. & T. Clark, 1960), p. 498.

[8] Barth, *The Humanity of God*, p. 39.

[9] *Ibid.*, pp. 45-46.

[10] Barth, *Church Dogmatics*, III/2, p. 247.

[11] Eugene Borowitz, "God-is-Dead Theology," in *Judaism*, XV, No. 2 (1966), 86.

[12] Williams, *Faith in a Secular Age*, p. 54.

CHAPTER NINE

Dietrich Bonhoeffer

When the name of Dietrich Bonhoeffer (1906-1945) is mentioned, one instinctively asks Godsey's question: "Why is it that his name is being mentioned in the same breath with such theological giants as Barth and Bultmann and Tillich?"[1] There appear to be two elements in an adequate answer to the question. First of all, Bonhoeffer died a martyr. He fulfilled in his own life what he saw the Christian life to mean: 'When Christ calls a man, he bids him come and die."[2] That sacrifice in witness to his belief lends a compelling urgency to what he writes. Men always listen more attentively to one who lives what he believes and dies willingly for it.

The initial attraction to Bonhoeffer then is the arresting testimony of his martyrdom. Once so drawn one finds, as he begins to read the man, the second reason for his present popularity. What he writes speaks to contemporary man of things that concern him in language he understands. What is the meaning of life is the question Bonhoeffer asks, and more specifically, what contribution has Christianity to make to life's meaning? As he formulates his answers to these questions over the years he speaks to two quite different audiences, the men of the church and the men of the world. To the first, his message is always the challenge to make the church what she is meant to be, "Christ-existing-as-community." To the second, his call is to maturity, to a life lived to its fullest in the development of all human potentialities, especially that of human freedom. The world is now, for the first time in its history, making such maturity a realistic possibility.

His ultimate object in that challenge to truthful living and that call to maturity is to bring both church and world to realize that if each is to fulfill its contemporary task each will find it has need of the other. To become what she ought to be the church needs to learn what contemporary man and his world are that she may serve them. Man needs to see that only the church can give him freedom from himself.

The central focus of Bonhoeffer's thought seems best caught in the view of his friend and editor, Eberhard Bethge, who sees that focus as a continually growing awareness of the concreteness of revelation.

> Bethge has shown how Bonhoeffer's passion for the concreteness of revelation provides an explanation for his distinctive attitudes and actions. It led to his interest in the *sociological* form of the church in *Sanctorum Communio,* his questioning in *Act and Being* of the dialectical theologians about how the revelation that is free and not at man's disposal ever becomes concrete revelation, his criticism that in his ethics Emil Brunner neglected to investigate whether the church must risk the proclamation of quite concrete commandments. It explains his continual plea at ecumenical conferences for the risking of a concrete commandment, his concern about the Sermon on the Mount and discipleship, his intransigent position in regard to the ecclesio-political decisions of the Confessing Church. Further, the question drove him to work on his *Ethics,* which asks how the reality of God becomes real on earth and answers that it is only in the context of real life that revelation becomes attached to the penultimate things, that there can be no static separation of the sphere of the world from the sphere of the church. Finally, it brought him to a denial that Christianity was a religion of salvation emphasizing release from this world, and to an affirmation of the "this-worldly" character of the Christian faith.[3]

The journey of his thought parallels the journey of his life. His earlier works, *Sanctorum Communio* (1928) and *Act and Being* (1930), as befits a professor and theologian, tend to concentrate on a theological analysis of the nature of revelation. He passes to a career as pastor, ecumenist, political activist, and finally prisoner and his thought moves ever more steadily in the direction of how revelation is to be related in concrete terms to life itself.

THE NATURE OF REVELATION

The very fact that God has chosen to reveal Himself to man speaks an important initial truth to Bonhoeffer. It says that "God is not free *of* man but *for* man." It says that God has "freely bound Himself to historical man," that He has "placed Himself at man's disposal." It means that "God is there, which is to say: not in eternal non-objectivity but . . . 'haveable,' graspable in His Word within the Church."[4]

Bonhoeffer's first book, his doctoral dissertation, *Sanctorum Communio* (*The Communion of Saints*), addresses itself to an analysis of what God's revelation of His availability means. His question is: what is the church? His answer is that God reveals Himself and thereby makes Himself available to men through Christ in the church.

God's availability, His being *for* man is aimed at meeting man's need. An analysis of what man is, leads Bonhoeffer to conclude that man is by nature essentially social. It is of his very being to be related. It is the divine plan, mirrored in man's nature, that man should live not in aloneness, but in community, *communio* with God and man. But the fall introduced sin into the human situation and sin for Bonhoeffer is separation, alienation, loneliness. From one made for union man became one who lives for self. "The reality of sin . . . places the individual in the utmost loneliness, in a state of radical separation from God and man."[5]

It is at this point that God's availability meets man's need. He reveals Himself as being *for* man; He speaks His Word, expressing Himself as one who loves man; He sends Christ as the expression of who He is and as the solution of mankind's need. The need is communal. There is a solidarity of all men in the fall and its consequent selfishness and separation. The redemption from this state is equally communal because the saving act of Christ is the creation of the community of the redeemed, a *communio sanctorum*, freed from the bondage of selfish existence because it lives by the same principle of life as he lives, love of the other, of God and of man. Thus Christ's task is to restore community to man. This he does by restoring at one and the same time the individual's unity with God and his community with other men.

> But as, when the primal communion with God was rent asunder, human community was rent too, so likewise when God restores the communion of mankind with himself, the community of men with each other is also re-established.[6]

Christ effects this double restoration of communion to man in the church which is most accurately described as "Christ-existing-as-community." It is thus the function of the church to be a communion and that in several senses. It is, first, the locus of humanity's restored community and in that sense the locus of the redemption. It stands, secondly, as the living expression of that which is the ultimate destiny of all humanity, communion with God and man restored in Christ. It is lastly the source from which the fruits of Christ's work are to flow to other men. By what it is and what is says, it speaks the Word, brings "Christ-existing-as-community" to other men.

Described in these terms the church is, of course, an object of faith. The Christian accepts the church thus portrayed as God's revelation of Himself in Christ. But the church may also be viewed from the sociological point of view because it takes shape in history. Viewed thus the ways in which the church has embodied herself in form and structure throughout history may be sociologically analyzed and light shed on what the church is existentially. There is value here but need for caution too for, after sociology has said all it has to say, it has not finally described the nature of the church. For the church is the Word of God active in history. There is that in it which transcends sociological categories.

Bonhoeffer sees also that overstress on the other view of the church, the theological view, is also open to danger. To see the church as only an object of faith runs the risk of seeing her as set apart from the world. Yet her whole function is to be in the world or more accurately to be Christ in the world. To forget that is to forget that the Word is meant to be fully incarnate, to be "Christ revealed as community."[7] Theology and sociology need each other's insights; they also need to be aware of each other's limitations.

Even as he wrote his thesis Bonhoeffer was undergoing a growing disenchantment with the church as he knew it to exist in his own experience. The thesis painted the church as it ought to be; meanwhile life was showing him the church in its real existence. Growing recognition of the gap between the ideal as he described it and its real embodiment led him over the years to a more and more radical criticism of the existing church. But for the present, his hope was that his analysis of the nature of the church would help to provide a vision of what the church ought to be working to become.

Bonhoeffer's next book, *Act and Being,* addressed itself specifically to the subject of revelation. The question he asked was: How is revelation to be conceived? He posits the problem this way:

> There has to be a theological interpretation of what the "being of God in revelation" means and how it is known, of what may be the interrelation of belief as act and revelation as being, and correspondingly of where man stands when seen from the standpoint of revelation. Is revelation merely what is "given" to man in the performance of a certain act, or is there such a thing for him in revelation as a "being"? What form is taken by the concept of revelation if we explain it in terms of the act, and what other form if in terms of a "being?"[8]

Godsey, in his study of Bonhoeffer's theology, summarizes the problem to which Bonhoeffer is addressing himself in these words:

> It should be theologically interpreted what "God's being in the
> revelation" means and how it is known, how faith as act and
> revelation as being are related and whether revelation is given
> to man only in the execution of an act or if there is a "being"
> in the revelation for him.[9]

By way of response to the question Bonhoeffer finds that certain types
of theologizing about the nature of revelation describe it in terms of act;
others prefer to see it in terms of being.

In the first view God is seen as having revealed himself to man in a
series of distinct historical events. He made Himself present to man in a
sequence of acts whereby He revealed Himself in history. Revelation is a
set of divine acts in relation to man. God reveals Himself in acting. Barth
would be a good example of this 'act theology.'

In the second view stress is laid on the continuity of revelation. Here
man is seen not so much as the recipient of a set of revelatory acts from
God; rather their existence itself (both God's and man's) is a 'being' in
revelation. Accent is put on realizing the continuity both of revelation and
of man, the continuity of man's possession of and being possessed by
revelation. Tillich exemplified this approach to God and to revelation. His
is a 'being theology.'

Bonhoeffer sees a certain value in the first kind of thinking. It preserves
God's freedom. Whether there will be revelation in His choice. He is not
"at man's disposal." If there is a revelation it is because He alone initiates
it. But, as we have already seen, God's freedom as He Himself has revealed
it is not a freedom *from* man; rather He has elected to exercise His freedom *for* man. He has chosen to enter into relationship with man. His
choice is to be in a state of being revealed. Thus Bonhoeffer's own prefer-
ence is for the second type of approach since he sees it as more accurately
reflecting not who God is in Himself but who He is in relation to man.

When these two ways of conceiving revelation are applied to the church
the question becomes: how is the church to be thought of? as a series of
acts or events in history wherein again and again man responds to revelation? or is it more correct to think of the church as existing in continuity
throughout history?

Bonhoeffer's answer is that in the church the value of both 'act' and
'being' thinking on revelation is bound together in a living unity. The
church depends for her existence on the act of faith in her and her possession of revelation on the part of the believer. Thus her existence is in one
sense contingent on a series of acts. Yet from another point of view it is
clear from her history that the church has a continuity of existence. She
has a being as the continuing revelation of God. Yet if one had to choose

which of the two approaches to the nature of the church is to be preferred, it is clear that Bonhoeffer's choice is for the church as being.

> The Christian communion is God's final revelation: God as
> "Christ existing as community"; ordained for the rest of time
> until the end of the world and the return of Christ. It is here
> that Christ has come the very nearest to humanity, here given
> himself to his new humanity, so that his person enfolds in
> itself all whom he has won, binding itself in duty to them, and
> them reciprocally in duty to him. The "Church" therefore has
> not the meaning of a human community to which Christ is or
> is not self-superadded, nor of a union among such as individu-
> ally seek or think to have Christ and wish to cultivate this
> common "possession"; no it is a communion created by Christ
> and founded upon him, one in which Christ reveals himself as
> ". . . the new man—or rather, the new humanity itself."[10]

The church is then a fellowship of persons. And within that fellowship
the saving act of Christ, his death/resurrection is proclaimed over and over
again in the act of preaching. The community bears the revelation, indeed
is the revelation (Christ existing as community) and thus the continuing
'being' of revelation is preserved. The community also speaks and hears the
revelation in each act of preaching and each conferral of the sacraments
and so the 'act' of revelation is continually reenacted. The church is revelation both in being and in act.

An analysis of faith leads to the same conclusion, that it too has the
characteristics of both act and being. Faith continues to be that which
sustains the community in existence. And within the community faith
finds, in the preaching and sacramental action, the acts which express its
own being. Thus Bonhoeffer finds that the church is at one and the same
time the continuous being of Christ's revelation and the place where that
revelation is made manifest in acts. In her, revelation reveals itself to be
both being and act.

As events in Germany became more and more critical, moving ever
more ominously towards war, they produced, in Bonhoeffer, a growing
disillusionment with the way in which the German Church was meeting
the crisis. It was all well and good to theorize about the nature of revelation and of the church. What was now ever more desperately needed was
thought and writing on the harsh demands that reality made on the church
to implement her thinking in practical action. His question therefore now
becomes: What are the practical implications of his thinking on revelation
and on the church? How do these realities affect life as it is to be lived in
the insistently critical present?

THE CONCRETENESS OF REVELATION

His next book, *The Cost of Discipleship* (1937), is a bridge book in his thinking. It moves away from the dense, abstract thinking of his earlier works and becomes more insistent on the need for an existential embodiment of thought in action. Yet for all of this it has not yet reached the radical religionlessness of his last writings.

The book addresses itself to the problem of grace, to the question: what difference ought its possession to make in a Christian's life? For too long the church has been emasculating grace of its meaning by the way she has preached it. It has become the badge of the comfortable and the self-satisfied. Once a man has accepted Christ as his Lord and Savior he has met the only demand that Christianity makes of him. He may then continue life untroubled by uncertainty about his final salvation. His confidence in Christ has solved that problem for him. So long as his faith remains strong he will be saved. Thus has Luther's principle of *sola fides* been corrupted to justify a life of self-satisfied mediocrity.

The church has corrupted the meaning of grace by converting it from a dearly bought and constantly demanding pearl of great price into a comforting guarantee of salvation without cost. She has transformed grace, which in its authentic form can only be costly, into a caricature of itself which Bonhoeffer labels "cheap grace."

> Cheap grace means grace as a doctrine, a principle, a system. It means forgiveness of sins proclaimed as a general truth, the love of God taught as the Christian "conception" of God. An intellectual assent to that idea is held to be of itself sufficient to secure remission of sins. The Church which holds the correct doctrine of grace has, it is supposed, *ipso facto,* a part in that grace. In such a Church the world finds a cheap covering for its sins; no contrition is required, still less any real desire to be delivered from sin . . . . Cheap grace means the justification of sin without the justification of the sinner. Grace alone does everything, they say, and so everything can remain as it was before.[11]

Over against this parody of grace stands the true grace, the grace that is costly.

> Costly grace is the gospel which must be *sought* again and again, the gift which must be *asked* for, the door at which a man must *knock.* Such grace is *costly* because it calls us to follow, and it is *grace* because it calls us to follow *Jesus Christ.*

It is costly because it costs a man his life, and it is grace
because it gives a man the only true life. It is costly because it
condemns sin, and grace because it justifies the sinner.[12]

Faced with this situation of a grace cheapened by the church and
inconsequential in the life of the individual Christian, Bonhoeffer calls
both back to Christian discipleship. First he paints a picture of the
demands that costly grace make on a man and then deals with how the
church must again become the place of discipleship.

GRACE AND DISCIPLESHIP

In her beginnings the church understood and paid gladly the price that
grace demanded. She gave herself to the total following of Jesus, the
discipleship that required of man his whole life in return for grace. Grace
and discipleship were seen and lived as inseparable. But as "the world was
Christianized and grace became its common property" men lost "the
realization of the costliness of grace" and only within monasticism did the
full price continue to be paid for grace. In his own good time God raised
up Martin Luther to recall once more to men's attention the two parallel
truths: (1) "The only way to follow Jesus was by living in the world,"[13]
and (2) grace costs a man his life. There is no grace without discipleship.
The church has allowed that vision to slip from her gaze. She needs now to
recover it.

The Church needs to relearn that the call to discipleship demands the
response of immediate obedience. Jesus simply says, Follow me. If
accepted, this willingness to follow produces the situation within which
faith can be given. It is at this juncture that the paradoxical quality of
faith becomes apparent. On the one hand, "only those who believe obey"
and on the other hand, "only those who obey believe."[14] It is when the
two come together and are lived that the obedient man of faith is produced.

As the Christian takes up the way of obedience he comes to learn that
discipleship means inescapably the cross. It calls for one "to be aware only
of Christ and no more of self, to see only him who goes before and no
more the road which is too hard for us."[15] The cross of discipleship, if it
is accepted, leads a man into loneliness and Christ demands this of his
followers in order that in their isolation they will come to fix their eyes
only on Him who leads. He cuts a man off from his world, from his father

and mother, wife, children and country, only that he may bring him back
to them through himself. This is true because the same Jesus who separates
us unites us in himself.

> ... The same Mediator who makes us individuals is also the
> founder of a new fellowship. He stands in the center between
> my neighbor and myself. He divides but he also unites.[16]

The long middle section of the book is devoted to developing three
characteristics of Christian ·discipleship: its extraordinariness, its hiddenness, and its distinctiveness. Extraordinariness means "living at the world's
level" but living as Jesus did and this means adopting his love as one's own.
"The cross is the differential" of that love. He loved through suffering up
to death itself. For the Christian disciple this can only mean a life of
suffering love.

Yet the exercise of love by the Christian must always be a hidden thing.
It must above all be hidden from one's self for as soon as "we want to
know our own goodness or love, it has already ceased to be love."[17]
Rather the Christian gives himself in faith to the life of the cross accepting
the paradox that such a way, the way of the cross, "is at once . . . the
hidden and the visible . . . ." way.[18]

Lastly the disciple by the life he leads will be different, yet again he
must not avert to the difference. He simply gives himself to following
Christ, clinging to his word and letting everything else go.[19] Thus he is
distinguished from, yet not set apart from, his fellows. Rather he comes
"to them with an unconditional offer of fellowship, with the single-
mindedness of the love of Jesus."[20]

THE CHURCH, THE PLACE OF DISCIPLESHIP

The demand that grace and discipleship makes on a man is death, death
to self and life, life in Jesus and for others. But if this is the essence of
Christianity why is a church needed? Cannot a man give himself to this life
as an individual? What is there about Christian discipleship that demands a
community, a church? It is to this question that the last section of the
book addresses itself.

The key to the answer to this question lies in a proper understanding of
the Incarnation. Christ did not become *this* man only, but man. He identified Himself with mankind, or as Godsey puts it, "Thus the incarnate Son

of God existed simultaneously as himself and as humanity."[21] Bonhoeffer himself explains in these words:

> As they contemplated the miracle of the Incarnation, the early Fathers passionately contended that while it was true to say that God took human nature upon him, it was wrong to say that he chose a perfect individual man and united himself to him. God was made man, and while that means that he took upon him our entire human nature with all its infirmity, sinfulness and corruption, the whole of apostate humanity, it does not mean that he took upon him the man Jesus. Unless we draw this distinction we shall misunderstand the whole message of the gospel. The Body of Jesus Christ, in which we are taken up with the whole human race, has now become the ground of our salvation.[22]

It is because Jesus Christ bears the new humanity in his body that we cannot find communion with him except in his body. Our fellowship with him is ". . . cleaving to him bodily."[23] This solidarity of ours with Christ in his Body, which is the church (Christ-existing-as-community) is the divine answer to the basic human problem which is also a problem which exists only in solidarity. Adam, created in order that he might be in the image of God, chose his own way to become like God. And this was not *a* man, but man himself who chose. In consequence,

> . . . with the loss of the God-like nature God had given him, man had forfeited the destiny of his being, which was to be like God. In short man had ceased to be man. He must live without the ability to live.[24]

God's answer to this was to come to man in a different image. He decided "to re-create his image in man."[25] This he does by assuming the image of fallen man. Christ in his image newly revealed. The image that Christ bears, however, is not the image of God which Adam first had.

> Rather, it is the image of one who enters a world of sin and death, who takes upon himself all the sorrows of humanity, who meekly bears God's wrath and judgment against sinners, and obeys his will with unswerving devotion in suffering and death, the Man born to poverty, the friend of publicans and sinners, the Man of sorrows, rejected of man and forsaken of God. Here is God made man, here is man in the new image of God.[26]

It is to this image, the "image of his shame," that we must be conformed before we can come to the possession of "the image of his glory." Our union with Christ in his Body allows us to enter this conformity with him. At the same time our communion with him delivers us "from that individualism which is the consequence of sin," and restores us to "solidarity with the whole human race" because "by being partakers of Christ incarnate, we are partakers in the whole humanity which he bore."[27]

Thus does Bonhoeffer see that the cost of discipleship which is union with Christ in his suffering love is the only price that can buy for men the restoration of their solidarity one with another. It is to the paying of this price that the church must once again learn to give herself.

With Bonhoeffer's last two books, *Ethics* and *Letters and Papers From Prison* (both published posthumously), we come to the final period of his life. These are the years of prison and death and the urgency of these experiences is mirrored in the subject matter of these books. Gone are the lofty theological discussions of his former writings. He has come, under the harsh realities of his life, to see that the church, if it is to survive, must come to grips with the agonizing day-by-day problems with which life presents every man. Urgency then is the first note of this period of his life and writing. The second note is harder to see but it is there under the surface. There is an optimism, a conviction always sustaining him, that his beloved church will finally learn her role in the new world coming to birth. Those who see Bonhoeffer writing off the church misread him. He is hard on her, brutally harsh in his criticism, but it is a cruelty which is always aware that the church's pathway must always be, as her Lord's is, through suffering and death. He wants her to suffer and die to all her old forms and ways of living but he wants this precisely that thereby she may be born again to serve the newborn world.

ETHICS

The *Ethics* is unfinished and fragmentary, sometimes difficult in its abstractness, yet like the grinder's sharpening wheel it throws off a series of brilliant sparks which light up his thought and illumine the direction in which it is moving. Rather than a book of a single, coherent argument it is a series of essays all bearing on the problem of what responsible and free Christian life means.

Bonhoeffer believes that we are beyond the day when men are liable to accept a theoretical ethical system. "Ethical fanaticism" too has collapsed, the view of the man who thinks he ". . . can oppose the power of evil with the purity of his will and of his principle."[28]

Today the man who wants to form and follow his conscience finds that he ". . . fights a lonely battle against the overwhelming forces of inescapable situations which demand decisions."[29] Two kinds of response tend to characterize modern man's answer to this situation. There is the man of duty. He does what he is commanded to do. But such a choice means a man loses the ability to place ". . . the deed which is done on one's own free responsibility, the only kind of deed which can strike at the heart of evil and overcome it."[30] Eichmann's plea at his trial that he did only his duty is the extreme example of where this choice can lead one. There are others whose choice is "private virtuousness." This one settles for an individual moral life. Beyond that he will not become involved. Such a one comes sooner or later to realize that this course does not free him from the disquiet he feels for failing to act responsibly in the world. He ends up in either self-destruction or phariseeism.

Faced with the multiplicity and complexity of today's ethical problems "reason, moral fanaticism, conscience, duty, free responsibility and silent virtue . . . ."[31] are reduced to the level of Don Quixote's weapons. They are powerless faced with today's world. Our rusty swords need replacement; we need a new ethical stance.

Bonhoeffer's suggestion is the man armed with wisdom and simplicity. The simple man fixed his gaze solely on God, hearing each day His commandments, His judgments and His mercies. He knows himself "not fettered by principles but bound by love for God . . . ."[32] And it is this simple man who is also wise. He ". . . sees reality in God."[33] He acquires the ". . . best possible knowledge about events . . . "[34] while at the same time realizes that "reality is not built upon principles but that it rests upon the living and creating God."[35] It is God he finds in all reality; it is on Him he relies and His will he follows.

This wise and simple man knows there is one place where God and His world are brought together in harmonious unity, one place where the world is used as God would have it used and that place is the person of Jesus Christ. To this person he gives himself in faith; in Christ he seeks the formation of his moral self. Bonhoeffer finds this moral formation to have three components. It is a conformation to Christ incarnate, crucified and risen.

Christ's incarnation he sees as an affirmation by God of the worthwhileness of the real world. He comes to realize that it must be as true of himself as it was of Christ that

God secures His love against any suggestion that it is not
genuine or that it is doubtful or uncertain, for He himself
enters into the life of man as man and takes upon Himself and
carries in the flesh the nature, the character, and the guilt and
suffering of man.[36]

The Christian is formed also in the likeness of the Crucified and so he
learns to die each day the death of the sinner, bearing the marks of the
wounds which sin inflicts on him. What suffering comes he bears willingly
knowing that thereby he is enabled to die to his own will that he may live
as Christ lives. Finally, he is conformed, too, to the Risen One and so "in
the midst of death he is in life."[37] He knows and lives in the knowledge
that in putting on the form of Christ he both confronts the world and
defeats it.

The church plays an indispensable part in this formation of man into
Christ because the church is not merely ". . . a religious community of
worshippers of Christ but is Christ Himself who has taken form among
men."[38] Thus it is much too narrow a view of the church to see her as
concerned only ". . . with the so-called religious functions of man . . ."[39]
Her concern is rather ". . . with the whole man in his existence in the
world with all its implications."[40] "What matters in the church is not
religion but the form of Christ, and its taking form amidst a band of
men."[41]

In the church, conformed to Christ, this form of Christ is the Christian's fundamental moral stance. How does the Christian proceed to
implement this posture, to reduce it to a concrete principle of life? As
Bonhoeffer sees it he begins by recognizing that Christ was not a theoreti-
cian of what is good; He was a practitioner of love. He affirmed reality,
things as they are, and it was with these that he dealt. The Christian should
then not speak about an ethical system, an ". . . attempt to define that
which is good once and for all. . ."[42] He needs rather to give himself as
Christ did to "the 'among us,' the 'now,' and 'here.' . . ."[43] He needs to
recognize that the form of Christ will take shape in him and must shape his
life ". . . in a manner which is neither abstract nor casuistic, neither pro-
grammatic nor purely speculative."[44] Life for him will mean "concrete
judgments and decisions . . . to be ventured here."[45]

Bonhoeffer is, however, quite aware of the danger of complete subjectivism in moral conduct which is attached to the view just presented. He
goes on to make it clear that morality always has an objective dimension.
One always lives his life in a context and that context determines in large
part the ways in which he will act and react.

> . . . By our history we are set objectively in a definite nexus of
> experiences, responsibilities and decisions from which we can-
> not free ourselves again except by an abstraction.[46]

For the true Christian the only truly ethical question is: what is the will
of God? Unfortunately the development of Western thought has brought
man to a situation where he finds it difficult to find that will. The development has left him with the problem of "thinking in terms of two spheres."
It has taught him to distinguish supernatural from natural, sacred from
profane. In consequence when he sets out to discover the will of God he is
unsure in which of these domains he is to find it and if he looks for it in
both he often encounters a conflict between them. Thus

> . .⸳. he abandons reality as a whole and places himself in one or
> other of the two spheres. He seeks Christ without the world,
> or he seeks the world without Christ. In either case he is
> deceiving himself. Or else he tries to stand in both spaces at
> once and thereby becomes the man of eternal conflict. . . .[47]

Bonhoeffer points out that such a view contradicts the view of Scripture which has always known only one reality ". . . and that is the reality
of God, which has become manifest in Christ in the reality of the
world."[48] The reality of Christ comprises the reality of the world within
itself. In Christ the world is found to have its beginning, its end and its
meaning. He created it; it becomes what it is meant to be; it will find its
final fulfillment in Him. And thus it is that by "sharing in Christ we stand
at once in both the reality of God and the reality of the world."[49] It will
be in seeking what Christ would seek that one finds the unity of natural
and supernatural.

Returning once again to the sole ethical norm: what is the will of God,
Bonhoeffer concludes that it is "nothing other than the becoming real of
the reality of Christ with us and in our world."[50]

To clarify further the way in which the Christian life is to be lived,
Bonhoeffer introduces the distinction between the last things and the
penultimate (things before last) things. The ultimate thing is justification,
God's saving of us in Christ. Yet before a man reaches that stage there is
much that must first be gone through. These are the penultimate things.
The penultimate, which is everything that precedes the justification of the
sinner by grace alone, must be taken seriously simply on account of its
relation to the ultimate.

In an attempt to grapple with the problem of salvation, Bonhoeffer
finds, men tend to choose one of two solutions. There is the radical

solution which sees only the ultimate, justification in Christ by grace and faith, as worthwhile. To the attainment of that end all else is sacrificed. In the light of the justice to be attained "everything penultimate in human behaviour is sin and denial."[51] This solution is in effect a total rejection of all things human. It is God alone and reaching Him that matters.

Equally extreme is the position of compromise. In this view the penultimate (perhaps one might say "the things of this world") retains its own right.

> ... there are still penultimate things which must be done, in fulfillment of the responsibility for this world which God has created. Account must still be taken of men as they are. The ultimate remains totally on the far side of the everyday . . . .[52]

In rejecting both efforts to solve the problem of salvation and of the nature of Christian life, Bonhoeffer reverts yet again to his basic position on the nature of morality. The Christian life means to be conformed to Christ, to the whole Christ. One cannot, therefore, construct a Christian ethic solely on the basis of the Incarnation; nor solely on the basis of the cross or the resurrection. Christ is not any one of these. He is all three: incarnate, dead, and risen. And it is only in the unity of this total view of him that conflict is resolved.

A certain measure of our faith and of our conformity to Christ is in the Incarnation. In that event we learn, and we learn to share, the love of God for His creation. We also believe in and are conformed to the crucified Christ and there ". . . we learn of the judgement of God upon all flesh . . ." We believe finally in the resurrection and in our conformity to Christ risen ". . . we learn of God's will for a new world."[53]

For the Christian then, neither radicalism nor compromise are the solution to life. The Christian life means rather

> ... being a man through the efficacy of the incarnation; it means being sentenced and pardoned through the efficacy of the cross; and it means living a new life through the efficacy of the resurrection. There cannot be one of these without the rest.[54]

Taking the penultimate seriously means, for Bonhoeffer, two things, being man and being good. In his perspective these things do not of themselves have ultimate value; a man gives himself to them in order that thereby he may prepare the way for the Word. For all of their lack of ultimate significance, however, being a man and being good must always be seen as having an intrinsic value in themselves and a man must always give himself to them with utmost seriousness.

Being a man and being good is not merely an inward process, a turning in on oneself to be sure that one has done all necessary to prepare oneself for the coming of the Lord. "It is [also] a formative activity on the very greatest visible scale."[55] This means a man must be dedicated also to producing the conditions which will allow other men to be men and to be good. One needs to see that taking the "next to last things" earnestly is a "charge of immense responsibility."

> The hungry man needs bread and the homeless man needs a roof; the dispossessed need justice and the lonely need fellowship; the undisciplined need order and the slave needs freedom.[56]

And if the hungry, homeless, dispossessed, lonely, undisciplined, and enslaved do not come to faith then the guilt falls on those who have not met their needs.

The one who takes the penultimate seriously comes to understand that "to provide the hungry man with bread is to prepare the way for the coming of grace."[57] But once again Bonhoeffer sounds the warning that the penultimate always looks to the ultimate. A man is helped to become a man so that having achieved this he may be laid open to the coming of God's grace. ". . . Ultimately it is not indeed a question of the reform of earthly conditions, but it is a question of the coming of Christ."[58]

The responsible Christian, aware of the importance of the penultimate and its relation to the ultimate, will come to conceive of his life in two basic categories: deputyship and responsibility. Deputyship will mean that one sees his life as necessarily modelled on Christ's life; hence it will involve the ". . . complete surrender of one's own life to the other man."[59] In the exercise of that selflessness the Christian relates to ". . . the man who is concretely his neighbor in his concrete possibility."[60]

In every concrete situation of relationship with his neighbor he does as Christ did, he sees ". . . what is necessary and what is 'right' for him to grasp and to do."[61] In so acting one observes, weighs up, assesses, and decides what the situation calls for. The future consequences of one's action, the motivation in one's heart, are also considered. And thus one is prepared ". . . to do what is necessary at the given place and with a due consideration of reality."[62] Having done all of this, having made one's choice and having acted, one is prepared to remain ultimately ignorant of one's own good and evil; to remain completely reliant upon grace. This is "responsible historical action."

Bonhoeffer calls responsibility the way in which we live our life of 'yes' and 'no.' Creation, atonement and redemption are the 'yes' of life. Condemnation and death are its 'no.' Or to put it another way, we are to say 'yes' to creation and redemption in life and 'no' to sin and death. It is in Christ that we learn the 'yes' and 'no' saying of life. For in him

> . . . is the 'yes' to what is created, to becoming and to growth, to the flower and to the fruit, to health, happiness, ability, achievement, worth, success, greatness and honour. . . .[63]

In Him we recognize too that ". . . 'no' means dying, suffering, poverty, renunciation, resignation, humility, degradation, self-denial. . . ."[64]

Saying 'yes' and 'no' to life as Christ did means that, for the Christian, life must be lived in responsible freedom. This will imply that

> the responsible man acts in the freedom of his own self without the support of men, circumstances or principles, but with a due consideration for the given human and general conditions, and for the relevant questions of principle. The proof of his freedom is the fact that nothing can answer for him, nothing can exonerate him, except his own deed and his own self. It is he himself who must observe, judge, weigh up, decide and act. It is man himself who must examine the motives, the prospects, the value and the purpose of his action. But neither the purity of the motivation, nor the opportune circumstances, nor the value, nor the significant purpose of an intended undertaking can become the governing law of his action, a law to which he can withdraw, to which he can appeal as an authority, and by which he can be exculpated and acquitted. For in that case he would indeed no longer be truly free. The action of the responsible man is performed in the obligation which alone gives freedom and which gives entire freedom, the obligation to God and to our neighbor as they confront us in Jesus Christ.[65]

And finally the Christian man is able to recognize that in every choice he makes there is a compound of freedom and of obedience as was true in Christ's life. He perceives that his selfless service to others is at once ". . . a blind compliance with the law which is commanded by him [by God] . . . ."[66] and an acquiescence ". . . in God's will out of his own most personal knowledge, with open eyes and a joyous heart . . . ."[67] He accepts gladly the paradox that "obedience without freedom is slavery; freedom without obedience is arbitrary self-will."[68]

Thus does Bonhoeffer conclude his portrait of the Christian moral life. The key to this life is Jesus and the Christian's conformity to Him. The heart of it is the taking seriously of the penultimate while never losing sight of its essential relation to the ultimate. One lives that life in responsible deputyship, with eyes always fixed on Christ, incarnate, dead and risen, the source and goal of all Christian life.

LETTERS AND PAPERS FROM PRISON

In his last book, *Letters and Papers from Prison,* Bonhoeffer takes up again his perennial themes, who is Christ and what is the church. This time, however, his treatment of them is far more radical than heretofore. The problem he is wrestling with first occurs in his letter of April 30, 1944. It becomes immediately clear that he is questioning the very possibility of the continuing existence of Christianity.

> The thing that keeps coming back to me is, what is Christianity, and indeed what is Christ, for us today? The time when men could be told everything by means of words, whether theological or simply pious, is over, and so is the time of inwardness and conscience, which is to say the time of religion as such. We are proceeding towards a time of no religion at all; men as they are now simply cannot be religious any more . . . . What does that mean for "Christianity"?[69]

Subsequent letters explore the reasons why he is so pessimistic about the future of Christianity. Basically his reasons are three: The traditional view of God is no longer an acceptable one; men are no longer interested in an other-worldly salvation; the church misconceives her role in the contemporary world. To meet the crisis he attempts to work out a view of God meaningful to men today, a this-world centered view of salvation and a church willing to adjust to a "religionless Christianity."

The Problem of God

Since the thirteenth century the men of the West have been gradually losing their belief in the traditional God of Christianity, learning how to get along without him. They have been "coming of age," reaching maturity. By now that process is virtually complete. Meanwhile the church in her attempts to deal with the problem has made two fundamental mistakes. She has first of all provided much too abstract a notion of God, stressing that He is the totally Other, the absolutely Transcendent, to be reached mainly by metaphysical speculation. Man's relation to God has been thought of as ". . . a religious relationship to a Supreme Being, absolute in power and goodness. . . ."[70] The church's other mistake has been to encourage men to think of God as a problem solver. He is the solution to death, suffering, pain, evil, sin, those areas of human life for whose meaning man does not have an explanation of his own.

It is now becoming apparent how serious these mistakes have been. Men now realize that if God is to make a difference in life He must be more than a concept, or a Supreme Being. He must somehow be a real experience in the midst of life. If He exists in a world apart, He is no longer of any significance. This world is all-absorbing.

The view of God as problem solver is equally doomed to extinction and that for a quite simple reason. Man is gradually learning to solve more and more of his problems for himself. Fewer and fewer questions remain to be answered by God; less and less is He needed. He will finally be edged out of the world.

> Religious people speak of God when human perception is [often just from laziness] at an end, or human resources fail: it is really always the *Deus ex machina* they call to their aid, either for the so-called solving of insoluble problems or as support in human failure—always, that is to say, helping out human weakness or on the borders of human existence. Of necessity, that can only go on until men can, by their own strength, push those borders a little further, so that God becomes superfluous as a *Deus ex machina*. I have come to be doubtful even about talking of "borders of human existence." Is even death today, since men are scarcely afraid of it any more, and sin, which they scarcely understand any more, still a genuine borderline? It always seems to me that in talking thus we are only seeking frantically to make room for God.[71]

To repair these past mistakes we need to refashion our thinking about God and the manner of our relating to him. The first step is to acknowledge that man has "come of age" and needs to be treated as such. The church must learn to accept the adulthood of man, to see him as capable of living his own life and solving his own problems. It is wrong to go on trying to keep man in tutelage to God; it is a mistake to try to save a place for God in the boundary situations of life.

The attack by Christian apologetic upon the adulthood of the world I consider to be in the first place pointless, in the second ignoble, and in the third un-Christian. Pointless, because it looks to me like an attempt to put a grown-up man back into adolescence, i.e. to make him dependent on things on which he is not in fact dependent any more, thrusting him back into the midst of problems which are in fact not problems for him any more. Ignoble, because this amounts to an effort to exploit the weakness of man for purposes alien to him and not freely subscribed to by him. Un-Christian, because for Christ himself is being substituted one particular stage in the religiousness of man, i.e. a human law.[72]

The next step is to ask and answer the question: Where then does God fit into human life? There are several elements in Bonhoeffer's answer. The first element is his conviction that God ought to be put at the center of life not at its borders.

I should like to speak of God not on the borders of life, but at its centre, not in weakness but in strength, not therefore, in man's suffering and death but in his life and prosperity. On the borders it seems to me better to hold our peace and leave the problem unsolved.[73]

. . . He must be found at the centre of life: in life and not only in death; in health and vigour, and not only in suffering; in activity, and not only in sin. The ground for this lies in the revelation of God in Christ. Christ is the centre of life, and in no sense did he come to answer our unsolved problems. From the centre of life certain questions are seen to be wholly irrelevant, and so are the answers commonly given to them. . . .[74]

The Problem of Salvation

The second element in Bonhoeffer's vision of a contemporary Christianity is to recognize that if God is to be put at the center of life we need also to review our understanding of what salvation means. For too long Christianity has defined salvation in other-worldly terms. Our ultimate fulfillment lies beyond this world; salvation is a process which will finally save us from this world and bring us to God. Such a view sees God as beyond the here and now, as an end to be achieved elsewhere. But it is precisely this God that contemporary man cannot accept. He is totally committed to this world, to living in it, to building it, to enjoying its happiness. The transcendent is neither thinkable nor desirable; thus neither is God.

But there is a view of salvation which speaks to man in a this-worldly framework. It is the Old Testament view which sees redemption and salvation as to be attained in this world and God as a God who leads man through the events in his history to a ". . . redemption on this side of death. . . . Israel is redeemed out of Egypt in order to live before God on earth."[75]

It is this view that the church needs to recover. She must learn that the real focus of Christian hope is not on the life that lies ". . . upon the far side of the boundary drawn by death."[76] Christians ought to be weaned from looking for ". . . a last refuge in the eternal from earthly tasks and difficulties."[77] Christian hope from this perspective is the realization that when one comes to faith in Jesus Christ he is then given the life of otherness that is the life of Jesus. In the power of that life he returns to earthly tasks and worldly goals, to community with other men in the building of their world. Thus "Christ takes hold of a man in the centre of his life."[78] Thus does He give him hope for the future of man in this life.

If salvation is so conceived it makes a radical difference in our view of God. No longer is He the totally Other, the absolutely Transcendent. Now in Christ and in the Christian's life of otherness in Christ, He becomes the "beyond in our midst." God in Christ is present in human relations and worldly tasks, in achievement and failure, in joy, happiness and suffering. Thus does it become true that "the transcendent is not infinitely remote, but close at hand,"[79] findable and haveable in the midst of human life.

The love of God that such a relation with Him produces also takes on a new dimension. Like the central theme or melody of a symphony God remains the *cantus firmus* in our life. ". . . God requires that we should love him eternally with our whole hearts . . . ."[80] Nevertheless, when the Christian puts on Christ's life of otherness he enters into a life where other loves and other melodies share place with his love of God. Indeed, "earthly affections" developed to the utmost of their limits provide the counterpoint for the love of God.

One last element enters into the vision of God and salvation that Bonhoeffer is building for his contemporaries. It strikes a paradoxical note in comparison with what he has said thus far. The God who can mean most to us is a suffering God. Faced with the enormities of life's demands and his own inadequacies to meet those demands a man may well lose heart. It is in this situation that he needs to make his own the final Christian paradox: God is strongest where He is most weak.

God allows himself to be edged out of the world and on to the cross. God is weak and powerless in the world, and that is exactly the way, the only way, in which he can be with us and help us. Matthew 8:17 makes it crystal-clear that it is not by his omnipotence that Christ helps us, but by his weakness and suffering . . . . The Bible, however, directs him to the power-lessness and suffering of God; only a suffering God can help. To this extent we may say that the process we have described by which the world came of age was an abandonment of a false conception of God, and a clearing of the decks for the God of the Bible, who conquers power and space in the world by his weakness. This must be the starting point for our "worldly" interpretation.[81]

The Problem of the Church

What is the church's role in the face of man's new vision of himself? She needs to recognize how badly she has corrupted the idea of religion. Then she needs to accept with equanimity (indeed Bonhoeffer seems to suggest that she should contribute enthusiastically to it) the advent of "religionless Christianity." Religion as the church has spoken of it and as traditionally practiced has been directed to the individual and he has been in consequence almost exclusively concerned with his own salvation and the development of his own personal prayer life. As a result the needs of the neighbor are forgotten, the problems of the world avoided. Religion in its traditional garb has also tended to be other-worldly, focusing the religious man's attention far more on the attainment of salvation in another world than on involvement in and concern for this world.

The church as the locus of religion has fought too for her position in the world, a segment of life reserved for her, a place to call her own. She has fought for self-preservation and forgotten that she is ". . . her true self only when she exists for humanity."[82] Last of all religion has preyed on man in his weakness. She has tried to keep a place for herself in men's lives where they feel most need. She has fought man's maturity.

Efforts are made to prove to a world thus come of age that it cannot live without the tutelage of 'God.' Even though there has been surrender on all secular problems, there still remains the so-called ultimate questions—death, guilt—on which only 'God' can furnish an answer, and which are the reason why God and the Church and the pastor are needed. Thus we live, to some extent, by these ultimate questions of humanity. But what if one day they no longer exist as such, if they too can be answered without 'God'?[83]

This is religion as Bonhoeffer sees it presently lived in the church and it is this he sees must be replaced by a "religionless Christianity." What he sees coming will be Christianity because Jesus as the man for others will be its focal point—and God as the beyond in our midst will be at its heart. But it will be religionless. This Christianity will replace religion's individualism with community and concern for others. For the metaphysical God in the heavens it will substitute God for the center of life. An otherworldly salvation will yield to redemption sought for, worked toward in this world. And it will be for the man of strength, not of weakness, of achievement not of failure. Yet this same man will find identity in his own experience with the God of weakness and suffering.

Thus in the end it turns out that the vision of "religionless Christianity," which is the heart of Bonhoeffer's thought in his *Letters and Papers,* is a challenge to the church to be what Christ is, one who lives for the selfless service of others. No more fitting conclusion to a study of Bonhoeffer can be found than a citation from the book he was planning to write on the future of Christianity. It is a passage that may well be the last words he had to say to his beloved church. In it he summarizes the work of his lifetime, his final answer to his two questions: What is the church and who is Christ?

> The church is her true self only when she exists for humanity. As a fresh start she should give away all her endowments to the poor and needy. The clergy should live solely on the free-will offerings of their congregations, or possibly engage in some secular calling. She must take her part in the social life of the world, not lording it over men, but helping and serving them. She must tell men, whatever their calling, what it means to live in Christ, to exist for others. And in particular, our own church will have to take a strong line with the blasphemies of *hybris,* power-worship, envy and humbug, for these are the roots of evil. She will have to speak of moderation, purity, confidence, loyalty, steadfastness, patience, discipline, humility, content and modesty. She must not underestimate the importance of human example, which has its origin in the humanity of Jesus, and which is so important in the teaching of St. Paul. It is not abstract argument, but concrete example which gives her word emphasis and power.[84]

CONCLUSION

Any definitive evaluation of Bonhoeffer attempted at present would be premature for two reasons. First of all, his work is only just beginning to be known and studied by Christian theologians. Sufficient time has not yet elapsed for them to assess adequately the impact which his work will ultimately have on the future of Christian thought. Secondly, the most influential portion of his thinking has been his last writings, the *Ethics* and the *Letters and Papers from Prison.* Both of these are only fragmentary and tantalizingly general statements of his thought. His "religionless Christianity," "man come of age," "Jesus as the man for others," will need a good deal more study and development by those who come after him before their real significance and impact can be judged.

Certainly, one thing is clear, Bonhoeffer was perhaps the first to see with complete clarity the almost total separation of religion from life in contemporary society. Joined to that insight was his other radical conviction that Christianity could not heal that separation in any of its traditional forms or any of its traditional ways of speaking about God or Christ or church.

Out of that double insight was born his major contribution and his chief appeal to present Christian thinkers. Any attempt to speak of what religion or Christianity means must begin with the world as it presently exists in all its concreteness and all its immediacy. An affirmation, hopeful yet clear-sighted, of man in his strength, his freedom, his technological mastery of nature and his own life, is the only possible base for the present and future survival of Christianity. It will survive, he was convinced, only if it accepts the death of the civilization and culture which has supported it for many centuries. Acceptance of the secular as the only viable form of human society is the only alternative to death for the Christian churches.

It is this fundamental conviction of Bonhoeffer's that would seem to guarantee the continuing impact of his thought. He accepted the radical transformation of society over the past few centuries as the fact that it is, and saw that Christianity must learn to live in, endorse, and serve this culture or die. In this sense his thought will be seminal for many years to come.

FOOTNOTES

[1] From *The Theology of Dietrich Bonhoeffer,* by John D. Godsey. The Westminster Press. W.L. Jenkins, 1960, p. 279. Used by permission.

[2] Dietrich Bonhoeffer, *The Cost of Discipleship,* paperback ed. (New York: The Macmillan Company, 1963), p. 99. Reprinted with permission of The Macmillan Company. Copyright 1955 by The MacMillan Company.

3Godsey, *The Theology of Dietrich Bonhoeffer,* pp. 264-5.

4Bonhoeffer, *Act and Being,* trans. Bernard Noble (New York & Evanston: Harper & Row, 1961), pp. 90-91.

5——*The Communion of Saints,* trans. H. Gregor Smith (New York & Evanston: Harper & Row, 1963), p. 106.

6*Ibid.*

7The phrase is used by William Kuhns, *In Pursuit of Dietrich Bonhoeffer* (Dayton, Ohio: Pflaum, 1967), p. 20.

8Bonhoeffer, *Act and Being,* p. 12.

9Godsey, *The Theology of Dietrich Bonhoeffer,* p. 55.

10Bonhoeffer, *Act and Being,* p. 121.

11——*The Cost of Discipleship,* pp. 45-46.

12*Ibid.,* pp. 47-48.

13*Ibid.,* p. 51.

14*Ibid.,* p. 74.

15*Ibid.,* p. 97.

16*Ibid.,* p. 112.

17*Ibid.,* p. 177.

18*Ibid.,* p. 176.

19*Ibid.,* p. 217.

20*Ibid.,* p. 204.

21*Godsey, The Theology of Dietrich Bonhoeffer,* p. 167.

22Bonhoeffer, *The Cost of Discipleship,* pp. 264-5.

23*Ibid.,* p. 266.

24*Ibid.,* p. 338.

25*Ibid.,* p. 339.

26*Ibid.,* p. 340.

27*Ibid.,* p. 341.

28Bonhoeffer, *Ethics,* trans. N. H. Smith, ed. Bethge, Paperback ed. (New York: The MacMillan Co., 1965), p. 66. Reprinted with permission of The Macmillan Company. Copyright 1955 by The Macmillan Company.

29*Ibid.,* p. 66.

30*Ibid.,* p. 66-67.

31*Ibid.,* p. 67.

32*Ibid.,* p. 68.

33*Ibid.*

34*Ibid.,* p. 69.

35*Ibid.*

36*Ibid.,* p. 72.

37*Ibid.*, p. 82.

38*Ibid.*, p. 83.

39*Ibid.*

40*Ibid.*, p. 84.

41*Ibid.*

42*Ibid.*, p. 85.

43*Ibid.*, pp. 86-7.

44*Ibid.*, p. 88.

45*Ibid.*

46*Ibid.*, p. 87.

47*Ibid.*, p. 197.

48*Ibid.*

49*Ibid.*

50*Ibid.*, p. 212.

51*Ibid.*, p. 127.

52*Ibid.*

53*Ibid.*, pp. 130-31.

54*Ibid.*, p. 133.

55*Ibid.*, p. 135.

56*Ibid.*, p. 137.

57*Ibid.*

58*Ibid.*, p. 138.

59*Ibid.*, p. 225.

60*Ibid.*, p. 227.

61*Ibid.*

62*Ibid.*, p. 233.

63*Ibid.*, p. 219.

64*Ibid.*

65*Ibid.*, pp. 248-49.

66*Ibid.*, p. 252.

67*Ibid.*

68*Ibid.*

69Bonhoeffer, *Letters and Papers from Prison,* trans. Reginald H. Fuller, ed. Eberhard Bethge, paperback ed. (New York: The Macmillan Co., 1965), pp. 162-63. Reprinted with permission of The Macmillan Company. Copyright 1953 by The Macmillan Company. ©1967 by SCM Press, Ltd.

70*Ibid.*, pp. 237-38.

71*Ibid.*, p. 165.

72*Ibid.*, pp. 196-97.

[73]*Ibid.*, pp. 165-66.

[74]*Ibid.*, p. 191.

[75]*Ibid.*, p. 205.

[76]*Ibid.*

[77]*Ibid.*

[78]Bonhoeffer, *Letters and Papers*, p. 206.

[79]*Ibid.*, p. 233.

[80]*Ibid.*, p. 175.

[81]*Ibid.*, pp. 219-20.

[82]*Ibid.*, p. 239.

[83]*Ibid.*, p. 195-96.

[84]*Ibid.*, pp. 239-40.

CHAPTER TEN

Rudolf Bultmann

The name of Rudolf Bultmann (*n.* 1884) dominated the theological scene in Europe during the period following Barth's ascendency and prior to the rise of Bonhoeffer's influence. He replaced Barth and was in turn replaced by Bonhoeffer in center stage. Where Barth's attention was fixed on the total otherness of God and the complete impossibility of man's knowing anything about Him unless God decides to reveal Himself, and as Bonhoeffer gave himself to exploring the concrete implications of that revelation for the man of today, Bultmann's focus was on the revelation itself, or more precisely on the vehicle of that revelation, the Scriptures. Bultmann's concern is the development of a manner of interpreting the Scriptures which will make its message comprehensible and meaningful to the modern world. As John Macquarrie puts it in one of his studies of Bultmann,

> ... the main theological interest in Bultmann lies in his attempt to interpret Christianity in such a way that one can be radically skeptical about the factual content of the gospel narrative and yet continue to believe in the essential message of the New Testament. Indeed, Bultmann would go further, maintaining that if the essential Christian message is to gain a hearing in the contemporary world, it must be disengaged from the form in which it is presented in the New Testament.[1]

Bultmann is convinced that the thought patterns which the biblical writers used to convey the message of revelation to their contemporaries are patterns which no longer make sense to Western man. If the Scriptures are to become contemporaneously intelligible then a double task is set for today's biblical scholars. First, the essential message of revelation, what God had to say to man, has to be disengaged from the thought patterns in which that message was first given. Then it needs to be clothed in twentieth century thought patterns and thereby rendered understandable to the men of this time.

The encounter which produces the possibility of Christian belief is always between God speaking and man hearing and answering 'yes'. Therefore the speech of God and the hearing of man must be brought into meaningful contact before faith can occur. Bultmann, in consequence, asks, first of all: Who is man today and how does he conceive of himself? Where does he stand; what situation is he in?

As his tool for answering these questions he chooses existential philosophy and in particular the existential philosophy of Martin Heidegger. He makes this choice because he feels that this is the type of philosophizing which most clearly analyzes the existence of man in his world and most nearly approaches satisfactory answers to the questions that man today asks about himself. It is to man in this situation that the Word of God must now speak.

With this task done Bultmann turns to the other half of his problem, God speaking. When He spoke to the men of the first century He spoke to them as they were situated, within the cultural framework in which they lived. What He wanted to say was embedded in their thought patterns. He accepted their world-view and spoke to them within it. The scholar needs, therefore, to understand the first century situation and its view of reality. Then he must search out and disengage from the Scripture, its vehicle of communication, the Word that God was speaking. What was said needs to be distinguished from how it was said. This process of disentanglement Bultmann calls "demythologizing."

With both these tasks accomplished Bultmann then turns to putting together again the Word of God and the hearing of man. Using existential categories he garbs the essential message of God in contemporary thought patterns. In the light of these remarks about Bultmann's method, what follows will discuss his thought in terms of these three aspects: the contemporary situation of man; the disengagement of the Word of God from its original thought patterns; and; the recasting of that Word in meaningful present day terms.

THE CONTEMPORARY SITUATION OF MAN

As Bultmann, following Heidegger, analyzes present day man, he sees him as both existing, and understanding that he exists, in a world where he is confronted with a variety of possibilities, a choice of ways to live out his life. The two most basic choices for living that face him are authentic or inauthentic existence. In authentic existence man chooses the fullest possible development of himself and all his potentialities whereas inauthentic existence means the choice of turning himself over to the world of things and the collective mass of men to be shaped and fashioned by them.

In Heidegger's view most men in the modern world make the second choice, the surrender of responsibility for one's individuality. It is by far the easier choice and the majority of men settle for it. It is simpler to become one of the collective, depersonalized mass, to consent to its way of life and settle for its values. Far harder is the choice of self-determination. Here a man takes full responsibility for shaping his own life, for choosing his own set of possibilities for living.

These are man's two possible choices for his life and he cannot avoid choosing one of them. Even the decision not to choose between them is a settling for inauthentic existence, a giving of oneself to life as it happens. One must choose either to shape his own life or let himself be shaped by other people and things.

The choice is not a single, once-for-all decision. Life is rather characterized by a constant necessity of choosing between authentic and inauthentic existence. ". . . Each 'now' is the moment of free decision. . . ."[2] And that insistent need for choice is what gives life its chief characteristic—anxiety. Man in his existence is always faced with being and making himself or being made by the world of things.

> For him (Heidegger) the chief characteristic of man's Being in history is anxiety. Man exists in a permanent tension between the past and the future. At every moment he is confronted with an alternative. Either he must immerse himself in the concrete world of nature, and thus inevitably lose his individuality, or he must abandon all security and commit himself unreservedly to the future, and thus alone achieve his authentic Being.[3]

If man makes the choice of inauthentic existence as his way of allaying the anxiety he feels about his existence, then he gives himself to the world, to an exclusive concern with things. His life becomes a quest for security by the acquisition and mastery of things. Yet the harder he struggles the more surely he falls under their domination. Seeking freedom he ends up in slavery. Things become the be-all and the end-all of his life, in a word, his master. In his refusal to see that it is his distinction from things that constitutes his self, he surrenders that distinct selfhood in a continually growing attachment to things. Thus does he become alienated from his true self.

This inauthentic being-in-the-world has its counterpart in an equally inauthentic life of relation with other men (being-with-others). This way of living, like the one just described, is the turning oneself over to the other; in this case to other men, to the collectivity. Here one identifies with our depersonalized society, ceases to accept personal responsibility for one's own existence and submits to being shaped by the group in all matters of decision, of value, of taste. Thus does an individual abdicate himself; thus does he become mediocre, just like everyone else. Thus does he escape the awful sense of insecurity that forever plagues him. He looks to others to give him security, but all they can do is prevent him from becoming himself.

Suppose, on the other hand, that a man, recognizing the two choices open to him, decides for authentic existence. What would this mean and how would he proceed to implement this choice in his life? Here it should be noted that for Heidegger, man is of himself able to implement his choice for authentic existence once he has made it. Bultmann, on the other hand, would hold that man is radically fallen and not able of himself to achieve authentic existence. For this he needs God's help.

The decision for authentic existence is a decision for freedom and that in several senses. It is first a decision for freedom from the world, from the slavery to things and from the tyranny of the collectivity. One decides to take full responsibility for making oneself. He opts for developing his own possibilities for being, rather than letting the other determine what possibilities for living he may actualize. He chooses detachment from the world that he may find his true self for himself.

It is, secondly, a decision for the future and thereby a decision to be free of the past and the slavery to which it has subjected one. The choice is made to give up the past's guilt and failure, and its alienation from the true self in subjection to the other. It means to commit oneself to responsibility for one's future. It is a refusal to accept the determination of the course of one's life by another, no matter what the past might have been. Bultmann is, of course, aware that there is a necessary and inevitable dependence upon the world; yet he believes that there is beyond this an essential self-determination that characterizes authentic existence. He describes the combination this way:

> Although biology and psychology recognize that man is a
> highly dependent being, that does not mean that he has been

handed over to powers outside of and distinct from himself. This dependence is inseparable from human nature, and he needs only to understand it in order to recover his self-mastery and organize his life on a rational basis. If he regards himself as spirit, he knows that he is permanently conditioned by the physical, bodily part of his being, but he distinguishes his true self from it, and knows that he is independent and responsible for his mastery over nature.[4]

In brief, the man who chooses authentic existence decides for true self-realization. He will determine to what things and people his self is given and how this will be done. He will make himself out of the possibilities of existence that are open to him.

THE DISENGAGEMENT OF THE WORD OF GOD

Such is one way of viewing contemporary man and the choices available to him. In addition to his search for authentic existence, this man is also equipped with a definite world view that has been forged for him by the scientific development of the last few centuries. For him ". . . the cause-and-effect nexus is fundamental."[5] Whatever happens in the world has a cause which science has already explained or will some day. Rain gods do not produce rain; atmospheric conditions do. Medicine or surgery cure, not miracles. Everything has its explanation and it is for man to discover that explanation without recourse to mystery or miracle or supernatural explanation of any sort. The natural is naturally explainable. The same is true of modern man's view of history. It is not fate or destiny that determines what will happen. Behind all of history there lies human decision and rational motivation. Thus "modern men take it for granted that the course of nature and of history, like their own inner life and their practical life, is nowhere interrupted by the intervention of supernatural powers."[6]

When this man is confronted with the world as it is described in the Bible he finds himself in a strange and unbelievable place and his tendency is to dismiss it as the dark, superstitious world of prescientific man. It has nothing significant to say to the present scientifically oriented world.

It is, in Bultmann's word, a world of myth." By this he means several different things. He means first of all the description of his world that man gives in order to explain his understanding of himself in that world.

Myth speaks of the power or powers which man supposes he experiences as the ground and limit of his world and of his own activity and suffering. He describes these powers in terms derived from the visible world, with its tangible objects and forces, and from human life, with its feelings, motives and potentialities . . . Similarly he may account for the present state and order of the world by speaking of a primeval war between the gods. He speaks of the other world in terms of this world and of the gods in terms derived from human life.[7]

Again, myth is man's way of saying that he believes that ". . . the origin and purpose of the world in which he lives are to be sought not within it but beyond it. . . ."[8] Myth is also the way man speaks to express his sense of dependence, the fact that he is aware of his finiteness and limitation. Lastly, ". . . myth expresses man's belief that in this state of dependence he can be delivered from the forces within the visible world."[9]

All of these meanings of myth and the beliefs they imply are expressed in the world view that is portrayed in the Scriptures.

The cosmology of the New Testament is essentially mythical in character. The world is viewed as a three-storied structure, with the earth in the centre, the heaven above and the underworld beneath. Heaven is the abode of God and of celestial beings—the angels. The underworld is hell, the place of torment. Even the earth is more than the scene of natural, everyday events, of the trivial round and common task. It is the scene of the supernatural activity of God and his angels on the one hand, and of Satan and his daemons on the other. These supernatural forces intervene in the course of nature and in all that men think and will and do. Miracles are by no means rare. Man is not in control of his own life. Evil spirits may take possession of him. Satan may inspire him with evil thoughts. Alternatively, God may inspire his thought and guide his purposes. He may grant him heavenly visions. He may allow him to hear his word of succour or demand. He may give him the supernatural power of his Spirit. History does not follow a smooth unbroken course; it is set in motion and controlled by those supernatural powers. This aeon is held in bondage by Satan, sin and death . . . and hastens towards its end. That end will come very soon, and will take the form of a cosmic catastrophe. It will be inaugurated by the "woes" of the last time. Then the judge will come from heaven, the dead will rise, the last judgment will take place and men will enter into eternal salvation or damnation.[10]

Such a world-view contemporary man finds unacceptable and he dismisses it as ridiculous. He concludes that whatever Scripture has to say belongs to a bygone day. It has nothing to say to today. It is at this point that Bultmann asks his question: Is the message of the New Testament so inextricably bound to the world-view in whose terms it is expressed that one is compelled to reject both the world-view and the message? Or, is it possible to discover an essential message in the Scripture that is valid for all ages of human history and to disengage it from its mythological framework? If this can be done then the possibility of expressing the message in terms of the present world-view arises and with it the hope that the New Testament still has something meaningful to say to our present world.

Bultmann's answer to the question is "yes," the myth and the message are separable. His life's work has been dedicated to "demythologizing" the message of the New Testament, separating myth from message, and then to finding the contemporary philosophical categories in which to express that message. The process of demythologizing is then an attempt to disengage the Word of God from its primitive setting.

As the first step in the process Bultmann makes a distinction between kerygma and myth. Kerygma is God's essential message to man; myth is the framework or world-view within which it is presented. Beginning with the story in which the message is set, i.e., the life of Jesus, Bultmann is quite sceptical about our ability to know anything certain of the life, words and deeds of the historical Jesus. The early Christian community quite soon made him a mythical figure. The facts of his life (whatever they might have been, they are now irrecoverable) underwent a transformation, in the thinking of the primitive Church, and the story of Jesus became the story of ". . . a great, pre-existent, heavenly being who became man for the sake of our redemption. . . ."[11] Conceived by the Holy Spirit and born of a virgin he atoned by his death for men's sins, died, rose, and ascended into heaven. "He will come again on the clouds of heaven to complete the work of redemption and the resurrection and judgment of men will follow. Sin, suffering, and death will then be finally abolished."[12]

Such is the story of Jesus as the New Testament tells it. To men of the present century it contains much of the mythological way of thinking which is simply unacceptable. Their scientific world view makes such thinking an impossibility. Bultmann sums up the contemporary reaction when he says,

And as for the pre-existence of Christ, with its corollary of man's translation into a celestial realm of light, and the cloth-

ing of the human personality in heavenly robes and a spiritual
body—all this is not only irrational but utterly meaningless.
Why should salvation take this particular form? Why should
this be the fulfillment of human life and the realization of
man's true being?[13]

But although the historical facts of the life of Jesus have been irretriev-
ably turned into myth Bultmann believes that it is possible, indeed
absolutely essential, for Christianity to discover in this mythologized story
a message of God to man which is of perennial validity. What is needed is
an attempt to say what the myth says in other terms more acceptable to
modern men. How is this to be done? How is the mythology of the New
Testament to be reinterpreted? What is the message of God for men contained in the New Testament that is still of value to modern man?

THE RECASTING OF THE WORD OF GOD

To uncover what the New Testament has to offer us we must learn to
ask it the proper questions, or put another way, we must know what
questions the Bible is intending to answer before we can ask it the right
questions. For Bultmann the central concern of the New Testament is to
communicate an understanding of human existence. "I think our interest
is really to hear what the Bible has to say for our actual present, to hear
what is the truth about our life and about our soul."[14] The questions to
be asked of it should, therefore, deal with the meaning of human
existence. Man has from his beginning puzzled over and asked himself
questions about the meaning of his existence. There is, therefore, in man a
natural inclination to find the subject matter of the New Testament a
topic of absorbing interest. To profit fully from the treatment of the
subject in Scripture, however, man should take this inbred inclination and
develop it by a personal reflection on his own existence. By so doing he
will bring to sharper focus the questions about himself which cause him
most concern.

Thus armed he will be able to ask the New Testament the proper
existential questions. Bultmann adopts Heidegger's method of inquiry into
the meaning of existence and his questions are derived from reflection
within that philosophical framework. What does the New Testament tell
me about the meaning of my existence? What has it to say about the two

possible ways of existence open to me: authentic and inauthentic? How does it propose that I can achieve authentic existence?

All that can be attempted here is to take a few examples of the way in which he asks questions of the New Testament and how it yields answers to questions asked this way. A further study of his method can best be pursued in his *The Theology of the New Testament,* (Scribners, 1952-55).

Let us limit ourselves to the person of Jesus and the events of his life and ask with Bultmann: What has this to say to me about the meaning of existence? Bultmann begins his answer by asking whether Heidegger's analysis of what authentic existence means is a sufficient answer to the problem of human existence. Is it enough to tell a man what he ought to be? The answer is, of course, no. He must also be told whether or not what he ought to be is an attainable goal. Can a man be what he ought to be, is a question that must be central to any serious discussion of human existence.

The New Testament answer to this question is an unequivocal no. Man is not of himself capable of fighting free of inauthentic existence, slavery to the things of this world. Such deliverance can only be effected by an act of God and this is the kerygma of the New Testament: God has so acted. As Bultmann puts it,

> ... Jesus Christ [is] the eschatological phenomenon. . . the Saviour through whom God delivers the world by passing judgement on it and granting the future as a gift to those who believe on him . . . .[15]

The New Testament says that man is given the real possibility of authentic existence only through the redemption wrought in Christ.

A man who reflects on his own human situation ought to know from his own experience how inauthentic his existence has been. He should also come, Bultmann would argue, to realize that,

> ... the life he actually lives is not his authentic life, and that he is totally incapable of achieving that life by his own efforts. In short, he is a totally fallen being.[16]

But, unfortunately, this does not happen, for self-reliance carries its own blindness with it. "For self-assertion deludes man into thinking that his existence is a prize within his own grasp."[17] One who has opted for security to be derived from things cannot be convinced of the emptiness of his choice. Thus it becomes apparent that the man who leads the inauthentic life needs to be "delivered from himself" if any possibility of authentic life is to be his. At this point the kerygma of the New Testament again asserts itself: "At the very point where man can do nothing, God steps in and acts—indeed he has acted already—on man's behalf."[18]

Christ is the event in which God acts. Once a man grasps this act as his own in faith he is made free. Freed from himself, he becomes capable of authentic existence. In the moment of this choice of faith this world comes to an end in the sense that man has been freed of it and the inauthenticity it imposes upon him. In this faith man passes over into the possibility of "eschatological existence," a life lived out of this world.

How then is one to view the event of Jesus Christ? In what sense is one to reject it as myth and in what sense is one to retain it as meaningful? In answering the question Bultmann feels ". . . the crux of the matter lies in the cross and resurrection."[19]

The cross is to be accepted as an historical event. Enough evidence exists to be able to fix the date of its occurrence. Its true significance, however, becomes evident when one relates it to the problem of one's existence. Viewed from this perspective one sees that

> to believe in the cross does not mean to concern ourselves with a mythical process wrought outside of us and our world, with an objective event turned by God to our advantage, but rather to make the cross of Christ our own, to undergo crucifixion with him.[20]

Acceptance of the cross means to turn from this world, to accept God's judgment on it and on oneself as belonging to it. It connotes giving up reliance on self which leads only to inauthentic existence in order to place one's reliance on God. In this sense it is a death to self, a crucifixion. It is the radical decision of faith, the commitment of self to God.

Once this choice of identification with the cross has been made one enters into a new life. Dead to sin and to concern with finding security in the things of this world, one has risen to a life of authentic existence. This is the significance of the resurrection, its existential meaning. Is the resurrection as an historical event a myth? Bultmann seems to regard it as such. He seems to understand it as giving final meaning to the cross in the sense that after death there comes life; by losing life new life is found. The New Testament treatment of the resurrection concentrates much more on its significance as the eschatological event than on its historical character.

> If the event of Easter Day is in any sense an historical event additional to the event of the cross, it is nothing else than the

rise of faith in the risen Lord, since it was this faith which led
to the apostolic preaching. The resurrection itself is not an
event of past history . . . . But the historical problem is not of
interest to Christian belief in the resurrection. For the historical event of the rise of the Easter faith means for us what it
meant for the first disciples—namely, the self-attestation of the
risen Lord, the act of God in which the redemptive event of
the cross is completed.[21]

The meaning of the cross/resurrection for the believer is that, through
Jesus who was a historical person, God Himself is speaking to man. What
He is saying is: Come, through belief in Jesus Christ, to the possession of
authentic existence. Bultmann believes that by this radical demythologizing of the story of the New Testament he has put the stumbling block, the
scandalon of Christianity where it belongs. The point at which man needs
to be challenged is not his willingness to accept the mythology of the New
Testament. He is to be challenged at the point where the New Testament
challenges him, at the point of his self-sufficiency. What modern man is
being summoned to accept by the Christian message, is not a three-level
universe of heaven, earth, and hell, but the fact that he does not have in
himself the power to be his true self. God, through Christ, offers to
remedy his radical self-insufficiency. This is what the kerygma of the New
Testament calls man to believe in. The response to that call has for Bultmann a triple aspect.

An affirmative response has three aspects: man embraces a
new understanding of himself as free from himself and
endowed with a new self by divine grace; he accepts the new
life which is founded on the grace of God; and he decides on a
new understanding of his responsible acting which sees it as
born of love.[22]

CONCLUSION

This brief account of how Bultmann proposes to demythologize the
New Testament, or perhaps more clearly, how he proposes to ask it to
answer questions which are existentially meaningful to modern man, will
be sufficient to indicate how controversial an approach to the Scriptures
his theological method would be to many Christian theologians.

One thing that surely can be said whether one agrees or disagrees with his method is that he has made the attempt to meet head on *the* religious problem of today, the making of Christianity relevant to today's world. Reginald H. Fuller summarizes Bultmann's positive contribution this way,

> It is generally recognized that Bultmann has rendered a great service by putting his finger on a real problem for the church today, one of which theologians were insufficiently aware during the recovery of biblical theology. That problem is, how to communicate the Christian message to modern man in such a way as to challenge him to a genuine decision.[23]

Granted this contribution, let us look at a few of the problems that his critics have found within his program for demythologizing.

The first set of objections centers around his method. As we have seen, Bultmann tries to translate mythology into existentially meaningful statements. But the problem that immediately arises is: Is the content of the New Testament meant only as an answer to man's existential questions?[24] If so, then much of the New Testament turns out to be meaningless. To take but two examples, St. Paul makes much of the fact that all of creation is fallen and in need of redemption and he looks forward to the time when this will finally be accomplished. But what existential significance can this have for an individual seeking authentic existence for himself?

Again, the New Testament has much to say about eschatology, the end of the world which lies in the future. Yet for Bultmann the most that eschatology seems to yield is the individual's passage from death to life in his choice by faith to enter authentic existence. With that choice he enters the last time. But there is surely a dimension in the eschatology of the New Testament to which such an interpretation does not do full justice. Much is made in St. Paul, for example, of the end of the world and the signs which will accompany it; the Gospels give a good deal of attention to the Last Judgment.

From these and similar objections brought against Bultmann's method it would seem legitimate to conclude that, although his demythologizing does offer a key for a richer understanding of some elements of the New Testament, it cannot by any means be the only method for determining what is of value in the New Testament. Fuller summarizes the force of this set of objections:

> There must then, it is admitted, be interpretation of the Christian myths all the time. But how are they to be interpreted? Bultmann says, existentially. This, as we have seen, is helpful

with those aspects of the New Testament language, of those myths which concern our appropriation of the saving act of God in Christ. But when it comes to speaking of the saving act itself, the use of existentialist interpretation results in the discarding or ignoring of some myths, and in the inadequate interpretation of others. Therefore, despite Bultmann's professed intention, we get elimination of significant areas of the New Testament proclamation. As we have seen, we hear nothing about the church as a corporate fellowship, or of the future, both cosmic and individual. Against this it must be insisted that, true to the professed program of demythologizing, *all* of the New Testament mythology must be retained, and all must be interpreted. And where the existential interpretation is inapplicable, some other kind of interpretation must be discovered. Only so will we avoid taking the witness of the New Testament to the Christ event *à la carte*.[25]

The second major problem that many have with Bultmann is his sense of history. Christianity has been traditionally considered a historical religion, that is, it is a set of beliefs founded finally on a series of historical events, specifically the life of Jesus Christ. Bultmann seems very pessimistic about how much actual historical fact we can know about Jesus. He would admit that there is continuity between history and kerygma, between the life of Jesus and the church's preaching of the meaning of his life. Beyond that, however, he seems unwilling to go. Thus history has been swallowed up in myth and cannot be retrieved. Most of his historical attention is fastened on the present, on what the Christ-event means here and now to the individual. He would characterize the "search for the historical Jesus" as futile. Bishop John Robinson finds that he cannot accept this historical scepticism. It is his feeling that such a stand is too radical a rejection of the tradition of the church. Two thousand years of belief have borne witness to the church's acceptance of the gospel events. The *quod semper et ubique creditur* (what has always and everywhere been believed) of the church cannot be lightly brushed aside. The life of Jesus as historical fact is central to Christianity.[26]

The same objection has been brought by others who have urged that Christianity as a religion needs some base in historical fact; otherwise it would collapse. Macquarrie puts the problem this way,

> Does the Christian message summon us to a pure speculative possibility of existence, or to a possibility which has been actualized under the real conditions of historical existence? We could have no confidence about embarking on the first of

these alternatives. So we come back to the question whether Christianity needs some minimum of factual history, and, if so, how much?[27]

These are two of the basic problems that are found in Bultmann's work by his critics. Most of them would agree nonetheless that Bultmann's contribution to theology has been enormous. For all of the problems involved in the use of his method, when it is used properly and with due caution, it can bring the message of the New Testament into much clearer perspective for the contemporary world. Most would subscribe to Alvin Porteous' final evaluation of his significance.

> If the church is to be renewed in our day, Christian beliefs must somehow "come alive" in some such way as Bultmann has tried to make them. The doctrine of sin must be seen as the self-made bondage of Everyman to the tyranny of worldly securities, rather than the poisonous legacy of a mythical first man. The doctrine of salvation must be seen as God's gift to us of authentic freedom to be our true selves in service of others, rather than the working out of some cosmic plan of redemption to which we are called upon to give our intellectual acceptance. Similarly, we cannot really claim belief in the cross of Christ without taking up our own crosses and following him; nor in his resurrection without exhibiting the power of a new life. And finally, we can articulate most convincingly our belief in the Kingdom of God, not by our ability to recite a timetable of events for the Last Day but by living constantly in "the dimension of the eternal," in momentary expectation of God's breakthrough into our lives in grace and judgement.

> When Christian doctrine has been translated into such existential terms as these, the search for the right scandal in the Bible has met at least with some degree of positive fulfillment.[28]

FOOTNOTES

[1]John Macquarrie, "Rudolf Bultmann," in *A Handbook of Christian Theologians,* Martin E. Marty and Dean G. Peerman, eds. Meridian Book edition (Cleveland & New York: The World Publishing Co., 1967), p. 460.

[2]Rudolf Bultmann, *Jesus Christ and Mythology* (New York: Charles Scribner's Sons, 1958), p. 56.

[3]H. W. Bartsch, ed., *Kerygma and Myth,* Torchbook ed. (New York: Harper & Row, 1961), pp. 24-25.

[4]*Ibid.,* p. 6.

[5]Bultmann, *Jesus Christ and Mythology,* p. 15.

[6]*Ibid.,* p. 16.

[7]Bartsch, *Kerygma and Myth,* p. 10.

[8]*Ibid.*

[9]*Ibid.,* p. 11.

[10]*Ibid.,* pp. 1-2.

[11]Bultmann, *Jesus Christ and Mythology,* p. 17.

[12]Bartsch, *Kerygma and Myth,* p. 2.

[13]*Ibid.,* p. 8.

[14]Bultmann, *Jesus Christ and Mythology,* p. 52.

[15]Bartsch, *Kerygma and Myth,* p. 117.

[16]*Ibid.,* p. 30.

[17]*Ibid.,* p. 31.

[18]*Ibid.*

[19]Bartsch, *Kerygma and Myth,* p. 35.

[20]*Ibid.,* p. 36.

[21]*Ibid.,* p. 42.

[22]S. Paul Schilling, *Contemporary Continental Theologians* (Nashville: Abingdon Press, 1966), p. 85.

[23]Reginald H. Fuller, *The New Testament in Current Study* (New York: Charles Scribner's Sons, 1967), p. 13.

[24]*Ibid.,* p. 21.

[25]*Ibid.,* pp. 23-24.

[26]John A. T. Robinson, *Honest to God* (Philadelphia: The Westminster Press, 1965), p. 35.

[27]Macquarrie, *Handbook of Christian Theologians,* p. 460.

[28]Alvin C. Porteous, *Prophetic Voices in Contemporary Theology* (Nashville: Abingdon Press, 1966), p. 95.

CHAPTER ELEVEN

Reinhold Niebuhr

Up until the beginning of the first World War the dominant note in theology both in Europe and America, as we have seen, was nineteenth century liberalism. There was a naive optimism about the inherent goodness of man and his possibilities for indefinite growth in goodness. Barring certain deplorable features like the poverty of the masses which human goodness and scientific know-how would soon erase, the culture and civilization which he had built were good and getting better. All that men needed to do to become what they ought to be was to give themselves unreservedly to the advancement of their world. Thus would they work out their own destiny. There seemed little place or need for the help of God's grace and the doctrine of man's sinfulness attracted scant attention.

World War I destroyed that world and its optimism about man. It laid bare the potential for evil that is always present in man. It exposed man's need for God. European theology was the first to react to the new situation. It did so in the work of Karl Barth with its insistence on the gulf that separated man from God and its stress on man's absolute need for God if he were to overcome his inherent tendency to evil. It was almost fifteen years before the first significant American contribution to the new mood of somberness and realism appeared. The contribution was Reinhold Niebuhr's *Moral Man and Immoral Society,* published in 1932. With its appearance Niebuhr (*n.* 1892) took and held for twenty years and more his position as America's foremost twentieth century theologian.

Yet, Niebuhr did not think of himself as a theologian. His field was rather ethics, or what is sometimes called apologetics, the application of the principles of Christian faith to the complex problems of present-day society. His thought as it developed came to be called Christian Realism. It was Christian because it was his conviction that only in the resources of Christianity could there be found the insights needed to explore and explain the full dimensions of man in both his individual and social nature. If such assistance to understanding man and his world could not be found in the biblical faith then that faith did not deserve to continue in existence.

His thought was at the same time a realism, a willingness to explore in painstaking detail all the complexities of today's human and social problems. Never was the light of faith applied to a situation until he had done all he could to uncover and analyze all its components. The penetration of reality to its depths was the object of his thinking. That thinking was realistic also in its acknowledgment that often the given problem did not allow for a simple, unqualified solution. He knew that man lives with ambiguities, that black and white are rare colors in human situations. His tool for handling this problem of ambiguity was dialectical thinking, the ability to see that every 'yes' calls for a responding 'no.' He became expert in the use of paradoxical statement, balancing one truth against another. He knew how to live with provisional answers, with for-now decisions. He was always aware

> . . . that the Christian is *"justus et peccator,"* "both sinner and righteous"; that history fulfills and negates the Kingdom of God; that grace is continuous with, and in contradiction to, nature; that Christ is what we ought to be and also what we cannot be; that the power of God is in us and that the power of God is against us in judgment and mercy; that all these affirmations which are but varied forms of the one central paradox of the relation of the Gospel to history must be applied to the experiences of life from top to bottom.[1]

His life's work was to know man in all his dimensions, individual and social, then search the Christian faith for the light it had to shed on man's life in his world.

This chapter will explore the nature of Niebuhr's Christian Realism, first searching out its origins in his own life experience, then uncovering its roots in his understanding of the nature of man as individual and in society, and finally exploring his Christology, especially his thought on the cross of Christ as that which gives meaning to man and history.

ORIGINS OF HIS CHRISTIAN REALISM

Niebuhr's early theological training, done at Yale Divinity School when liberalism was at its height, produced a minister who took seriously the providence of God, affirmed the natural goodness and perfectibility of man, believed that Christian love of neighbor offered the practical solution to all problems of human relationships, and who looked forward optimistically to the Kingdom of God that man would soon definitively establish on earth.

His first assignment was to a parish in Detroit where he had thirteen years to observe at its heart the sprawling growth of American industrialism. It was those years which tempered his optimism and his idealism. He came to learn a number of things. First, he discovered how futile was the preaching of moral idealism. Preaching would never change social inequities. These could only be fought after one had learned first-hand the hurt, the exploitation, the tragedy that industrial society inflicted on so many of its members. Only then would Christian love see the need for getting down to practical involvement in the harsh realities of modern life. It was only through first-hand experience, also, that preaching could learn to sharpen its weapons for a realistic criticism of contemporary society.

First-hand knowledge of what human nature is really like also came to him in those years. Industrialists and auto workers alike made it clear to him that self-interest is a basic motivation in human life. Moreover, for the protection of that self-interest, men will develop a variety of self-deceptions and of social hypocrisies.

Finally he was brought to recognize that self-interest's main instrument in protecting and advancing itself is what he calls "the will to power." The more wealth and power one can amass the greater is one's security against the other. Nothing preserves the self so surely as the possession of power over other men. And since power is so important, the development of whatever means will procure it becomes life's driving force.

The process of disillusionment with liberalism was a gradual one but by the time Niebuhr left Detroit to teach at Union Theological Seminary in 1928 the process was complete. He had become a realist in his view of society and of the way man, on the one hand, was crushed by it and, on the other, manipulated it for his own self-aggrandizement.. He himself had become more truly Christian, too, in his discontent with the churches and their failure to make any impact on the society they supposedly served, and in his recognition that many of them had bowed to the hard facts of the need for survival by blessing the *status quo*. His own course would run in the opposite direction, in the direction of an almost cynical exposure of the ills of man and his society. He had become a Christian realist and was ready to begin work on what would remain the major preoccupation of his life, the study of man in himself and in his relation to society.

THE NATURE OF MAN

Niebuhr's mature analysis of the nature of man is contained in his two-volume work, *The Nature and Destiny of Man.* This is his presentation of the Christian view of man. He finds that this view has three major emphases which he summarizes as follows,

> ... (1) It emphasizes the height of self-transcendence in man's spiritual stature in its doctrine of 'image of God.' (2) It insists on man's weakness, dependence, and finiteness, on his involvement in the necessities and contingencies of the natural world, without, however, regarding this finiteness as, of itself, a source of evil in man. In its purest form the Christian view of man regards man as a unity of God-likeness and creatureliness in which he remains a creature even in the highest spiritual dimensions of his existence and may reveal elements of the image of God even in the lowliest aspects of his natural life. (3) It affirms that the evil in man is a consequence of his inevitable though not necessary unwillingness to acknowledge his dependence, to accept his finiteness and to admit his insecurity, an unwillingness which involves him in the vicious circle of accentuating the insecurity from which he seeks escape.[2]

Thus Niebuhr finds man is created and therefore finite and dependent. He stands over against God the infinite and the transcendent who has nonetheless entered into an intimate relation with man. This creature, man, is a compound of nature and spirit.

> ... Man is a child of nature, subject to its vicissitudes, compelled by its necessities, driven by its impulses, and confined within the brevity of the years which nature permits its varied organic form. ... The other less obvious fact is that man is a spirit who stands outside of nature, life, himself, his reason and the world.[3]

Within the Christian perspective ". . . man's insignificance as a creature, involved in the process of nature and time, is lifted into significance by the mercy and power of God in which his life is sustained."[4] This dependent yet significant, limited but loved, creature is endowed with the priceless gift of freedom. It is this freedom that chooses the course of his life; it decides what view of reality and what exercise of his being, man will make his own. Freedom elects the relationship between nature and spirit which will characterize man's life.

It is when man comes to exercise that freedom that Niebuhr finds Scripture once more asserting a truth about man. He is a sinner. He will "inevitably but not necessarily" choose to use his freedom wrongly. Because man is nature and spirit there is an ambiguity in his existence. He is at once bound and free, limited in his nature and unlimited in his ability to transcend nature. He stands in and yet above nature.

This ambiguity gives rise to a tension, an anxiety in man, a desire for security in place of the uncertainty of the ambiguity. It is for freedom to resolve the ambiguity, allay the anxiety, provide the security man seeks. Man's freedom may choose to dispel the anxiety in either of two ways. Both the right and the wrong choice are within its power and so man does not choose the wrong necessarily.

The right choice, as Niebuhr sees it, would be for man to accept his creatureliness and his dependence on God. In this choice he elects the transcendent God as the ultimate center of reality. His decision is to accept himself for what he is, weak, finite, ignorant and to trust in God who, revelation tells him, is good, to give him the security he seeks. This is the way of faith, the finding of meaning and security outside the self in God. And it is a real option; the choice is available. "The ideal possibility is that faith in the ultimate security of God's love would overcome all immediate insecurities of nature and history."[5]

But though the ideal possibility is at hand to be chosen it is the message of the Bible that freedom inevitably chooses the other alternative. Man elects to seek security in himself. He denies his creatureliness and becomes his own god. He overestimates his freedom, pretending it is unlimited. He exaggerates his wisdom, stripping it of its relativity. This choice is sin, the refusal to accept finiteness.

Scripture is constant in its description of what constitutes the state of sin. In the myth of the Fall it tells the story of Everyman. Adam is the symbol of each man who chooses his unfettered freedom over his dependence upon the Creator. The prophets of the Old Testament also saw what the essence of sin was.

> The real evil in the human situation, according to the pro-
> phetic interpretation, lies in man's unwillingness to recognize
> and acknowledge the weakness, finiteness and dependence of
> his position, in his inclination to grasp after a power and
> security which transcend the possibilities of human existence,
> and in his effort to pretend a virtue and knowledge which are
> beyond the limits of mere creatures.[6]

And for Saint Paul in the New Testament, "the sin of man is that he seeks to make himself God. . . ."[7]

This seeking to transcend his finiteness which is man's basic sin is essentially the sin of pride which, Niebuhr finds, takes several forms. In its first form man, anxious about his insecurity, tries to overcome it by seeking power over other people and over things. This is pride of power. It is the sin of the man who, being already in possession of some degree of social power, has come to believe himself secure. He does not find it necessary, therefore, to acknowledge the contingency and dependence of his life. He has deluded himself into believing he is molder of his own destiny, judge of his own values, author of his own existence.[8] But this form of pride is also the sin of the man who has little or no power. The absence of power is the source of his insecurity and he lusts for it and drives toward having it. His pursuit of it will inevitably be at the expense of others. Thus both power and its absence corrupts.

Pride occurs also in the form of intellectual pride.[9] Here man whose knowledge is always finite, makes pretensions to total or final knowledge. It is the sin of the thinker who imagines his own explanation of the meaning of reality to be the final one. It often happens too that this form of pride is used to bolster pride of power. Thus, to use Niebuhr's example of the relations between majority and minority racial groups,

> . . . The majority group justifies the disabilities which it imposes upon the minority group on the ground that the subject group is not capable of enjoying or profiting from the privileges of culture or civilization.[10]

In this kind of wisdom, power and privilege should be reserved to the group wise enough to use it well.

Finally, pride can take a moral form, the form of self-righteousness.[11] Here what seems good to me is by that fact objective moral value. Those who disagree are wrong since their view does not conform to what is objectively right. The pride involved here is the pretentiousness of the finite creature who finds the absolute in his own relative judgments of right and wrong. The classic example is the Pharisee, or perhaps in today's terms, the racist.

Pride is man's primary sin and most men are guilty of it in one or another of its forms. But Niebuhr finds that, in addition to those who allay their insecurity by abusing their freedom, turning a relative into an absolute freedom, there are also those who solve the problem of insecurity by refusing to accept the burden of freedom. Such a one tries to escape from the ". . . responsibilities of self-determination. . . ."[12] by abandoning himself to impulse or desire. Life's problems are not faced; they are evaded in ". . . sexual license, gluttony, extravagance, drunkenness and abandonment to various forms of physical desire . . . ."[13] Niebuhr finds combined in this type of sin both an excessive self-love and at the same time an attempt to escape from the self. He finds too that society visits much sterner penalties on this form of human sin than it does on sins of pride. Yet, in his view, pride is the far more dangerous and destructive form of selfishness.

MAN IN SOCIETY

Sin is not only an individual phenomenon; it has its social dimension too. The components of that social dimension are explored by Niebuhr in his *Moral Man and Immoral Society*. The thesis of this book is that it is possible for the individual to come through faith to a realization that, as a Christian, love should be the dominant factor in his life. Furthermore, the individual is able to express love in his own personal relations with other men. Thus individual man can be moral. The further question is whether society can be moral, whether the love that governs interpersonal relationships can be made an operative principle in inter-societal relationships. The second half of the title indicates Niebuhr's response to the question. The bulk of the book is devoted to explaining why he feels society must be immoral in the sense that the highest moral value, love, cannot be made its basic law of operation.

It is obvious from his doctrine of sin and from his conviction that sin is a universal human phenomenon that Niebuhr, in saying individuals can be moral, is not equating morality with sinlessness. What he does mean is that

> Individual men may be moral in the sense that they are able to consider interests other than their own in determining problems of conduct, and are capable, on occasion, of preferring the advantages of others to their own. They are endowed by nature with a measure of sympathy and consideration for their kind, the breadth of which may be extended by an astute social pedagogy. Their rational faculty prompts them to a sense of justice, which educational discipline may refine and purge of egoistic elements until they are able to view a social situation, in which their own interests are involved, with a fair measure of objectivity.[14]

The same claim, however, cannot be made for groups.

> In every human group there is less reason to guide and to
> check impulse, less capacity for self-transcendence, less ability
> to comprehend the needs of others and therefore more unre-
> strained egoism than the individuals, who compose the group,
> reveal in their personal relationships.[15]

The basic reason for the difference he finds is in the strength of the
"collective egoism" of the group. Pride and the will-to-power over others
may be mastered by the single person. There is a cumulative pride in a
society which is far more resistant to control, far less capable of being
brought under ". . .the dominion of reason or conscience."[16]

It is for this reason that appeals to love of neighbor will never effect
social reform nor will the love ethic suffice to settle disputes between
nations. This being so, differences between groups and the social injustices
which feed on these differences will not yield to ". . . moral and rational
suasion. . . ."[17] In a conflict of interests ". . . power must be challenged
by power."[18] The norm of a society made up of diverse groups, each with
its own will-to-power, cannot be love. It must be justice. And justice is
effected by coming to a reasonably acceptable harmony between the conflicting parties. What man must make his goal for the foreseeable future is

> . . . not the creation of an ideal society in which there will be
> uncoerced and perfect peace and justice, but a society in
> which there will be enough justice, and in which coercion will
> be sufficiently non-violent to prevent his common enterprise
> from issuing into complete disaster.[19]

There will be those who believe injustice can be eliminated by an increase of reason and intelligence and they have some measure of truth on
their side. But ultimately reason cannot overcome the selfishness of an
entire class or nation and those who enjoy privilege will cling to it with or
without the support of reason. Religion, too, must be aware of its limitations when it attempts to provide resources for mediating inter-group
conflict. It can motivate the individual but its effect is considerably less on
the group either that has or that wants privilege.

Nation, class, privileged group, unprivileged proletariat, all are scruti-
nized and the same judgment is passed on all of them. Self-interest is their
breath of life and it is the wise man who recognizes this and who, while
striving to live the ethic of love in his own life and to infuse its spirit into
the groups to which he belongs, is also prepared to work toward the

reasonable compromise which will give to the parties in conflict as close an approximation to justice as the concrete situation allows.

The Christian who is aware of the nature of society and conscious too of the demands of unselfishness which his faith makes on him will view the situations with which life in society will confront him as a series of "impossible possibilities." In each of them he is challenged to live an absolute, the law of love. Because he is a sinner and because society's problems do not yield easily to a solution dictated by love, he is called to an impossibility. Yet, at the same time, if the faith he professes gives him anything it gives him the trust that the possibility somehow exists of implementing love in his society. As William Hordern puts it:

> While there is no situation in which the love-ethic can be applied perfectly, there is no situation in which we cannot come closer to fulfillment of the ideal than we have yet done.[20]

Man is at once and paradoxically the servant and the master of the society he lives in.

CHRIST THE MEANING OF MAN AND HISTORY

Niebuhr's view of man the individual and man in society is a somewhat pessimistic view as we have thus far seen it. The emphasis lies more on man's potentiality for sin than on his possibility for good. For the dimension in his thought that restores the balance and gives the optimism of Christian hope to his thinking one needs to turn to his treatment of Christ. Christ is for Niebuhr both the answer to human sinfulness and key to the meaning of human history.

As we have seen, freedom is an essential component of man's nature. Equally characteristic is the universal misuse he has made of that freedom. Man's action in time, his choices and their effects, are the stuff of which human history is made. Because Niebuhr views man's use of his freedom as both corrupted and corruptive he sees his history as filled with ambiguities and inequities. It is written in a series of crooked lines. Yet Christian faith sees God as writing straight with these crooked lines. It is the divine love for man and God's decision that human history will come out right at its end that casts light on that sinfulness and that history and enables man to find meaning and hope amid all the contradictions, not by the light of his reason but under the illumination of his faith.

The fact of history which faith sees as central and which it uses to shed light on man's sinfulness and history's ambiguities is the fact of Christ and especially the fact of his cross. The cross of Christ has in Niebuhr's thought what Paul Lehmann calls a ". . . pivotal significance . . . both for the human situation and as the clue to the person and work of Christ. . . ."[21]

The cross stands as proof of the presence and power of evil in the world. God is overcome and killed by that evil. Yet it stands, too, for the even stronger presence and power of redeeming grace in the world. In dying God overcomes evil and offers man the same power to overcome. ". . . . It is God's nature to swallow up evil in himself and destroy it."[22] He takes upon Himself the full force of human evil, suffers to death under its impact and thereby conquers its power over man.

This is one meaning and perhaps the deepest and ultimately the most hopeful of its meanings. Yet there are other meanings also. The cross contains a lesson of despair because it points to the sinfulness of man and his hopelessness when left to himself. It is the world that kills God and the world is all of us and so we are all implicated in this rejection of God. As a lesson of optimism the cross reminds that the one who dies is a man, or mroe correctly, *the* man, the second Adam from whom we all descend and with whom we are all identified. And the fact that he is man ". . . proves that sin is not a necessary and inherent characteristic of life. Evil is not . . . a part of essential man."[23]

To clarify further these various meanings of the cross of Christ, Niebuhr makes use of the concepts of the cross as the wisdom of God and the cross as the power of God. The essential message of the Christian Gospel is that in the cross of Christ both the wisdom of God and His power are made available to man; ". . . which is to say that not only has the true meaning of life been disclosed (wisdom) but also that resources have been made available to fulfill that meaning (power). In Him the faithful find not only 'truth' but 'grace'."[24]

First of all, how does the cross reveal the wisdom of God? It is in the cross that man can come to understand the full meaning of the power of God and how its two components, justice and mercy, wrath and forgiveness are reconciled. God cannot love without justice; nor can He be just without mercy. Both these demands of his power are fulfilled in Christ. His justice demands that the evil inherent in man and his history be punished. God's relation with man is not a matter of merely forgiving the sins of man. The divine justice must be fulfilled. "There can be no simple abrogation of the wrath of God by the mercy of God."[25] That justice is fully fulfilled in the death of Christ.

But that death of Jesus Christ who is the Son of God also reveals that God "... has a resource of mercy beyond His law and judgment ...."[26] The complete fulfillment of the law of divine justice is at the same time an act of surpassing mercy because, once the penalty is paid, man is free of punishment. It is in taking upon Himself the full rigor of the law that God annuls the necessity of man bearing that rigor. "He has a resource of mercy beyond His law and judgment but He can make it effective only as He takes the consequences of His wrath and judgment, upon and into Himself."[27] Thus is the wisdom of God made manifest, His ability to reconcile the apparently irreconcilable divine justice and mercy.

The cross manifests another revelation of the wisdom of God and this one relates to human experience. The human is able to abuse its freedom and thereby produce evil. It is not, however, able to right the situation it thus creates. The problem of sin and its effects in human history, though humanly produced, is not humanly solvable. Man can cause the damage; he cannot repair it. Nor can God simply repair evil by forgiving it. The situation can be righted only if the demand of evil that it be fully punished be first met. In this line of thought Niebuhr finds the lesson of the cross for men. "The fact that God cannot overcome evil without displaying in history His purpose to take the effects of evil upon and into Himself, means that the divine mercy cannot be effective until the seriousness of sin is fully known."[28] That is to say, the cross is meant to induce first despair and only then, hope. Man must first recognize the radical seriousness of his plight. He must see he has created a situation which he cannot solve and thus be brought to despair.

It is at this point that Niebuhr introduces the notion of the cross as the power of God. It is only when a man has come to despair of discovering in himself the resources to solve his situation that he can produce the sorrow and the turning to God for help which is the condition for the gift of divine forgiveness and divine assistance.

> It is in this contrition and in this appropriation of divine mercy and forgiveness that the human situation is fully understood and overcome. In this experience man understands himself in his finiteness, realizes the guilt of his efforts to escape his insufficiency and dependence and lays hold upon a power beyond himself which both completes his incompleteness and purges him of his false and vain efforts at self-completion.[29]

Thus does man come to appropriate both the wisdom and the power of

God that is present in the cross. His recognition of his need for the power of God is at the same time his realization of the wisdom of God. And his appropriation of the power of God is simultaneously the acceptance of His wisdom.

The appropriation of God's power by man has a double meaning. It means, first of all, the presence of God's power in him. In accepting Christ he acknowledges his own inability to save himself, or put another way, he accepts his own sinfulness. It is only on this condition that the empowering presence of Christ becomes his. But when Christ is present the power of new life is also present.

Over against this power of God in us must be set the power of God over us. So long as a man lives and history lasts human pride will continue to set itself against the will of God. Pride will go on introducing corruption into the world. And the power of God will go on condemning human sinfulness, standing in judgment over it.

These two aspects of the power of God need to be kept in continuous tension in a man's life, that God forgives and yet man sins, that grace can lead man to new life and yet at every stage in that life there are present new possibilities for human evil. Every new level of virtue achieved is a new level of possibility for sin.

Life remains, then, forever ambiguous, and the same is true of history. It does not yield itself to an easy understanding of its meaning. Indeed as long as it lasts it will not have its final meaning. What the cross makes clear is that human life and human history do not contain within themselves their own ultimate significance. That is only to be found in Christ and so in God. And God will be found only at life's end and history's completion. Meanwhile the human situation remains always ambiguous.

In his understanding of the meaning of history Niebuhr rejects both the liberal view and the tragic view. Liberal Christianity reads the meaning of the cross in essentially optimistic terms. It sees in what happened there the introduction of vicarious love as ". . . a force in history which gradually gains the triumph over evil. . . ."[30] In this view ". . . the power of love in history, as symbolized by the cross, begins tragically but ends triumphantly. It overcomes evil."[31]

But Niebuhr has learned from his own experience to beware of the optimism of liberalism. He knows that the facts of history give the lie to the thesis of a gradual growth in human goodness. Evil is still very much with us. Along with goodness it too grows as man advances. History has a much more tragic dimension to it than liberalism would allow.

There is another view of the cross which does fuller justice to its meaning. Here the tragedy of history is more heavily accented. For this view the vicarious love that Christ introduced into history does not triumph. It goes unto the end being defeated by human sinfulness. Yet, for all that, it continues to be and to offer to man the true meaning of life. The triumph of Christ's love is not in its victory but in its truth.

> But the idea of the suffering servant in history may also mean that vicarious love remains defeated and tragic in history; but has its triumph in the knowledge that it is ultimately right and true.[32]

Niebuhr finds this explanation of the meaning of history equally unsatisfactory. There is abundant evidence of human goodness. The effect of what Christ did is manifestly present in the world. Both explanations are rejected because neither seems to do full justice to the fact that Jesus is both God and man. He is God and it is as God that he suffers for man's evil. This means that ". . . the contradictions of history are not resolved in history; but they are only ultimately resolved on the level of the eternal and the divine."[33] Yet it is equally true that what Christ did was done as a man in history and for man in history. ". . . God is engaged and involved in history, and is not some unmoved mover, dwelling in eternal equanimity."[34]

For the man of faith there is goodness in history and the power of God is able to effect change for the better in his own life and in society. He is called to responsible action in the world and he is meant to be confident that such action can be effective of good. Yet always he has need of caution. The judgment of God lies on all human action. That action will remain, until the end, a compound of good and evil. No final stage of human goodness is possible in history. Man's task is to strive for the possible and the better but never to settle for what he has achieved as the final coming of the Kingdom of God. That final coming as the title and thesis of one of Niebuhr's books suggests is *Beyond Tragedy,* beyond the ambiguities and contradictions of man's life in this world.

CONCLUSION

Niebuhr's thinking has been an unremitting attempt to apply the insights of the Christian faith to the complexities of contemporary society. The style he has chosen to embody this attempt has been, rather consistently, a devastating analysis of human pretensions and human inadequacies. What he does most expertly is to uncover the danger of a naive optimism regarding man's possibilities and his future. And he does this for the most part without falling into the opposite danger of an unrelieved pessimism about man. From this point of view his realism is just that; it is real. He perceives and describes the good and the bad, the hopeful and the to-be-regretted in man. And one somehow senses that he is right, that the real man is this compound of opposites.

He has had his share of critics, however, and we will close by looking at two major points of criticism brought against him. There are, first of all, among his critics those who would criticize his view of the church and the function it is to play in human life. They would agree that he ". . . is rightly critical of the sentimentalities, the tyrannies, the obscurantism, and the self-righteousness of the 'churches' in history."[35] But they would question whether for all of its deficiencies, he has given sufficient emphasis to the fact that it is in the church that God's revelation of his relationship with men has been preserved. And by the fact that it does preserve this revelation, it stands in continuing witness against the evil in man and in his society. It stands too as witness that God relates to man in community, not in individuality. It is a people he saves, not individuals. The church for all its failings is the embodiment of divine revelation and relation to man.

By way of answer to one expression of this criticism Niebuhr makes this response,

> I think I have increasingly recognized the value of the Church as a community of grace which, despite historic corruptions, has the "oracles of God," as St. Paul said about Israel. The Church is the one place in history where life is kept open for the final word of God's judgment to break the pride of men and for the word of God's mercy to life up the broken-hearted.[36]

He is quick, however, to add as a qualifying caution the reason which originally led him to criticize the Church.

> But when I see how much new evil comes into life through the pretension of the religious community, through its conventional and graceless legalism and through religious fanaticism, I am concerned that my growing appreciation of the Church should not betray me into this complacency.[37]

His critical spirit will not allow him to exempt from warranted criticism any aspect of life, including the religious aspect, in which humanity is involved. Institutions, especially, must be open to continuing critical appraisal lest the prideful humanity in them should corrupt them.

Another area of his thought which has also drawn sharp negative reaction has been his analysis of human sinfulness. There are those who see in this analysis so pessimistic a view of human nature that it is hard to conceive how a human nature so constituted could even aspire to goodness. Such a view, they contend, tends to paralyze human effort. Others, approaching it from another perspective, see his sketch of human nature's sinfulness as being done in such dark colors that it is hard to imagine how even God could extricate man from the position into which he has put himself.

Others, less extreme in their criticism, find fault with the categories to which he reduces all sin, either pride or sensuality. They would contend that for many men neither category is suitable, or perhaps better, both categories tend to be far too dramatic to describe the state in which they live. Such, for example, are the ones who live quiet, placid lives, undisturbed by the problems around them, unwilling or unable to see any reason why they should show concern or accept responsibility for other men and their needs. Life, except in its individual dimension, is almost a moral vacuum. Yet they are neither proud nor sensual. This segment of humanity is surely as guilty before God as the proud man is. And certainly they are just as dangerous as the man of pride, for they are the ones who create or permit the conditions in society which invite the proud to move in and take over.

To all of these criticisms of his doctrine on sin Niebuhr's response would be, I think, that for him the basic human sin is self-regard. Call it what you will, it is concentration on the self which characterizes all human sinfulness and, unless man has the help of God to overcome this, his situation is helpless. Finally it is in his ruthless dissecting of human self-concern and it corruptive influence on society and on history coupled with his insistence that only divine wisdom and divine power can solve this most fundamental of man's problems, that he has made his lasting contribution.

FOOTNOTES

[1] Reinhold Niebuhr, *The Nature and Destiny of Man*, vol. II, *Human Destiny*, Paperback edition (New York: Charles Scribner's Sons, 1964), p. 204. Copyright 1941, 1943 Charles Scribner's Sons. Reprinted by permission of the publisher.

[2] Niebuhr, *Nature and Destiny of Man*, vol. I, *Human Nature*, p. 150.

[3] *Ibid.*, p. 3.

[4]*Ibid.,* p. 92.

[5]*Ibid.,* p. 183.

[6]*Ibid.,* p. 137.

[7]*Ibid.,* p. 140.

[8]*Ibid.,* pp. 188-89.

[9]*Ibid.,* pp. 194-98.

[10]*Ibid.,* p. 198.

[11]*Ibid.,* pp. 199-203.

[12]*Ibid.,* p. 186.

[13]*Ibid.,* p. 228.

[14]Reinhold Niebuhr, *Moral Man and Immoral Society*, Paperback edition (New York: Charles Scribner's Sons, 1960), p. xi.

[15]*Ibid.,* pp. xi-xii.

[16]*Ibid.,* p. xii.

[17]*Ibid.,* p. xv.

[18]*Ibid.*

[19]Niebuhr, *Moral Man and Immoral Society*, p. 22.

[20]William Hordern, *A Layman's Guide to Protestant Theology, Paperback ed. (New York: The Macmillan Co., 1962), p. 160.*

[21]Paul Lehmann, "The Christology of Reinhold Niebuhr," in *Reinhold Niebuhr: His Religious, Social and Political Thought,* eds. Charles W. Kegley and Robert W. Bretall, paperback ed. (New York: Macmillan Co., 1961), p. 255.

[22]Reinhold Niebuhr, *Beyond Tragedy,* paperback edition (London: James Nisbet & Co., 1937; New York: Charles Scribner's Sons, 1937), p. 168.

[23]*Ibid.,* pp. 167-68.

[24]Niebuhr, *Human Destiny,* p. 98.

[25]*Ibid.,* p. 56.

[26]*Ibid.,* p. 55.

[27]*Ibid.*

[28]*Ibid.,* p. 56.

[29]*Ibid.,* p. 57.

[30]*Ibid., p. 45.*

[31]*Ibid.*

[32]*Ibid.*

[33]*Ibid.,* p. 46.

[34]*Ibid.*

[35]William J. Wolf, "Reinhold Niebuhr's Doctrine of Man," in *Niebuhr:His Thought,* p. 248.

[36]Niebuhr, "Reply to Interpretation and Criticism," in *Niebuhr: His Thought,* p. 436.

[37]*Ibid.*

CHAPTER TWELVE

Paul Tillich

Twentieth century Protestant theological thought has, in the main, run along three lines. The first of these, begun by Karl Barth, has concentrated on explaining divine revelation as that revelation is found in the Word of God. Emphasis is placed in this approach on the need for man to hear God as He speaks and to respond in faith and obedience. The second line of development, typified by Rudolf Bultmann, has been essentially biblical in its orientation. The attempt is made to find in Scripture what it is that God wants to say to man. To achieve this purpose Scripture is interpreted in terms of what it has to say to man's existential questions: Who am I, what can and should I be?

In Paul Tillich (1886-1965) we come to the main representative of the third line of development, the philosophical understanding of Christian revelation. It will be noted immediately that Tillich's option for a philosophical approach to Christianity is the exact opposite of Barth's. He himself notes the basic difference. Theology, he believes, can be approached in two ways. If the theologian opts to stress the unchangeableness, the perennial truth, of the Christian kerygma rather than the importance of making that message meaningful to man in his situation, then he produces a kerygmatic theology, one which is principally interested in the preservation of the Christian faith in its purity. He believes that Barth's choice is for a theology of this kind and he acknowledges that it keeps Christian truth from the dangers of relativization which are always present when attempts are made to adapt that truth to the contemporary situation. Tillich's choice, on the other hand, is for an "answering theology." In this approach one listens first to the questions that man is asking then frames the Christian message in terms that answer man's questions.

Tillich is well aware that the danger of the first kind of theology is irrelevance and of the second an adaptation which results in distortion and dilution. But it is his own conviction that religion must speak to culture as it is if religion is to make itself present to man. He chooses to run the risk of distortion rather than that of irrelevance.

Tillich is then a philosopher-theologian, that is to say, he believes that philosophy is the instrument to be used in probing the most fundamental of human questions. Once those questions have been uncovered and the human situation implicit in them has been laid bare, then, but only then, does it become possible for the theologian to speak of what Christianity has to say to those questions and that situation.

THE METHOD OF CORRELATION

Tillich speaks of his method of theologizing as the method of correlation. He explains, "the method of correlation explains the contents of the Christian faith through existential questions and theological answers in mutual interdependence. . . ."[1] Unlike Barth who begins with the divine answer, Tillich's point of departure is the human question. His probing for what is the human question carries him over a broad range of human culture because he believes that man best reveals himself in the cultural forms with which he surrounds himself and through which he expresses himself, his interests, his concerns, and his anxieties. For Tillich, painting, theatre, politics, history, sociology, science, depth psychology, literature, philosophy, patterns of life, all of these are grist for the mill of his analysis of the human situation. At the end of that investigation of culture he is in a position to know what questions man asks. Only then does he proceed to theologize, to match divine answer to human question, to show how religion, and specifically Christianity, can help man answer his questions.

Put another way, Tillich views his life work as living in a "boundary situation," on the boundary between philosophy and theology, religion and culture. His task is to understand both and to work for their correlation or better their mutual interpenetration. Underlying this view of the theologian's task is Tillich's conviction that "as the substance of culture is religion, so the form of religion is culture."[2] By this he means that a study of any civilization's cultural forms will uncover either its religious concerns or its lack of such. Or, put the other way around, if religion is present in a culture, it will manifest its presence in all the forms of that culture; if it is not present, the culture will be void of any religious implications.

THE HUMAN SITUATION

Faithful to his method of correlation Tillich's theology is first of all an analysis of man's contemporary situation. He asks: Who is present-day man? How does he conceive of himself? How does he view the meaning of his existence? He answers: For man today as for man in the past the basic question to be asked is, What is the meaning of life?

As man ponders the answer to this question he becomes aware of the basic human condition of finitude. His possession of existence is a very limited one and even that possession is continually threatened by nonexistence. His being is precarious. He could at any moment just as well not be as be. Man knows that he is from moment to moment confronted by the threat of nonbeing. Faced by this threat, how does man give meaning to his life? He needs to find somewhere "the courage to be," to assert that life is worth living in spite of its precariousness.

Put another way, man's awareness of the insecurity of his existence gives rise to anxiety, "the existential awareness of non-being," a concern that perhaps existence does not have a meaning but is rather an absurdity. As Tillich reads the various forms of contemporary cultural expression in psychology, in existentialism, in art and poetry, and in the facts of history and politics he finds ample evidence to support his belief that this anxiety has led modern man to view his human situation as meaningless. His reaction to this meaninglessness has been in terms of despair, apathy, a tendency to self-destruction and a general sense of lack of worthwhileness in life. Out of this anxiety as well as out of this realization of life's limitedness if not pointlessness the same problem arises: where does man find the courage to be, how does he allay his anxiety about life's meaning?

It is Tillich's contention that man chooses to express his courage to be through his freedom. He elects to give life meaning by using his freedom to make the choices that make life meaningful. The basic choice that is made is of self and the freedom inherent therein as the sole source of meaning in life. Implicit in such a decision is a rejection of the essential human condition of finitude. Man decides that he gives rather than finds meaning. Put another way, the choice of self as the source of meaning in life means acting in terms of a denial of what man is, finite, dependent, limited. Thus does man, in his choice of that which will give him the courage to be, deny what he is and separate himself from his true situation. He elects a state of alienation. This state is, for Tillich, the state of sin. In this choice, man at one and the same time makes himself his god and denies who he is, a finite, limited being.

The consequence of this freely chosen state is a sense of separation from one's true being and an ensuing loneliness. Man is estranged from himself and from the One who is really the Ground and Source of his being. It is to this fundamental misuse of freedom in the search for the courage to be that Tillich traces much of the sickness of the men of his time, their sense of despair, emptiness and cynicism, their acceptance of life as meaningless.

> Thus, the state of our whole life is estrangement from others and ourselves, because we are estranged from the Ground of our being, because we are estranged from the origin and aim of our life. And we do not know where we have come from or where we are going. We are separated from the mystery, the depth, and the greatness of our existence. We hear the voice of that depth; but our ears are closed. We feel that something radical, total, and unconditioned is demanded of us; but we rebel against it, try to escape its urgency, and will not accept its promise. We cannot escape, however. If that something is the Ground of our being, we are bound to it for all eternity, just as we are bound to ourselves and to all other life. We always remain in the power of that from which we are estranged. That fact brings us to the ultimate depth of sin: separated and yet bound, estranged and yet belonging, destroyed and yet preserved, the state which is called despair. Despair means that there is no escape. Despair is "the sickness unto death." But the terrible thing about the sickness of despair is that we cannot be released, not even through open or hidden suicide. For we all know that we are bound eternally and inescapably to the Ground of our being. The abyss of separation is not always visible. But it has become more visible to our generation than to preceding generations, because of our feeling of meaninglessness, emptiness, doubt and cynicism—all expressions of despair, of our separation from the roots and the meaning of our life. Sin in its most profound sense, sin as despair, abounds amongst us.[3]

From this state of primal separation from the Ground of his being man is unable to extricate himself. Every effort he makes in that direction is rooted in his chosen condition of estrangement and thereby doomed to failure. Thus all of man's social and political strivings for betterment, his own personal reaching for moral growth, even his practice of religion are of no avail so long as they come from his alienated self.

This is Tillich's analysis of the human situation. As he reads the cultural expressions of that situation he sees these also reflecting the human state of separation from its authentic being. Behind it all he glimpses man asking what has always been his fundamental question: who am I, what is the meaning of my life? At this juncture he is ready to turn from the human question to the divine answer.

THE DIVINE ANSWER

The beginning of an answer lies in man's coming to know himself for what he is, finite and therefore dependent in his being. This admission leads in its turn to an acknowledgment of the One upon Whom man depends and from Whom he has separated himself. This One is not a being among other beings; he is rather the Ground of all being, Being-Itself, the ultimate reality. Thus Tillich names God: "The name of this infinite and inexhaustible depth and ground of all being is *God*. That depth is what the word *God* means."[4]

Tillich believes that an acknowledgment of God as the Ground of being is within the grasp of every man because every man is capable of, indeed has, an ultimate concern. God and ultimate concern are synonyms. Tillich explains,

> ... If that word (God) has not much meaning for you, trans-
> late it, and speak of the depths of your life, of the source of
> your being, of your ultimate concern, of what you take
> seriously without any reservation. Perhaps, in order to do so,
> you must forget everything traditional that you have learned
> about God, perhaps even that word itself. For if you know
> that God means depth, you know much about Him. You can-
> not then call yourself an atheist or unbeliever. For you cannot
> think or say: Life has no depth! Life itself is shallow. Being
> itself is surface only. If you could say this in complete serious-
> ness you would be an atheist; but otherwise you are not. He
> who knows about depth knows about God.[5]

A further clarification of what Tillich means by ultimate concern is found in his sermon on the Gospel story of Martha and Mary. The two sisters are used as symbols of the two possible views that a man can take of the meaning of life.

> Martha is concerned about many things, but all of them are
> finite, preliminary, transitory. Mary is concerned about one
> thing, which is infinite, ultimate, lasting.[6]

As it is with Martha and Mary so it is with every man.

> Man is concerned about many things: food, shelter, knowl-
> edge, art, social problems, politics—with varying degrees of
> urgency. But a concern becomes ultimate only when it
> demands total surrender and promises total fulfillment. Ulti-
> mate concern is unconditional, total, and infinite. Any
> concern less than this is a preliminary concern, for it is condi-
> tional, partial, and finite.[7]

All men, then, in Tillich's analysis of the human situation have something about which they are ultimately concerned, something that is all-
important to them, something for which they are willing to give their lives.
Ultimate concern is a universal human phenomenon. It follows then that
all men are believers because the name God is the symbol for what concerns a man ultimately.

It would appear that Tillich, in speaking of God as both Ground of
being and ultimate concern, is attempting to throw light on the notion of
God from two different but allied points of view. God is, to begin with,
seen as the depth dimension in life. One meets Him as one plunges below
the surface of reality, where all is superficial and transitory, to the level of
things that really count in one's life. The deeper one drives into the heart
of reality, the closer one comes to what is of final and decisive concern in
one's life. When that point is reached, one has come to that which gives
both being and final meaning to all reality; one has attained to the Ground
of being; one has encountered God.

Tillich now moves to his next point, his contention that, in the Christian message, this God speaks to man as he is in his existential situation of
separation, alienation, and despair. That man yearns for something which
will give him meaning and hope in his life. To that man God speaks in His
Word, Jesus Christ. To that man He holds out in Christ the promise of
"New Being."

THE NEW BEING

In the person of Jesus as portrayed in the New Testament one sees a
man not subject to the separation from the Ground of being that plagues
one's own life. As a man Jesus lived as other men do, in all the circumstances of the human situation. Like other men he too exercised his
freedom, but always within the clear context of who he was, a dependent,

finite and therefore limited being. As such he lived in an uninterrupted acknowledgment of the Ground of his being. In him there was that which Tillich calls perfect "God-manhood." This is man as God intended him to be, man transparent to the depths of being itself. Fully human though he was, he lived not separated from but continuously united with God. He embodied the complete overcoming of all separation from ultimate reality. In a word, he lived what he was, accepting reality for what it was.

Here, in Jesus Christ, lies the power of man's renewal, his reconciliation with himself and with God. Here is the New Being, the principle of human salvation. ". . . reuniting that which is estranged, giving a centre to what is split, overcoming the split between God and man, and man and his world, man and himself."[8] United with him man comes to share the power of that New Being. In the strength of that power he can be liberated from his misuse of freedom; he can be freed from the separation that curses his human existence; he can participate in God-manhood.

But how does man come to participate in this New Being? Christianity says, in a puzzling paradox, man needs only accept the fact that he is accepted. He need only believe and trust that in Christ God gives him the New Being.

> . . .it is as though a voice were saying: "You are accepted. . . .
> Do not try to do anything now; perhaps later you will do
> much. Do not seek for anything;. . .*Simply accept the fact
> that you are accepted*![9]

J. Heywood Thomas neatly paraphrases this Tillichian notion of faith when he says,

> . . . faith is paradoxical in character. It is accepting and being
> accepted, accepting acceptance. Faith accepts the fact that he
> who is separated is accepted.[10]

Once a man has come to this belief and trust he is able to accept himself for what he is: sinner but saved, separated but united to the divine ground. Out of this being accepted he comes to self-acceptance. Thus is he healed. Thus in the power of the New Being does the divine answer reply to the human question: What is the meaning of life.

RELIGION AND CULTURE

A further aspect of Tillich's thought calls for comment, his lifelong interest in the relationship between religion and culture.

A man is religious if he is ultimately concerned, or, put another way, if he affirms that all being has its source and ground in God, Being-Itself. A culture is that complex web of structures, relationships, forms and expressions with which man surrounds himself and through which he expresses who he is and what meaning he gives to life.

The relation between religion and culture, as Tillich reads history, is a dialectical one in which at one point in history each interpenetrates the other and at another time one rejects or stands over against the other. The process by which this relationship expresses itself in history moves through three stages, one replacing and negating the other, only, in its turn, to be negated and replaced. The process is at once cyclic and forward moving like a wheel in motion.

The first type of relation between religion and culture, Tillich calls "theonomy" or a "theonomous culture." In such a period of history man is at peace with himself and at one with the "unconditional." It is a culture which ". . . expresses in its creations an ultimate concern and a transcending meaning not as something strange but as its own spiritual ground."[11] Man reads reality and he accepts his place in it as one who is free, yet finite, capable of unlimited growth yet within a context of limitation. God's law as it manifests itself in the order of things is seen to be in harmony with man's own nature. The culture that such a man creates manifests this acceptance of reality in all of its cultural expressions. All these expressions speak of ultimate concern and of a relationship between man and God and man and man which is integral and authentic. Man is at home in the world because he has found his real place in it. He is very much involved in penetrating and understanding reality yet his expression of that understanding is always in terms of things as they really are. Tillich would cite the early Middle Ages and the beginning period of the Reformation as times in history when such a theonomous culture existed, when God was present in all of society.

But the same history that displays theonomous cultures evidences also a type of culture to which theonomy seems inevitably to yield. This is "heteronomy," the "heteronomous culture." Thus, for example, the high

Middle Ages yielded to the barren externalism and the deadening weight of legalism of the late Middle Ages; the Protestant Reformation gave way to Protestant orthodoxy when the dynamic, living insights of the Reformers were replaced by the systems and codes and laws of their seventeenth century successors.

Heteronomy is a period when a shift occurs in the source from which man draws his awareness of the Ground of being and his relationship to that Ground. In theonomy the source of the awareness is man's own self, particularly his reason assenting to reality as it presents itself to him. Reason and things as they are coincide. But in heteronomy the understanding of reality is imposed upon man from outside himself. "Heteronomy asserts that man, being unable to act according to universal reason, must be subjected to a law, strange and superior to him."[1 2]

The momentum of a theonomous society continues its existence beyond the time when its cultural forms were the natural expression of how man saw reality. But in heteronomy inner vision, as the source of culture and the root of an authentic view of reality and man's place in it, is replaced by external authority.

Either church or state sets itself up as the arbiter of what a man is to believe and how he is to act. Religion or state validates its authority by claiming to speak for God. Human freedom and cultural creativity are stifled. The external cultural trappings of a theonomous culture continue but the authenticity has gone out of them. They no longer spring from man's own inner vision but are derived from and imposed by law and authority. Sooner or later man rebels against such an externally determined culture. He will not for long accept a meaning of life and an explanation of who he is that is imposed from outside himself.

When the limit of man's tolerance of heteronomy is reached, the stage is set for the movement of history to a third cultural form, "autonomy" or the "autonomous culture." Such a culture is always reactionary, a reaction against the external forces that have imposed a world-view and a culture. It is a movement in the direction of human self-assertion, the insistence that man himself must control the building of his cultural environment. Man becomes the center of all things, the determiner of meaning and its manifold expressions in his society. He lives by his own rationality, making his own laws. It is an autonomy because there is no openness to reality as it is in itself, as is the case in theonomy. Rather the rupture of harmonious correlation between man's vision of meaning and the meaning inherent in reality of itself, which was introduced by heteronomy, is continued. Man does not accept the meaning present in reality. He rather decides what meaning he will allow reality to have and what cultural expression he will give to that meaning. Autonomy, then, is a culture dominated by man's reason. In it man is ultimately concerned about himself. Cultural forms are void of any reference to the ultimate. There is only the here and now, the "conditioned." Tillich sees the Renaissance as an example of autonomous man's rejection of the heteronomy of the late Middle Ages; in eighteenth-century rationalism he reads reason's rejection of Protestant orthodoxy; finally he regards contemporary society as the latest example of an autonomous culture.

KAIROS

At this point Tillich introduces another of his characteristic ideas to describe how one culture comes to pass over into another. This is his notion of *kairos,* a Greek word which, in literal translation means: 'the right or acceptable time.' The term in its general sense refers to the passage from one form of culture to another. In a very particular sense it is used to refer to the coming of Jesus Christ, the New Being. This is the unique *Kairos,* in human history, unique because it has universal significance for all mankind. Apart from this meaning, there is one final use that Tillich makes of the idea. There is only one *Kairos,* but throughout history there have been other *kairoi,* other acceptable times. These are the points in history at which autonomy is ripe for a movement into theonomy.

Tillich believes our own age to be on the verge of such a *kairos.* As he reads the cultural signs of our time, autonomy has just about exhausted itself. Man appears to have come to the point of no return in his attempt to impose his own meaning on the world. The legacy of that attempt has been meaninglessness, absurdity, despair. Life seems to have no depth or meaning. All indications seem to point to the return of religion to culture. As Tillich would put it, autonomy is entering a *kairos* for its return to theonomy. The "acceptable time" appears to be once again present for man to realize the sterility and lack of fulfillment inherent in his self-centered view of reality. Tillich looks forward to a proximate return of man and his culture to a world where the ultimate meaning of things is rooted and grounded in God.

Toward the beginning of our treatment of Tillich, reference was made to his conviction that "as the substance of culture is religion, so the form of religion is culture." The statement offers a convenient vehicle for a final summary of his ideas on religion and culture. In a theonomous culture, religion and culture are closely interrelated. Culture expresses religion's concern with the ultimate and religion gives meaning to all cultural forms. But when theonomy yields to heteronomy, the relation of religion to culture is distorted. Religion dominates in this culture. In such a culture it is not ultimate concern rising up out of man's own inner being that forms and fashions culture. Rather the finite replaces the infinite as the source and ground of culture. A finite authority imposes its own conception of the meaning of reality. Thus the culture becomes an expression of the 'demonic,' a substitution of the conditioned for the unconditional. A distorted religion falsifies the cultural forms.

The passage from heteronomy to autonomy represents another kind of distortion, another dislocation of the right relationship between religion and culture. Culture now rises out of man's self-sufficiency and cannot therefore be a reflection of reality as it truly is. Culture is false in that it is wrongly grounded. Balance and cohesion is only restored when by a return to theonomy, religion is rightly restored to its role as the substance of, as that which gives unconditional meaning to, culture. Culture reassumes its authentic function as the expression in conditioned forms of the true understanding of reality which is based on man's acknowledgment of his relation to God, the Ground of all being.

CONCLUSION

When one comes to an appraisal of Tillich's thought, one is brought face to face with the quandary in which today's Christian thinkers find themselves. Two alternatives seem to be open to them in their attempt to present Christianity to contemporary man. The choice of either alternative appears to involve almost insoluble problems. On the one hand, Barth's choice, a presentation of the Christian faith with accent on God as wholly Other and as standing in judgment on all human achievement, strikes no responsive chord in the heart of modern man. His view that God reveals Himself to man in the Scriptures and that man's only way to God lies in the obedience of faith to this revelation is unacceptable to a generation that has grown up in a world where evidences of man's self-sufficiency grow ever more impressive. Christianity, as Barth presents it, seems to them quite unnecessary.

Tillich opts for the other alternative, to start with man where he is, to analyze the existential situation of man and then show how Christian faith can help man to cope with problems arising out of that situation. By so choosing, Tillich opens himself up to charges from both Christian theologian and secular man.

For the theologian, Tillich's interpretation of the Christian message is open to serious question. To begin with, they say, God, as Tillich describes Him, bears little likeness to the God of traditional Christianity. Tillich's God is not personal since person is a category that can only be used of a being and God is beyond being. He is its Ground. What then, they ask, becomes of the God of Abraham, the Father of our Lord Jesus Christ and the personal God Christian faith has believed in for two millenia?

The theologians also find serious difficulty with Tillich's understanding of Jesus. For Tillich, Jesus was human, not divine. He was the man in whom man's primal separation from the divine ground of being was completely healed. In this sense he was a unique man, but a man, nonetheless. What does this portrait do to the biblical affirmations of his divinity?

Thus the two linchpins of the whole Christian faith, the traditional Christian personalist theism and the divinity of Christ, seem to be unfastened by Tillich. If this is true, what then remains of Christianity? The charge of the theologian, then, is that Tillich has sacrificed the integrity of the Christian message for the sake of contemporary relevance.

On the other hand, Tillich is likewise rejected by contemporary man. Harvey Cox voices that rejection in these terms.

> Tillich's approach has no place for pragmatic man. It is built on the assumption that man by his very nature *must* ask these "ultimate" or existential questions. . . . The difficulty, however, is that they are obviously *not* questions which occur to everyone, or indeed to the vast majority of people. They especially do not occur to the newly emergent urban-secular man.[13]

For all of his attempts to speak contemporaneously, the charge is, Tillich uses the language of nineteenth century idealism. He speaks of a world where the structures of being correspond to the laws of man's reason. His universe of thought is heavy with philosophical terminology, with the tension between being and nonbeing, with the challenge to man to pass from existential separation to union with the Ground of being. But,

> The appeals of Tillich and others of his generation to the "depths of life" invoked by the "meaning" of the old myths are expressions of beliefs and sensibilities that we no longer share.[14]

Man today does not ask the questions that Tillich says it is natural for him to ask. If this charge be true then Tillich's answers fall on unhearing ears. Tillich's method of correlation, it would seem, fails of its purpose. The men of the two worlds he would bring together for mutual enlightenment both find serious fault with his attempt to correlate them.

Protestant Christian thought has traveled a long road from Luther and Calvin to Barth and Tillich. In some eras the road has passed mostly through the land of Christian revelation. At other times the road's environ has been the landscape of human experience with Christian revelation as the sun illuminating the highway. And sometimes the road has run along the boundary between the sacred and the secular. The present question, on which the future depends, is: how is to possible to build that road into the future in such a way that it runs between irrelevance and adaptation? We are only at the beginning of tentative probings toward an answer to that question.

FOOTNOTES

[1] Paul Tillich, *Systematic Theology* 3 vols. (Chicago: University of Chicago Press, 1951) I, 60.

[2] ———, *The Interpretation of History* (New York: Charles Scribner's Sons, 1936), p. 50.

[3] ———, *The Shaking of the Foundations,* paperback edition (New York: Charles Scribner's Sons, 1948), pp. 159-60.

[4] *Ibid.,* p. 57.

[5] *Ibid.*

[6] Tillich, *The New Being,* paperback edition *(New York: Charles Scribner's Sons, 1955), p. 152.*

[7] Carl J. Armbruster, S. J., *The Vision of Paul Tillich* (New York: Sheed and Ward Inc., 1967), p. 25.

[8] Tillich, *Systematic Theology,* II, 192.

[9] ———, *The Shaking of the Foundations,* p. 162.

[10] J. Heywood Thomas, *Paul Tillich* (Richmond: John Knox Press, 1966), p. 14.

[11] Tillich, *The Protestant Era,* paperback abridged edition (Chicago: University of Chicago Press, 1957), p. 57.

[12] *Ibid.,* p. 56.

[13] Harvey Cox, *The Secular City* (New York: Macmillan Co., 1965), p. 79.

[14] John Charles Cooper, *The Roots of the Radical Theology* (Philadelphia: The Westminster Press, 1967), copyright ©1967, The Westminster Press. Used by permission. p. 135.

Bibliography

Reformation

Bainton, Roland, *The Reformation of the Sixteenth Century*. Boston: The Beacon Press, 1952.

Bouyer, Louis, *The Spirit and Forms of Protestantism*. Westminster, Md.: The Newman Press, 1956.

Chadwick, Owen, *The Reformation*. Baltimore: Penguin Books, 1964.

Dillenberger, John and Claude Welch, *Protestant Christianity*. New York: Charles Scribner's Sons, 1954.

Dolan, John, *History of the Reformation*. New York: Desclee Co., 1965.

Lortz, Joseph, *The Reformation: A Problem for Today*. Westminster, Md.: The Newman Press, 1964.

Pauck, Wilhelm, *The Heritage of the Reformation*. New York: Oxford University Press, 1968.

Van de Pol, Willem , *World Protestantism*. New York: Herder and Herder, 1964.

Whale, J.S., *The Protestant Tradition*. Cambridge: Cambridge University Press, 1959.

Martin Luther

Bainton, Roland, *Here I Stand: A Life of Martin Luther*. New York: The New American Library, 1955.

Boehmer, Heinrich, *Martin Luther: Road to Reformation.* New York: Meridian Books, 1957.

Bornkamm, Heinrich, *Luther's World of Thought.* St. Louis: Concordia Publishing House, 1965.

Dillenberger, John, *Martin Luther: Selections From His Writings.* Garden City: Doubleday and Co., Inc., 1961.

Green, V.H.H., *Luther and the Reformation.* New York: Capricorn Books, 1964.

Kerr, Hugh T. (ed.), *A Compend of Luther's Theology.* Philadelphia: The Westminster Press, 1943.

Rupp, E.G., *Luther's Progress to the Diet of Worms.* New York: Harper & Row, 1964.

Rupp, E.G., *The Righteousness of God.* London: Hodder and Stoughton, 1953.

Todd, John, *Martin Luther.* Westminster, Md.: The Newman Press, 1965.

John Calvin

Harkness, Georgia, *John Calvin: The Man and His Ethic.* New York & Nashville: Abingdon Press, 1958.

Kerr, Hugh T. (ed.), *A Compend of the Institutes of the Christian Religion by John Calvin.* Philadelphia: The Westminster Press, 1964.

McNeill, John, *The History and Character of Calvinism.* New York: Oxford University Press, 1954.

Olin, John (ed.), *A Reformation Debate: John Calvin and Jacopo Sadoleto.* New York: Harper & Row, 1966.

Wendel, Francois, *Calvin.* London: William Collins, Sons & Co. Ltd., 1965.

Anabaptism

Bainton, Roland, *The Travail of Religious Liberty*. New York: Harper & Row, 1957.

Estep, William., *The Anabaptist Story*. Nashville, Tenn.: Broadman Press, 1963.

Hershberger, Guy F. (ed.), *The Recovery of the Anabaptist Vision*. Scottdale, Pa.: Herald Press, 1957.

Lecler, Joseph, *Toleration and the Reformation*. New York: Association Press, 1960.

Littell, Franklin, *A Tribute to Menno Simons*. Scottdale, Pa.: Herald Press, 1961.

————, *The Origins of Sectarian Protestantism*. New York: The Macmillan Co., 1964.

Williams, George, *The Radical Reformation*. Philadelphia: The Westminster Press, 1962.

Williams, George and Angel Mergal, (eds.), *Spiritual and Anabaptist Writers,* vol. XXV. *Library of Christian Classics*. Philadelphia: The Westminster Press, 1957.

Anglicanism

Dickens, A.G., *The English Reformation*. New York: Schocken Books, Inc., 1964.

Hughes, Philip, *The Reformation in England* (3 vols.). London: Hollis and Carter, and New York: The Macmillan Co., 1950-54.

Neill, Stephen, *Anglicanism*. Baltimore: Penguin Books, 1958.

Parker, T.M. *The English Reformation to 1558*. London: Oxford University Press, 1950.

Ridley, Jasper, *Thomas Cranmer.* Oxford: The Clarendon Press, 1962.

Rupp, E.G., *Studies in the Making of the English Protestant Tradition.* Cambridge: Cambridge University Press, 1966.

Wand, J. W. C., *Anglicanism in History and Today.* New York and Toronto: Thomas Nelson and Sons, 1962.

Puritanism

Haller, William, *The Rise of Puritanism.* New York: Harper & Row, 1957.

————, *Liberty and Reformation in the Puritan Revolution.* New York: Columbia University Press, 1955.

Knappen, M. M., *Tudor Puritanism.* Chicago: University of Chicago Press, 1939.

Morgan, Edmund, *The Puritan Dilemma.* Boston: Little, Brown and Co., 1958.

Perry, Ralph, *Puritanism and Democracy.* New York: Harper & Row, 1964.

Schneider, Herbert, *The Puritan Mind.* Ann Arbor, Mich.: University of Michigan Press, 1958.

Simpson, Alan, *Puritanism in Old and New England.* Chicago: University of Chicago Press, 1955.

Methodism

Burtner, Robert and Robert Chiles, (eds.), *A Compend of Wesley's Theology.* Nashville, Tenn.: Abingdon Press, 1954.

Cragg, G.R., *The Church and the Age of Reason 1648-1789.* Baltimore: Penguin Books, 1960.

Curnock, Nehemiah (ed.), *The Journal of John Wesley.* New York: Capricorn Books, 1963; G.P. Putnam's Sons.

Davies, Rupert, *Methodism.* Baltimore: Penguin Books, 1963.

McConnell, Francis, *John Wesley.* New York and Nashville: Abingdon Press, 1939.

Rack, Henry, *The Future of John Wesley's Methodism.* Richmond, Va.: John Knox Press, 1965.

Todd, John, *John Wesley and the Catholic Church.* London: Hodder and Stoughton, 1958.

Williams, Colin, *John Wesley's Theology Today.* London: Epworth Press, 1960.

Nineteenth Century Liberal Protestantism

Barth, Karl, *Protestant Thought: From Rousseau to Ritschl.* New York: Harper and Brothers, 1959.

Niebuhr, Richard, *Schleiermacher on Christ and Religion: A New Introduction.* New York: Charles Scribner's Sons, 1964.

Reardon, B.M.G. (ed.), *Religious Thought in the Nineteenth Century.* Cambridge: Cambridge University Press, 1966.

Schleiermacher, Friedrich, *On Religion: Speeches to Its Cultured Despisers.* New York: Harper and Brothers, 1958.

Schweitzer, Albert, *The Quest of the Historical Jesus.* New York: The Macmillan Co., 1961.

Vidler, Alec, *The Church in An Age of Revolution 1789 to the Present Day.* Baltimore: Penguin Books, 1961.

Karl Barth

Barth, Karl, *The Humanity of God.* Richmond, Va.: John Knox Press, 1966.

————, *The Word of God and the Word of Man.* New York: Harper & Row, 1957.

Casalis, Georges, *Portrait of Karl Barth.* Garden City: Doubleday and Co., Inc., 1964.

Hamer, Jerome, *Karl Barth.* Westminster, Md.: The Newman Press, 1962.

Hartwell, Herbert, *The Theology of Karl Barth: An Introduction.* Philadelphia: The Westminster Press, 1964.

Willems, Boniface, *Karl Barth: An Ecumenical Approach to His Theology.* Glen Rock, N.J.: Paulist Press, 1965.

Dietrich Bonhoeffer

Bonhoeffer, Dietrich, *Ethics.* New York: The Macmillan Co., 1965.

————, *Letters and Papers From Prison.* New York: The Macmillan Co., 1962.

————, *Cost of Discipleship.* New York: The Macmillan Co., 1963.

————, *No Rusty Swords.* New York: Harper & Row, 1965.

Godsey, John, *The Theology of Dietrich Bonhoeffer.* Philadelphia: The Westminster Press, 1960.

Kuhns, William, *In Pursuit of Dietrich Bonhoeffer.* Dayton, Ohio: Pflaum Press, 1967.

Marty, Martin (ed.), *The Place of Bonhoeffer.* New York: Association Press, 1962.

Moltmann, Jürgen and Jürgen Weissbach, *Two Studies in the Theology of Dietrich Bonhoeffer.* New York: Charles Scribner's Sons, 1967.

Robertson, E.H., *Dietrich Bonhoeffer.* Richmond, Va.: John Knox Press, 1966.

Vorkink, Peter (ed.), *Bonhoeffer in a World Come of Age.* Philadelphia: Fortress Press, 1968.

Rudolf Bultmann

Bartsch, Hans (ed.), *Kerygma and Myth.* New York: Harper & Row, 1961.

Bultmann, Rudolf, *Jesus and the Word*. New York: Charles Scribner's Sons, 1934.

————, *History and Eschatology*. New York: Harper & Row, 1962.

————, *Jesus Christ and Mythology*. New York: Charles Scribner's Sons, 1958.

Fries, Heinrich, *Bultmann-Barth and Catholic Theology*. Pittsburgh, Pa.: Duquesne University Press, 1967.

Macquarrie, John, *An Existentialist Theology*. New York: Harper & Row, 1965.

————, *The Scope of Demythologizing*. New York: Harper & Row, 1966.

O'Meara, Thomas and Donald Weisser, (eds.), *Rudolf Bultmann in Catholic Thought*. New York: Herder and Herder, 1968.

Reinhold Niebuhr

Carnell, Edward, *The Theology of Reinhold Niebuhr*. Grand Rapids, Mich.: W.B. Eerdmans Publishing Co., 1951.

Harland, Gordon, *The Thought of Reinhold Niebuhr*. New York: Oxford University Press, 1960.

Kegley, Charles and Robert Bretall, (eds.), *Reinhold Niebuhr: His Religious, Social and Political Thought*. New York: The Macmillan Co., 1961.

Niebuhr, Reinhold, *The Nature and Destiny of Man*. 2 vols., New York: Charles Scribner's Sons, 1941-43.

————, *Moral Man and Immoral Society*. New York, Charles Scribner's Sons, 1932.

————, *Beyond Tragedy*. New York: Charles Scribner's Sons, 1937.

————, *The Children of Light and the Children of Darkness*. New York: Charles Scribner's Sons, 1944.

Paul Tillich

Adams, James, *Paul Tillich's Philosophy of Culture, Science and Religion.* New York: Harper & Row, 1965.

Armbruster, Carl, *The Vision of Paul Tillich.* New York: Sheed and Ward, 1967.

Brown, D. M., *Ultimate Concern: Tillich in Dialogue.* New York: Harper & Row, 1965.

Kegley, Charles and Robert Bretall, (eds.), *The Theology of Paul Tillich.* New York: The Macmillan Co., 1962.

Martin, Bernard, *The Existentialist Theology of Paul Tillich.* New Haven: College and University Press, 1964.

McKelway, Alexander, *The Systematic Theology of Paul Tillich.* Richmond, Va.: John Knox Press, 1964.

Tavard, George, *Paul Tillich and the Christian Message.* New York: Charles Scribner's Sons, 1962.

Tillich, Paul, *The New Being.* New York: Charles Scribner's Sons, 1955.

————, *The Shaking of the Foundations.* New York: Charles Scribner's Sons, 1948.

————, *The Religious Situation.* New York: Meridian Books, 1956.

————, *The Theology of Culture.* New York: Oxford University Press, 1964.

————, *The Protestant Era.* Chicago: University of Chicago Press, 1948.

Index